The Art of Astrology

A comprehensive contemporary textbook designed to
enable anyone to set up a birth chart with professional
accuracy.

By the same author
ASTROLOGY AND HEALTH

The Art of Astrology

A Complete Course in the Working Techniques
of Natal Astrology

by

Sheila Geddes D.F.Astrol.S.

THE AQUARIAN PRESS
Wellingborough, Northamptonshire

First published 1980
First Paperback Edition 1981
Second Impression 1982
Third Impression 1983

British Library Cataloguing in Publication Data

Geddes, Sheila
  The art of astrology.
  1. Astrology
  I. Title
  133.5   BF1708.1

  ISBN 0-85030-207-2
  ISBN 0-85030-250-1 Pbk

Printed and bound in Great Britain

CONTENTS

LIST OF ILLUSTRATIONS

INTRODUCTORY NOTE

In this book, I have departed from the form of traditional textbooks in some fundamental ways.

In particular, I have not thought it necessary to plunge readers into the intricacies of the solar system and time/space problems before they have set up their first birth chart.

Most students of astrology start with a desire to set up and interpret birth charts, and these remain the fundamental purposes of practising astrology for the majority of us. Since these can both be done without any knowledge of astronomy, it has seemed ridiculous to me that students should be required to learn a mass of quite complicated facts, at the very outset, which have nothing to do with the interpretation of a birth chart.

Having said that, however, I must make it clear that I hold the opinion that any astrologer worthy of the name should understand the workings of the solar system on which our discipline is based. It is far more satisfactory to know why one is doing certain calculations than to do them blindly. More than this, the study is, in itself, fascinating and absorbing, giving insights into the way in which all living things develop in accordance with the ever-changing pattern of the planets. For myself, this has become more meaningful as I have continued to develop as an astrologer. Far from 'forgetting it once the exams are over', I have found that once astrological techniques become second nature, the mind is free to understand more of the underlying meaning of the 'stars in their courses'.

Of course, there is nothing to stop the scientifically-minded student from learning the basic astronomy first. I am only concerned that enthusiasm should not be blunted at the outset by a feeling that everything is too complicated and likely to be too difficult—especially in the case of those who may prove to be very good interpreters but who are not scientifically oriented.

Information which I have felt to be irrelevant to the beginner has been included in Chapter 10, at the end of the book. It is suggested that this be read through when the reader has some experience of interpreting charts.

Finally, and by request, I have included an interpretation of the aspects between planets as an appendix to the book. It has not been included in the text because students do not become astrologers by learning interpretations parrot fashion, and the ones given should be regarded as nothing more than guidelines. As always, the clues are in the psychology of the native as represented by the *whole* birth chart and only increasing experience uncovers the secrets concealed therein.

ACKNOWLEDGEMENTS

I wish to acknowledge, with thanks, the permission given by Hodder and Stoughton Ltd to quote from Lyall Watson's *Supernature* and by W. Foulsham and Company to reproduce various pages from their *Raphael's* ephemerides.

My thanks are also due to the following:

John Filbey, D.F.Astrol.S., F.F.Astrol.S., for checking the chapter on astronomy, for giving me permission to use his methods of calculating the noon date and progressed sidereal time and the interpolations in Chapter 7, and for checking all my computations.

Alice Back, D.F.Astrol.S., for redrawing and checking all my charts.

My sister, Rosemary Langford, for typing and proof reading.

My husband, Alexander Geddes, who as a non-astrologer has worked patiently through all the examples.

This book is dedicated to the astrologers, past
and present, to whom I owe so much, and to the
astrologers of the future, in the hope that they
will see our discipline back in its rightful place
—in the syllabuses of the Universities.

When I consider thy heavens, the work of thy fingers, the moon and the stars, which thou hast ordained; What is man, that thou art mindful of him?

Psalms, 8:3-4

If the world down there took heed to the foundation nature layeth, and followed it, it would have satisfaction in its folk. But ye wrench to a religious order him born to gird the sword, and make a king of him who should be for discourse, wherefore your track runneth abroad.

Dante, *Paradiso*

There are some mystical things about Astrology, but there is nothing supernatural about the way it works. Man is affected by his environment according to clearly defined physical forces, and his life, like all others, becomes organized by natural and universal laws. To believe otherwise is tantamount to assuming that the *Encyclopaedia Britannica* was thrown together by an explosion in the printing works.

Lyall Watson, *Supernature* (Hodder and Stoughton, 1973)

INTRODUCTION

Astrology is the study of a lifetime. Even if it were desirable, it would not be possible to provide all the information available between the covers of one book or, indeed, of many books. This book has been written primarily for the serious student, and it has been compiled to cover the syllabuses of most of the teaching bodies that hold examinations leading to a recognized qualification as an astrologer.

It is also a book for anyone who wants to learn how to interpret a birth chart. There is no shortage of astrologers who will set up a chart and leave the client to do his own interpretation. However, it is very simple to learn how to erect a chart by 'rule of thumb', without knowing the reasons for the various calculations. Although this knowledge is necessary for examination purposes, it can be left until after the student has learnt some basic interpretation.

The book has been arranged so that the reader can begin interpreting charts almost immediately (Chapters 1, 2, 3 and 5). He can then learn how to erect a chart simply (Chapter 4). Chapters 6, 7 and 8 take the serious student on to a knowledge of the astronomy underlying the calculations and to a more precise use of them, both in setting up a birth chart and in dealing with future trends. A chapter on the history of astrology follows and further information on a wide variety of subjects is given in the final chapter.

It is hoped that the reader, whether a potential examination candidate or not, will learn from this book how to help himself in working out his own life pattern and how to give practical help to others.

Astrologers are fond of quoting the apocryphal reply of Newton to Halley, when challenged on his belief in astrology, 'Sir, I have studied it. You have not.' An even better quotation is from Herbert Spencer: 'There is a principle which is a bar against all information, which is proof against all arguments, which cannot fail to keep a man in everlasting ignorance; that principal is contempt, prior to investigation.'

The Validity of Astrology

With this thought in mind, it is suggested that the student of astrology need not be concerned with the scoffers. Truths are for seekers. I have not attempted in this book, therefore, to 'justify' astrology. These who would like to study this aspect of the subject are referred to *The Case for Astrology* by John Anthony West and Jan Gerhard Toonder (see Appendix IV).

The Basis of Astrology

Astrology is based on the movements of our own solar system—the Earth itself on its journey round the Sun, the Moon, our satellite, and the other planets which circle the Sun.

From the earliest times right up until the seventeenth century there was a general assumption that the world as we know it was governed by the movement of the heavens and the celestial bodies. This was the universal law and it was believed that the great store of energy originating from the heavens was projected onto Earth and affected all living things. The birth and growth of every living thing on Earth was attributed to 'Celestial Virtue'. In effect, the Earth mirrored the heavens: 'As in the macrocosm, so in the microcosm.'

Although the so-called Age of Reason virtually 'threw out the baby with the bath water', there was always a nucleus of astrologers who continued to practise by interpreting the planetary movements.

Modern Astrology

Today, we regard astrology as an interpretive art. We are concerned with where we fit in to the cosmic pattern. A modern astrologer is able to tell a client what he has brought into life with him (in terms of psychology) and advise him on making the most of his potential.

Every birth chart shows a great deal of potential which is very seldom used to its full. It is the astrologer's role to advise the client of all his many talents and to indicate areas of difficulty and how even these may be made a vehicle for growth. It is no part of an astrologer's job to tell a client what to do.

Benefits of Studying Astrology

The study of this discipline should result in a greater understanding of ourselves and others and in more tolerance (since 'To understand all is to forgive all'). It will also enable us to make the most of our own talents and opportunities and, in many cases, it leads to increased intuition. Finally, it is a fascinating study which never becomes boring since the patterns are ever changing, never repeated exactly and always beckoning us forward into the unknown future.

CHAPTER 1

THE PLANETS

Aids to Learning

If you have not already done so, please go back and read the Introduction, which contains some necessary preliminary information.

You are about to embark on a study which is inexhaustible. This book will tell you some of the astrological characteristics of the planets and of the zodiacal signs, but you will learn much more by wider reading and from studying the characters, together with the birth charts, of people who are well-known to you. I suggest, therefore, that you start a notebook where you can summarize your own findings under the various headings. A loose-leaf book is most useful for this purpose.

A useful mnemonic is provided by the keywords, which were originally compiled by Margaret Hone. These have been in use for over a quarter of a century and so many people have found them helpful that I have included similar keywords here. These, also, can be tabulated, but you should regard them as mere skeletons which you are going to clothe with flesh as you add to your knowledge.

*Astrological
Definitions*

Every profession has its jargon, and astrology is no exception. Here are definitions of some of the more common terms employed. Further definitions will appear in the appropriate sections of the book.

The *birth chart* is a diagram showing the position of the planets, plus the Sun and Moon, at the time and place of birth.

The *horoscope* is another name for the birth chart, although it is often used to describe the birth chart and the interpretation (or analysis) of the chart.

The *native* is the person for whom the birth chart is *erected* (or 'set up' or 'cast'). He is also referred to as 'the subject'.

The Lights. This phrase refers to the Sun and Moon. They are often included in the term 'planets', although astrologers are well aware that they are not planets.

The *signs of the zodiac* (or zodiacal signs) are names given to the segments of the sky against which the Sun appears to move, as seen from the Earth. In the past, these segments roughly corresponded to the positions of the constellations of stars whose names they bear, but this is no longer true (see the chapter on

17

atronomy). When the Sun appears to be against the background of the part of the sky known as Aries, it is said to be 'in' Aries, and the native is said to have an Arian 'Sun sign'.

Ascendant. This is the sign and degree of the zodiac rising on the eastern horizon at the time and place of birth. It appears on the birth chart as the beginning of the first 'House' and is a very important point in the interpretation of a chart.

The *Midheaven.* This is also known by its Latin name of *Medium Coeli* and often abbreviated to MC. It signifies the sign and degree of the zodiac which is culminating (see Chapter 6). In a birth chart, it gives some indication as to the type of career that is likely to be attractive to the native.

Rulership. A sign of the zodiac is often said to be 'ruled' by a planet and the planet 'ruling the Ascendant' is said to be the 'ruler of the chart'. One sometimes also hears a person described as being ruled by the sign which contained the Sun at the time of birth. This is simply astrological shorthand and it does not mean that astrologers believe that the planet or sign directly influences the native. The usual explanation given is that there is a correlation between the characteristics attributed to the signs and planets and the character of the native.

It may be that we shall shortly begin to take a different view, since modern scientific thought and discoveries are tending to confirm that the planets directly influence all life on Earth. It seems unlikely, however, that we would ever adopt the idea that this rulership was present to such an extent that we were not able to control our own destinies.

It may be as well at this stage to say a word about free will, since most astrologers experience this as a perennial question. My own answer to such a question is that we are only free within limits. For instance, we cannot decide for ourselves in what country we will be born nor what family we will have. Neither can we always prevent the things which happen to us during our lives. Nevertheless, we have absolute freedom in the way in which we meet our circumstances, whether they be difficult or easy. We all know the type of person who becomes a complete invalid at the first signs of any trouble and also severely incapacitated persons who refuse to regard their condition as a handicap and continue to do exactly what they always intended to do. It is with this in mind that we should deal with clients who come to us for an astrological consultation.

The Sun, Moon and Planets

The interest in 'newspaper astrology' has focused attention on the Sun sign for no better reason than that everyone knows the sign which they were 'born under', i.e. the sign in which the Sun appeared at the time of birth.

The Sun, however, represents only one facet of life, though an important one. A complete birth chart may show that the Sun's characteristics have been weakened for some reason. This explains why some people reject astrology on the grounds that they are not like the descriptions usually given for natives of their Sun sign.

The Lights and each of the planets correlates with a different facet of the psychology of the native. Oken has described this as the 'what' of astrology, the zodiacal signs being the 'how'. In other words, the principles expressed by the various planets will operate differently in each of the zodiacal signs.

The basic interpretation of the Sun, Moon and planets follows. As you study the subject more deeply, you will build on the basic information and you will come to understand how each planet 'works' in the different signs of the zodiac. Here is the first keyword summary which should be noted and learned.

KEYWORD INTERPRETATION OF THE LIGHTS AND PLANETS

⊙ SUN—Vitality. Power. The true, vital self.
☽ MOON—Basic impulses. Responses.
☿ MERCURY—Communications. Mentality.
♀ VENUS—Harmony. Relationships.
♂ MARS—Drive. Energy.
♃ JUPITER—Expansion. Maturity.
♄ SATURN—Limitation. Responsibility. Discipline.
♅ URANUS—Change. Personal Freedom.
♆ NEPTUNE—Intuition. Nebulousness.
♇ PLUTO—Regeneration. Purification.

The Sun ⊙

Without the Sun there would be no life on Earth and it is interpreted astrologically as the creative principle. It is the centre of being, the 'I AM' of life. In the birth chart, it is usually the dominating feature signifying the potential of the individual.

The zodiacal sign in which it manifested at the time of birth will show the type of personality and the way in which the native expresses himself fully. Most people will, therefore, show the characteristics of the Sun sign very strongly.

The Sun was worshipped in ancient times as the Great God and it embodies the principle of fatherhood and typifies the Source of our Being.

In astronomy, it is the centre of our solar system round which the other planets revolve.

Psychologically, it can be said to correspond to the basic self, which is the centre of all other aspects of the personality of the native.

Physically, being the heart of the solar system, it is given rulership over the heart and the spine.

Zodiacal sign. The Sun is the ruler of Leo, and is considered to be a masculine planet. It also rules the fifth house (see Chapter 3).

The glyph ⊙ (or sign) for the Sun represents the circle which expresses a complete whole with a dot in the centre representing the life seed.

Words which apply to the Sun: regal, dignified, powerful, dramatic, generous, lively, creative, loving (see also the related words under the heading of Leo).

The Moon ☽

The Moon, being a satellite of our Earth, and much nearer to us than any of the other planets, has a very direct effect on our lives. We are aware that it is responsible for the ebb and flow of the tides and, in fact, it is now established that the Moon exerts its pull on even quite small bodies of water. Since water is the largest constituent of our bodies, it is not difficult to accept that the Moon's movements directly influence us.

In the same way that it causes tides to ebb and flow, so astrologically, the Moon governs our subconscious reactions and feelings, and the variations (or moods) which we experience in them. Basic impulses are shown by the Moon's position in the birth chart.

Psychologically, it often gives a clue to the life decisions which people may have made as young children (usually as the result of the characters of their parents). It often gives an indication of the character of the mother or the wife of the native, as well as indicating his own type of emotional reactions.

The very first impression which we make on others is often a clue to the Moon's position in our own birth chart.

Physically, it relates to the breasts, stomach and digestive system.

Zodiacal sign. Since the Moon influences all plant life on Earth, it is associated with fertility. It is not surprising that it is considered astrologically as ruling the sign of Cancer, which is strongly maternal.

The glyph ☽ for the Moon is the crescent moon.

Words which apply to the Moon: home-loving, moody, changeable, responsive, imaginative, sensitive, receptive, intuitive. Other related words will be found under the heading of Cancer.

☿ *Mercury*

In mythology, Mercury was the messenger of the Gods. The planet rules communications of all kinds, speech, writing, travelling, learning, etc. Its position in the birth chart indicates the type of mentality of the native.

Psychologically, it represents the urge to know and then to communicate the knowledge.

Physically, it rules the nervous system (nerves are *messengers* who carry *communications* to and from the brain), lungs, brain and thyroid gland. Mercury's position in the birth chart will indicate the type of mentality and the type of nervous system.

Zodiacal sign. It has rulership over the signs of both Gemini and Virgo.

The glyph ☿ for Mercury is said to represent the half-circle (human spirit or mind) over the whole circle (divine spirit—the complete whole) and the cross (earthly matter) below both. Until you are familiar with all the signs, it may be easier to remember it as the same sign as for the planet Venus, with the addition of the 'wings' of Mercury's winged helmet.

Words which apply to Mercury: adept, clever, cool-natured, expressive, intelligent, perceptive, critical. Other related words will be found under Gemini and Virgo.

♀ *Venus*

Venus was the goddess of love to many different nationalities and under many different names. All were agreed that her influence was that of a loving and sensuous woman. In the birth chart, the position of Venus will indicate the type of personal relationships which will be made by the native. The feelings are accentuated (contrast Mercury, where the mentality dominated) but the love is not only erotic but also signifies the need for warmth and affection and the desire to bestow them.

The love of beauty and connotations with art and music are all indicated by the planet's position. The desire to possess beautiful things and for the luxuries of life generally is a very Venusian trait.

Psychologically, the position of Venus indicates our necessity to relate to others and to live in harmony with them.

Physically, Venus rules the throat, kidneys and parathyroids.

Zodiacal sign. Astrologically, Venus rules Taurus and Libra.

The glyph ♀ for Venus is the circle joined to a cross below. This is the symbol used in medicine and biology to denote 'female'.

Words which apply to Venus: artistic, graceful, peace-loving, diplomatic, friendly, beauty-loving, companionable. Other related words will be found under Taurus and Libra.

Mars ♂

The 'God of War' is the planet of initiative and energy. Its position in the birth chart indicates the degree of drive and vitality in the native. As one would expect from the mythology attaching to Mars, it indicates pioneering instincts, health, leadership and passion in all its forms. Astrologically, one would consider the position of Mars together with that of the Sun to judge the health and vitality of the native.

Psychologically, its position in the birth chart will show the way in which the energies will be directed. This gives a very good clue to what the native really wants from life.

Physically, it rules the sex glands, the muscular and urogenital systems and adrenal glands.

Zodiacal sign. Astrologically, it rules the sign of Aries.

The glyph ♂ for Mars is the sign used in medicine and biology for 'masculine'. The arrow head expresses the forcefulness and drive of this planet.

Words which apply to Mars: direct, decisive, energetic, forceful, pioneering, passionate, impulsive. Other related words will be found under Aries.

Jupiter ♃

In mythology, Jupiter (or Jove) was the Father of the Gods. To him was attributed the power of dispensing justice and upholding the law. He was most powerful and controlled all the great things (the little details were beneath his notice). Astrologically, Jupiter's influence represents the expansion of consciousness, aspirations and spiritual development.

The alternative name of Jove reminds us that Jupiter is also portrayed as a jovial character, generous and expansive and the bestower of all good things. Astrologically, Jupiter is often called 'the great benefic'.

Psychologically, its position in the birth chart will show the way in which the native will seek his own pleasure and relaxations (or expansion) as well as his own spiritual growth. Perhaps more than any of the other planets, Jupiter's influence appears to have a more spiritual significance but it should not be forgotten that the whole of the birth chart can be interpreted on that level. Maturity is also attributed to Jupiter and it may help you to remember this if you think of material expansion and growth being achieved when plans mature.

Physically, this planet rules the liver and the pituitary gland.

Zodiacal sign. Astrologically, it rules the sign of Sagittarius.

The glyph ♃ for Jupiter is the half-circle at right angles to the cross.

Words which apply to Jupiter: broadminded, optimistic, generous, expansive, mature, fortunate, aspiring, philosophical. Other related words will be found under the sign of Sagittarius.

♄ *Saturn*

In his *Planets Suite,* Holst described Saturn as the 'bringer of old age'. In some ways, this description is apt. Saturn is a 'cold' planet and influences us by limitations and responsibilities, some of which are extremely frustrating and impose a lot of discipline on the native, all of which tends to make people age, or at least grow up, more quickly.

Saturn is often referred to as malefic (in contrast to Jupiter, the great benefic) but this is to ignore the capacity for achievement and overcoming of our troubles which are only learned by the difficult lessons of life. Saturn is the great teacher.

Psychologically, the position of Saturn in the birth chart will indicate the native's attitude to responsibility, the amount of practicality in his make-up and his capacity to meet difficulties. This planet is said to represent the father, as well as showing the native's own capacities and it may be helpful to think of it as the Victorian 'heavy father' who was a strict disciplinarian but only for the good of the child.

Physically, it rules the skin and bones (in itself a good description of old age, when the flesh appears to shrink and one becomes prone to bone ailments, such as rheumatics), also the teeth and gall bladder.

Zodiacal sign. Astrologically, it rules the sign of Capricorn.

The glyph ♄ for Saturn has been described as 'Father Time's sickle'.

Words which apply to Saturn: just, controlled, practical, disciplinary, responsible, reliable, patient, ambitious. Other related words will be found under the sign of Capricorn.

The Outer Planets

The planets already described were known to the ancient astrologers and for many centuries it was thought that our planetary system ended with Saturn.

The three outer planets which have now been discovered are so far out and move so slowly that they stay in the same zodiacal sign for long periods. For this reason, they are regarded, astrologically, as affecting a whole generation rather than a particular person. There are times when this is not true because a particular planet is considered to be 'strong' and to directly affect the native. For instance, if Uranus was in its own sign of Aquarius, or if the Sun was in that sign, this would make Uranus an important planet for the particular native.

22

Herschel identified this planet in 1781. It was originally called by his name and it still appears as Herschel in some books. Further details are given in Chapter 6.

Uranus ♅

At the time that it was discovered, there was a great deal of change and revolution going on in many parts of the world. People were seeking personal freedom and were banding together to achieve it, as shown by the growth of the Trade Union movement in Britain. New nations were being formed, or were breaking away from their old loyalties.

Psychologically, this urge towards personal freedom (even resorting to revolution to achieve it) seems to be mirrored in the way in which the planet 'works' in a birth chart.

The position of it in the chart, by zodiacal sign, will give an indication of the native's ability to make changes and the degree to which personal freedom is necessary to him. It also shows the desire to act impulsively and unconventionally.

Physically, Uranus rules the circulatory system and probably the pineal gland.

Zodiacal sign. Astrologically, it rules the sign of Aquarius.

The glyph ♅ for Uranus looks like an 'H' for Herschel with the addition of a small circle. The complete sign is rather like the old type of television aerial. Television, being a new scientific invention, is associated with Uranus.

Words which apply to Uranus: magnetic, original, freedom-loving, humanitarian, friendly, inventive, unconventional, independent. Other related words will be found under Aquarius.

The discovery of this planet in 1846 was not from a direct sighting but by an assumption of its probable position, which was exerting a pull on the planet Uranus and causing it to move erratically. This was a strange way to discover a new planet and, no doubt, this is what gave rise to Holst's description of it as 'The Mystic'.

Neptune ♆

At this time, esoteric practices such as mesmerism and hypnotism were beginning to be used and the Spiritualist movement had just started.

Mythologically, Neptune was the God of the Sea (which was then, more than now, the great unknown element, and which was often described as 'boundless'). This planet seems to corrolate with that idea and it is for this reason that the keyword for Neptune has been given as 'nebulousness'.

Psychologically, its position in a birth chart will show the way in which the intuition or inspiration will be used. It also seems to correlate with the need to escape from confining conditions. An element of deception may also be indicated.

Physically, this planet rules the thalamus, the spinal canal and the mental and nervous systems.

Zodiacal sign. Astrologically, it rules the sign of Pisces.

The glyph ♆ for Neptune is like the trident of the Sea God.

Words which apply to Neptune: intuitive, boundless, sensitive, imaginative, adaptable, idealistic, spiritual. Other related words will be found under Pisces.

℗ *Pluto* This planet was not discovered until 1930, after the death of Percival Lowell, who had done most of the work to calculate its probable position.

In mythology, Pluto was the god of the Underworld and the correlation in the birth chart appears to be that of the unknown—death and life beyond death. Scientifically speaking, there has been little time since 1930 to observe the effects of this planet in birth charts but there seems to be no doubt that:

Psychologically, it refers to the unconscious. It is surely no accident that its discovery has coincided with the development of psychology and psychoanalysis.

The position of Pluto in the birth chart will show the way in which the native can 'bring to light' the hidden forces in his subconscious which can then be used or discarded according to their nature.

Pluto appears to function best where there is a necessity to make an ending and a new beginning: 'As one door shuts, another opens.' It has a 'refining' significance, purging out all that should be discarded if the native wants to continue to progress.

Physically, Pluto rules the reproductive system.

Zodiacal sign. Astrologically, it rules the sign of Scorpio.

There are two *glyphs* for Pluto which are commonly used. One is a combination of the initials of Percival Lowell (℗) the other is more often found in American books and is the symbol of the trident with the circle as its middle point (♇). If you decide to use this, be careful not to confuse it with the glyph of Neptune.

Words which apply to Pluto: elimination, regeneration, refining. Other related words will be found under Scorpio.

The descriptions of the Planets have been kept concise at this stage. A fuller meaning of each will become apparent as we consider the signs of the zodiac in the next chapter. It will then be seen how the *principle* of each Planet works in the *manner* of the sign over which it has rulership.

CHAPTER 2

THE SIGNS OF THE ZODIAC

In this chapter, a description of the characteristics of each sign is given. You will add greatly to your knowledge of each by reading as widely as possible and by studying the birth charts of people you know well. I would remind you again that this is a lifetime's study and you can go on clothing the bare bones of the interpretation for as long as you wish.

There are no 'good' and 'bad' signs in astrology. In every case, the potential represented by each sign can be used for good or evil, so that, for instance, the Arian capacity for leadership can result in the native becoming a Prime Minister or the leader of a gang of criminals. All qualities which are admirable if used rightly can be become faults by misuse or over-stress—hence the phrase 'I am *firm*. You are *obstinate*. He is *pigheaded*.'!

With the signs, as with the planets, there is a tendency towards a 'masculine' or 'feminine' nature. The masculine signs describe those who are outgoing, or extravert by nature. We shall refer to these as 'positive' signs. The feminine signs describe those who are inward looking, or introvert, and these are called the 'negative' signs. It would be a mistake to think of them as describing people who are introvert or extravert to the point of imbalance—they merely indicate a tendency to one more than the other.

The zodiacal signs also fall into categories according to the *elements* which rule them. These are fire, earth, air and water. The *fire* and *air* signs are all *Positive*. The *earth* and *water* signs are all *Negative*.

These elements are called the *Triplicities* and you will note that each category contains *three* signs.

THE TRIPLICITIES (OR ELEMENTS)

Fire
Aries, Leo, Sagittarius. The *nature* of fire is to be enthusiastic, energetic and positive.

Earth
Taurus, Virgo, Capricorn. The *nature* of earth is to be static, practical and negative.
Air
Gemini, Libra, Aquarius. The *nature* of air is to be intellectual, communicative and positive.
Water
Cancer, Scorpio, Pisces. The *nature* of water is to be emotional, impressionable and negative.

Signs which are in the same triplicity will 'work' in harmony. The reason for this will be explained in Chapter 3.

THE QUADRUPLICITIES (OR QUALITIES)

There is a further category, known as the *Quadruplicities* (or Qualities) in which each group contains *four* signs. The qualities are cardinal, fixed and mutable.
Cardinal
Aries, Cancer, Libra, Capricorn. The *quality* of the cardinal signs is to be active.
Fixed
Taurus, Leo, Scorpio, Aquarius. The *quality* of the fixed signs is to be *cautious*.
Mutable
Gemini, Virgo, Sagittarius, Pisces. The *quality* of the mutable signs is to be *adaptable*. The mutable signs are also referred to as the 'common' signs, but the word 'mutable' is preferred here, as being more expressive of the quality of adaptability.

Signs in the same quadruplicity do *not* work well together. The reason for this will also be explained in Chapter 3.

Figure 1 shows both the triplicity and the quadruplicity which contains each sign of the zodiac.

	FIRE (positive)	EARTH (negative)	AIR (positive)	WATER (negative)
CARDINAL	ARIES ruled ♂	CAPRICORN ruled ♄	LIBRA ruled ♀	CANCER ruled ☽
FIXED	LEO ruled ☉	TAURUS ruled ♀	AQUARIUS ruled ♅	SCORPIO ruled ♇
MUTABLE	SAGITTARIUS ruled ♃	VIRGO ruled ☿	GEMINI ruled ☿	PISCES ruled ♆

Figure 1. Triplicity and Quadruplicity of Zodiacal Signs.

If the chart is memorized, together with the following keywords, you will find that you have a good foundation on which to build your interpretation of the various signs. The keywords show how the principle of a planet will function in each of the signs.

In ARIES: with ENERGY and INITIATIVE
In TAURUS: with POSSESSIVENESS and PERMANENCE.
In GEMINI: with ADAPTABILITY and VERSATILITY.
In CANCER: with PROTECTIVENESS and SENSITIVITY.
In LEO: with CREATIVITY and POWER.
In VIRGO: with PRECISION and DETAIL.
In LIBRA: with HARMONY and DIPLOMACY.
In SCORPIO: with INTENSITY and PASSION.
In SAGITTARIUS: with FREEDOM and TOLERANCE.
In CAPRICORN: with PRUDENCE and ASPIRATION.
In AQUARIUS: with INDEPENDENCE and UNCONVENTIONALITY.
In PISCES: with INTUITION and ADAPTABILITY.

It is important that, as you learn the functions of the various signs, you keep in mind the mixture of quadruplicity and triplicity, together with the ruling planet. These will give you a very good idea of the zodiacal sign on which to base your further understanding.

It is traditional to start with the zodiacal sign of Aries, because the spring equinox begins when the Sun enters this part of the heavens at about 22 March each year. Further explanation is given later, but at this stage it is only necessary to know that the Sun enters the zodiacal sign between the 20th and the 23rd of each month, depending on the year. It should be understood that the *dates given for each sign are approximate.*

Aries (The Ram) ♈

The Sun is in this sign from 22 March to 20 April. A reference to Figure 1 will show that Aries is of the *fire* triplicity and the *cardinal* quadruplicity. This already tells us quite a lot about the personality of the Arian native. Since the nature of fire is to be *enthusiastic, energetic* and *positive* and the cardinal quality to be *active,* the birth chart which shows a strong Arian influence will represent a person who is all of these things. Further, as Aries is ruled by Mars, all the Martian attributes are emphasized—again *energy, initiative* and qualities of *leadership.*

The words describing the fire element, the cardinal quality and the Mars rulership are all similar, and this means that the Arian is an uncomplicated character. His personality, mentality and feelings are 'all of a piece' and make him easily recognizable. He is self-orientated, so you may expect that his great energy will be devoted to his own ends.

As the first sign of the zodiac, we can think of him as being at the first stage of life—the baby, whose instinct is directed to his own needs and who is largely unconcerned with other people except as they affect him.

The Arian is a pioneer and he loves to start new things. When they are running smoothly, he loses interest quickly and will cheerfully hand over his projects to someone else (probably a Taurean) to do what he would consider the boring, mundane work necessary to keep them going.

He is impulsive and quick in action and thought, brave and daring. He enjoys dangerous situations which bring out his best points, calling for quick action, courage, leadership and initiative.

He can also be quick tempered—but not for long. In fact, nothing lasts very long with him—life is too short and there are always so many new things to try.

Mentally, he is quick-witted, but can be illogical. He is good at taking rapid decisions and reacts well under stress. He puts his great energy into studying anything in which he is really interested, and will cheerfully disregard everything else.

Emotionally, he makes a stimulating companion provided he is not required to be tactful or patient. Although he can be childish and pugnacious if he fails to get his own way, he is able to inspire the respect of others in positions which call for his leadership, due to his undoubted qualities in such situations. As one would expect of such a lively and exuberant person, his sexual nature is strong.

Psychologically, he feels the necessity to assert his own rights. This can result in rebelliousness for its own sake, especially if the Moon is in Aries.

Spiritually, the evolved Arian may sacrifice himself for the good of others. Positions of leadership in pioneering conditions offer the opportunity for this. (It is thought that Jesus may have been an Arian.)

Health is generally good with much vitality. As the ruler (Mars) also rules the adrenal glands, so in Aries, the action of the adrenalin is seen, resulting in quick reactions and abundant energy. The *head* is part of the body which is ruled by Aries and the phrases 'head first' and 'head strong' may be remembered in this connection as they describe the typical Arian.

The tendency to rush around and, generally, to undertake too much renders the Arian accident prone. Headaches, migraines, cuts and burns are the most likely causes of trouble. It is essential that both physical and mental relaxation should be practised daily by the Arian to keep him healthy.

Physically, Arians are often red complexioned and red haired, with well-marked eyebrows and strong features. (Care should be taken in identification from appearance, as it is common for people to have the facial characteristics of their Ascendant or Moon sign rather than their Sun sign.)

Suitable Careers will be those that represent a challenge and where the Arian can be the leader. Explorers and pioneers of all types, surgeons, professional sportsmen, soldiers, racing drivers, and all related professions where energy and initiative are required will be suitable.

Because of the relationship to the head, Arians often make good psychologists and psychiatrists.

The *Glyph* ♈ for Aries, the Ram, resembles the horns of the ram. The 'butting' action in which the animal charges 'head first' is again typical.

Words which are associated with Aries: anger, impulse, energy, courage, sharpness, leadership, wit, redness, iron, acid and all the Martian words.

The above description will apply substantially to anyone who has Sun, Moon or Ascendant in Aries. It will also apply to anyone with Mars in Aries (Mars is then said to be 'strong' in its own sign), but other planets in Aries will *modify* the traits according to their own principles.

For instance, the planet Saturn in the sign of Aries would exert limitation and discipline—in many ways, the direct opposite of the Arian character. If it appeared to work well in the particular birth chart being studied, the astrologer's interpretation might be as follows:

Despite your natural instincts to act impulsively and energetically, you are able to channel your energies into disciplined and responsible ways.

Remember that the *principle* of the planet will work in the *nature* of the sign in which it falls.

Taurus (The Bull)
♉

The Sun is in this sign from 21 April to 21 May.

Taurus is of the *earth* triplicity and the *fixed* quadruplicity. Remembering that the nature of Earth is to be *practical, static* and *negative* and the fixed quality is to be *cautious,* thus, (as with Aries), the element and quality are compatible so that the character is uncomplicated. Venus is the planet which rules Taurus and this contributes the principles of harmony and relatedness.

If we think of the Taurean as being at the second stage of growth—the young child—it will help to illustrate the character. At this stage, the child is conscious of others and wants to make happy relationships and friendships. It still needs much reassurance of love and so tends to cling to the parents. It is not very adventurous yet and prefers the places and people who are familiar and with whom it feels secure. The child has now become conscious of its own toys and possessions and continually seeks to acquire more.

In the same way, the Taurean needs the feeling of security and seeks it in money and the things which it can buy. He feels safe when he has a comfortable home, beautiful possessions, and a little more money than he really needs.

He has, in fact, a flair for money (not only his own) and Taureans are found in the world of finance and big business. They are not afraid of responsibility and, being practical and reliable people, they handle it well.

The Taurean is patient and determined but can also be obstinate and tends to resist changes.

As one would expect with the influence of Venus, he loves luxury, all the good things of life and is attracted to art, music and beauty in all its forms. The Taurean often has artistic ability in one of these realms.

Despite the obvious correlation with the planet Venus, Taurus is the most 'earthy' of the Earth signs. He is usually a nature lover, often a very good gardener, a connoisseur of good food and wine (earthly comforts) and has a very 'down to earth' attitude. He often likes to put his money into land or real estate.

Mentally, Taureans are 'plodders'. They do not learn quickly, but they learn thoroughly. They are constructive and practical, methodical and deliberate. They do not enjoy debate, since they are not quick witted and also because, having made up their minds, they are not likely to change them.

Emotionally, as children of Venus, they need to establish stable relationships, but they tend to be possessive, both with friends and in closer relationships. They are much appreciated, however, for their warm nature and affection. Their sexual nature is sensual, as they appreciate the body and its pleasures. They can easily fall into the trap of jealousy, wanting to keep their friends and lovers very much to themselves, in the same way that they are possessive about their belongings. Where the Arian is inclined to say 'me' the Taurean is inclined to say 'mine'.

Psychologically, the Taurean has a great need to feel safe. Difficulties in this

29

direction are likely to come from his grasping attitude (sometimes even downright meanness) and he needs to learn that there is no such thing as material security.

Spiritually, he needs to free the self from the domination of things. To quote Tolkien, 'He that cannot throw away a treasure at need is in fetters.'

Health. The throat and the thyroid glands are ruled by Taurus. There is a tendency to throat infections, goitre and overweight conditions. The body tends to retain excess water. Moderation in food and wine intake is necessary to keep the Taurean healthy.

Physically, the Taurean is often thick set and sturdy. His movements are deliberate. The full neck, which is typical of so many singers (bull neck), is a Taurean characteristic.

Suitable careers will be found in financial fields, for example as a stockbroker, banker, economist, accountant, treasurer, or in the construction industry as a builder, architect, surveyor, in natural surroundings as a nurseryman, florist, gardener, or farmer, or in the art world as a musician, singer, painter, etc.

The *glyph* ♉ for Taurus resembles the head and horns of the bull—a nicely rounded bull, like a true Taurean!

Words which are associated with Taurus: possessions, land, houses, beauty, music, gardens, singing, money, art, affection.

This description will apply substantially to anyone who has the Sun, Moon, Ascendant or Venus in Taurus. Other planets will modify these traits. Mars, which supplies *drive* and *energy,* will function in Taurus with *possession* and *permanance.* The interpretation of this position in a birth chart might be:

> Your energy will be mainly devoted to the making of permanent relationships and to acquiring possessions. You may need to overcome a tendency to become possessive with friends and lovers.

♊ Gemini (The Twins)

The Sun is in this sign from 22 May to 22 June.

Gemini is of the *air* triplicity and the *mutable* quadruplicity. As the nature of air is to be *communicative, intellectual,* and *positive,* and the mutable quality is *adaptable,* so Gemini will be all of these things. In addition, the sign is ruled by the planet Mercury representing *communication* once again and *mentality.* As with the first two signs of the zodiac, these expressions are all compatible and so the Geminians are not complex characters.

We can think of Geminians as being at the later stage of childhood, anxious to know, to learn, to communicate what they have learned, and intent on acquiring a wide range of skills and interests. At this stage of their lives, they seem to be perpetually 'busy' and anything new has a strong attraction for them.

People who have Gemini 'strong' in their birth charts are mentally orientated. Like their ruler, Mercury, the Messenger of the Gods, they appear to be 'here, there and everywhere'. Intelligent, adaptable, quick in mind and movement, they bear a resemblance to Puck—'I'll put a girdle round about the Earth in forty minutes.'

The Geminian nature is well represented by the sign of 'the Twins', as they appear to have a dual nature. For instance, they are often equally good at using their hands and their brains. They frequently run two or more projects at the same time and some of them appear to enjoy the variety of having two totally different careers. One thing which they do not like at all is routine conditions. Nothing could be worse, to them, than office routine with its 'set' hours and obligations.

The restlessness which is such a part of the Geminian's character makes him enjoy the type of career where he can travel and which may give him the opportunity to plan his day's work for himself. Unfortunately, too many activities often lead to a situation where he becomes 'a jack of all trades and master of none'.

Mentally, Geminians are all that has already been described, for they appear to consist almost entirely of mind.

Emotionally, they are rather cold. If other placings in the chart suggest that this is not so, they may still give the impression of 'stand-offishness'.

They like to flirt in a lighthearted way and the partner (or, more likely, partners) will be made well aware that the affair is not to be taken seriously. Despite an apparent lack of emotion, however, they tend to remain close to their family and particularly to their siblings.

Psychologically, Gemini really needs variety. Air must move or it stagnates—so Geminians tend to feel threatened and 'hemmed in' by any situation which is restrictive. Such conditions make them restless and nervous.

Spiritually, because the mind is valued about the heart, the Geminian tends to judge others in terms of their own mental capabilities. There is a need to be more thoughtful for others and to value them for their own worth.

Health. Gemini rules hands, arms, lungs and nervous system. Respiratory diseases and complaints of nervous origin are the most likely causes of trouble. The restless excitability of Geminians needs to be balanced by periods of rest and by the channelling of their energies in physical activities which result in healthy exhaustion.

Physically, Geminians are usually slender, wiry and quick of movement. They keep their youthful looks provided that nervous strain is avoided. Their eyes often reflect the liveliness of their minds.

Suitable careers will be in the field of communications, especially where there is opportunity to run the career in their own way. Employment as news reporter, courier, despatch rider, travel agent, chauffeur or commercial traveller, are suitable and self-employment as a journalist, author, dramatist or broadcaster would also be congenial. Careers in direct communications such as telephonist, teacher, lecturer and linguist will all be likely choices for the Geminian.

The glyph Ⅱ of Gemini is the Roman numeral for two, signifying the dual personality.

Words which are associated with Gemini: telephone, radio, roads, railways, letters, books, reports, speech, dexterity, handicrafts and all Mercurial words.

This description will apply substantially to anyone who has the Sun, Moon, Ascendant or Mercury in Gemini.

Venus in Gemini will show its principle of *harmony,* and *relationship* with *adaptability* and *versatility.* The interpretation of such a position might be as follows:

Your attitude to personal relationships is adaptable and versatile. This makes for fun and lightheartedness in flirtations, but suggests that you would find it difficult to be faithful to one. Your partner needs to be someone who appreciates your versatility in lovemaking and is not too worried about your roving eye!

♋ Cancer (The Crab)

The Sun is in this sign from 23 June to 23 July.

Cancer is of the *water* triplicity and the *cardinal* quadruplicity. The nature of water is to be *intuitive, emotional* and *negative*. The cardinal quality is *active*. Here we have the first complex sign of the zodiac. The ruler of Cancer is the *Moon*, which expresses *basic impulses* and *responses*.

The Cancerian is essentially the mother figure. Caring for a young child makes the Cancerian protective. *Active* in her role of Mother, she is bound by *emotional* ties to her child, *responsive* to his needs, and feeling *intuitively* what he requires of her. The desire for motherhood is a *basic impulse* in many women. This shows how all the ingredients in the mixture combine perfectly in the maternal type. The male Cancerian also enjoys jobs in which he is looking after other people as well as his own family and often feels protective towards his own pet projects.

It should be noted that this first complex sign of the zodiac is also the first where other people are considered by the native, albeit only the close relations and the family. Cancerians whose 'babies' are threatened are fiercely protective and tenacious, reminding us of the Crab with all the claws out, clinging on fiercely and ready to nip anyone who disturbs it.

As the Moon goes through its various phases causing fluctuations here on Earth, such as the ebb and flow of the tides, so the Cancerian swings from one mood to another. Kindness suddenly becomes 'crabiness', sensitivity and sympathy become hypersensitivity and self pity, and the children must then tread softly until mother is in a good mood again.

Cancerians are good home-makers and are not happy without a home of their own. They love their families 'warts and all' and will brook no criticism of them from an outsider. Although they appear to be tough, they are actually sensitive and easily hurt, but they are more likely to retaliate on behalf of a member of the family than they are for themselves.

They love collecting things and have a great feeling for anything to do with the past, so that they often collect antiques, or silver (the Moon metal), but sometimes all they collect is 'clutter' because they hate to throw anything away. It is hardly surprising that they have the reputation of being untidy.

Mentally, they have good memories, intuition and imagination. They tend to be unoriginal in their opinions and to adopt other people's ideas—a typical result of being a water sign (water adopts the shape of the container which holds it). They are great worriers, over both big and small issues and do not seem to be able to differentiate between the two.

Emotionally, they look for partners who will make good parents. They will make a comfortable home and be protective towards the partner as well as the family. They are romantic and warmly affectionate, despite their moodiness which may cause difficulties at times. They tend to give themselves much trouble in fussing over people simply because they enjoy looking after them. (It is often the

Cancerian mothers and fathers who continue to worry about their grown-up children, or who refuse to recognize that they are adults and entitled to run their own lives.)

Psychologically, Cancerians have a great neccessity for establishing a 'base'. Once this is achieved and they can settle down they are usually very stable characters, but a Cancerian without a home is lost and lonely. In the same way, there must be someone or something to 'look after' or they feel that life is not worth while.

Spiritually, they grow by cultivating a degree of detachment from others, by letting their loved ones be free and by learning to 'hold close with open hands'.

Health. The breasts, stomach and alimentary canal are ruled by Cancer. The digestive system is easily upset, probably due to the habit of worrying. Like all the water signs, Cancerians often tend to retain fluid and have weight problems.

Physically, Cancerians are round-faced (or 'moon-faced') and their features often show the tension lines of the confirmed worrier. A Cancerian Sun native will often resemble the Moon sign rather than the Cancerian Sun sign.

Suitable careers are all those which entail looking after people such as nursing, catering, domestic science, teaching and running hotels, also jobs connected with the sea or with the past such as fishing, sailing, auctioneering, being a historian, a curator or an antique dealer.

The glyph ♋ for Cancer has been described as resembling the breasts and also as the claws of the Crab. One could hardly think of two things which had so little in common, so the student should choose his own mnemonic.

Words associated with Cancer: motherhood, protectiveness, memory, home, food, tides, antiquity and all the Moon words.

The above description will apply substantially to all who have Sun or Moon in Cancer. Other planets will express *themselves* in this sign with *tenacity, sensitivity* and *protectiveness.*

The Sun is in this sign from 24 July to 23 August.

Leo (The Lion)
♌

The *fire* element with the *fixed* quality seems like a contradiction in terms, since fire is *enthusiastic, energetic* and *positive* while fixity is *cautious.* Unlike Aries (which was all fire, in effect), Leo has enough practicality to harness his enthusiasm and turn it to good use. The Sun is the ruler, emphasizing *vitality* and *power* which are characteristic of the Leo native.

The Sun was worshipped as a god and the lion is known as 'The King of the Forest', so it is not surprising the Leo natives instinctively feel that their place is at the top. Those who have learnt to use their power wisely have little difficulty in achieving positions of authority. They often have the kind of charisma which draws people to them, and this, combined with an optimistic and warm-hearted nature, ·means that they are never short of friends. They are natural leaders, and the practicality of the fixed quality makes them born organizers. Once this is recognized, Leos are not allowed to 'hide their light under a bushel' (even if they wanted to, which does not often happen) so they are often thrust into the prominent positions which they fill so well.

Self-orientation is not as brash as in the Arian, but Leo has a great sense of his own dignity and importance, which can develop into an arrogant and domineering attitude if it is not corrected in early life.

Leo natives have a great sense of drama and tend to be 'a little larger than life' but do not be put off by their effusive manner—the affection and warmth are quite genuine. They always have an urge to do things in a big way, and they can be wildly extravagant at times.

They are consummate actors, and though Fate may be twisting the Lion's tail quite severely, his courage, dignity and acting ability will hide the fact from the world.

It is interesting to note that the Leo native shares the quality of courage with the Arian (another fire sign), but where the Arian will *go out* to fight (cardinal), the Leo will *stand his ground* and *refuse to be moved* (fixed), in situations of danger.

This sign represents the age at which the father is head of the family—king in his own castle, caring for the weaker ones (his subjects) and expecting their adulation in return. If he does not get it, he can be crushing in his attitude, adopting a regal air and making the offender feel small.

Leos expect 'the lion's share' of all good things, but will provide generously for everyone else (whether they can afford it or not).

They are more easily hurt than they show, especially if they feel that they are not receiving their due amount of appreciation.

Mentally, the Leo has the conservatism of the fixed signs, as his opinions, once formed, remain unchanged. However, he is a constructive and practical thinker. Like all the fire signs, his ideas are on a large scale and he is not too concerned with details—he will 'organize' other people to see to them and will make sure they are not overlooked. He has a breadth of vision which again shows his courage—he is not afraid of tackling anything because of its size. This is one of the characteristics which helps Leo natives to become prominent in the world of theatre as producers and impressarios. Pageantry appeals to their sense of occasion, the desire to dress flamboyantly and to the sheer thrill which comes from staging something on a grand scale. Once they are committed to a project it will be carried through and be magnificently done.

Emotionally, Leos have the sexuality associated with all the fire signs, together with genuine and warm affection. They are intensely loyal to partners and friends and it is comparatively rare to find a lion without a mate. They are genuinely loving people and it is very important to them to feel that they are appreciated by others.

Psychologically, they feel the necessity of being in the limelight. Usually, they get their way by their sheer charm of manner and undoubted capability. However, difficulties arise when they are in subordinate positions.

Spiritually, the Leo native grows by learning to respect the qualities of others and to love them enough to place them on a equal footing with himself.

Health. The heart and the back come under the 'rulership' of Leo. Health is usually good, as vitality is high, but Leos tend to crowd their day with so much that there is no time for relaxation. They over-drive themselves and put strain on the heart. They will often take on too much and then cope with it, refusing all offers of help (which would be an affront to their dignity). This may give their ego a boost, but does nothing for their health, and it is easy to see why 'top' businessmen so often suffer from coronaries.

Physically, Leos are often immediately recognizable by their 'sunny' looks, and their positive reactions to meeting new people. They have a dignified manner and walk and the hair is often framed round the face and a little unruly (like a lion's).

Suitable careers are any where organization and breadth of vision are necessary, and, of course, positions of authority. Leos are found as managing directors, chairmen of companies and public relations officers in the business world. In sport as professional sportsmen of all kinds, in the theatre as actors, producers and impressarios and also in the luxury trades, especially as goldsmiths and jewellers.

The glyph for Leo ♌ is said to resemble the lion's tail.

Words associated with Leo: regal, warmth, fire, kingship, fatherhood, jewels, gold, drama, sunshine, happiness, courage, breadth, creativity and all 'Sun' words.

The above description will apply substantially to anyone who has Sun, Ascendant or Moon is Leo. Other planets in Leo will manifest in their own particular way, but with *power* and *creativity.*

Virgo ♍ (The Virgin)

The Sun is in this sign from 24 August to 23 September.

It is of the *earth* element and *mutable* quality. This gives a mixture of *practicality, reliability* and *negativity,* with the *adaptability* of the quality. Like Gemini, Virgo is Mercury-ruled so it is *communicative.*

Where two signs share the same rulership, it is interesting to see how the planet works with different mixtures of elements and qualities. We saw in Gemini, a 'pure' Mercurial type, with the air element enhancing the communicative nature. Here, in Virgo, the emphasis is still on communications and the mentality, but the Gemini 'airy-fairy' attitude has gone and the practicality of earth gives Virgo the means to use Mercury's gifts in material ways. Office routine, which was anathema to the Geminian, will be liked by the Virgoan, and, in general, the mind is more disciplined.

The chief characteristic of the Virgoans is the faculty to deal with detailed and intricate work. They are the people you will find working to thousandths of an inch. Such work is *critical* and they will bring all their considerable powers of concentration and their dexterity to it. The corollary of this is that they become critical and fussy over details in other areas of their lives. Precision is important to them. Their minds need to know how things work and they will often take immense trouble to find out. They always strive for perfection and only give up such tasks with difficulty as they hate being beaten or accepting anything less than the best.

The connection with the Virgin is shown in many ways and there is a desire for purity, wholesomeness of food and sometimes obsessive tidiness and cleanness. Most Virgo natives can not bear to have anything wrong with them—it 'niggles' at them and they can not let it alone until things are right again—so they often have a great interest in hygiene, diet and all matters connected with health.

We can think of Virgo as the spinster aunt of a few generations ago, who stayed at home looking after her parents, became an unpaid servant, in effect, and eventually a fussy 'old maid'. The desire to serve their fellow-men is very important to Virgoans and almost all of them accomplish this, either in their work or in a part-time activity. They prefer to work in the background, being too shy to be happy in the limelight. Like Martha, they are 'careful and troubled about many things' and the impossibility of getting all the little details just right probably accounts for an apparent lack of self-confidence. However, most of them have a very good (and justified) opinion of their own capabilities and their thorough attitude to hard work. As a result, they find it difficult to delegate work to others, obviously believing that it will not be done so well as they would do it themselves. They then become critical and fault-finding in a 'nit-picking' way which others find irritating.

No doubt it is this which keeps so many Virgoans in subordinate positions, as there is no doubt of their capacity to put in a more-than-adequate day's work. Virgoans have to be perpetually busy and Mercury seems to supply them with abundant nervous energy. It is true that a lot of it is dissipated in an attempt to get every chore done (some of which would seem quite unnecessary to anyone but a Virgoan).

Mentally, the Virgoan has the sharp, critical faculties which enable him to assess and analyse. The Mercurial quickness to learn is balanced by the retentiveness of earth, so that he is able to communicate what he has learnt to others. However, he finds it difficult to envisage large projects and because of his obsession with details, he can lose sight of the main objective—in effect he 'can't see the wood for the trees'. Not for him, then, the organizing ability of Leo—but if Leo will organize the occasion Virgo will be his right hand man.

Emotionally, the Virgoan never lacks appreciative friends, who benefit from his kindness and genuine desire to help others. Despite this, he often finds it difficult to appreciate others because he can see all their faults. He is reserved and this can make him appear cold at times (another Mercurial trait). Sexual feelings are not strong and his partner will need to come to terms with his desire for perfection. (The Venus and Mars positions will show the sexual feelings more clearly than the Sun sign.)

Psychologically, the Virgoan finds difficulty in coming to terms with his own imperfections. Although he is highly critical of others, he is also critical of himself. Never measuring up to his own standards, he can use his targets as a challenge to enable him to get as near to perfection as possible, or he can see them as being forever inaccessible and become discouraged and frustrated.

Spiritually, he progresses by cultivating tolerance—both to his own weaknesses and to those of others. Exercises in 'putting himself in the other's place' can be invaluable in overcoming the tendency to see things only from his own point of view.

Health. Virgo 'rules' the hands (like Gemini), the nervous system (Mercury) and intestines. Illnesses tend to be of the nervous type, caused by over-anxiety and the compulsion to have everything just right, also by the habit of self-criticism. Such anxiety affects the digestion and gives rise to intestinal troubles.

Physically, they tend to keep their youthful looks. They usually have a kindly expression and the eyes are often the best feature.

Suitable careers are found in matters connected with health, such as a naturopath, dietician, public health officer, social worker; in the communications media as broadcaster, teacher, lecturer, drama critic; in precision work of all kinds and as analyst and statistician and in business as secretary or civil servant. Craftsmanship of all types is indicated by manual dexterity, especially that which requires attention to detail.

The glyph ♍ for Virgo is said to resemble the coils of the snake that brought about the downfall of Adam and Eve, ending in a characteristic female symbol (compare Scorpio).

Words associated with Virgo: work, natural, harvest, diet, corn, animals, health, teaching, precision, criticism, analysis, handiwork and the 'Mercury' words.

This description will apply substantially to anyone who has Sun, Ascendant, Moon or Mercury in Virgo. Other planets in Virgo will manifest according to their own nature but with *detail* and *precision*.

Polarity

We have now reached the half-way stage in our descriptions of the various signs. Each one of the first six signs has its opposite number among the second six. If you look at the diagram (Figure 2), you will see that the pairs oppose each other across the chart and are said to be 'in opposition'. (You will learn more about this in the chapter on Aspects.) They are also described as being *in polarity* since they are in the same relationship as the North Pole is to the South Pole (see Figure 2). They balance each other, in many ways, one of which is that of health; e.g. Arian headaches may well originate from kidney troubles (the part of the body ruled by Libra which is in polarity to Aries).

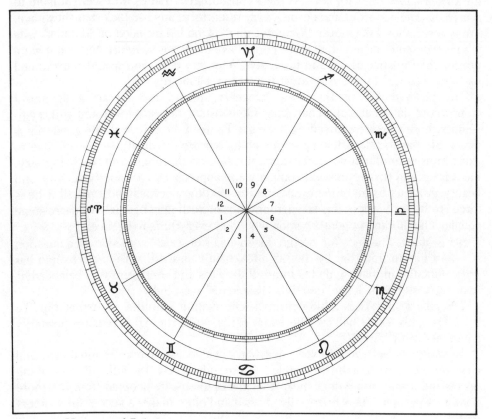

Figure 2. Houses and Polarity.

The first six signs represented types who in general terms, are mainly concerned with their own personal activities. The second six signs are more concerned with their relationships with others and they tend to act in a wider sphere. This will become more apparent as we study the meanings of the 'Houses' later.

♎ *Libra (The Scales)*

The Sun is in this sign from 24 September to 23 October.

The mixture is the *air* element combined with the *cardinal* quality; in other words, *communicative, intellectual* and *positive* elements with an *active* quality. The rulership of Venus adds *harmony* and *relationships* are emphasized.

Venus is another planet which 'rules' two signs. In Taurus the earth element showed Venus manifesting in practical and cautious ways. The Taurean wants to 'hold close' those with whom he forms a relationship, seeing them as *his* belongings. The Libran, with the air element prominent, brings to the Venusian relationship a need to *communicate* with the partner. He seeks for a *balanced* partnership, and desires harmony with one special person above all. He tends to feel unfulfilled in life if he fails to make such a relationship.

Libra is the sign of the Scales (or the Balance), and the feeling for justice is strong in the native. A negative use of this trait sometimes causes Librans to be full of self-pity—'It's not *fair*', is their constant cry. They often seem unable to accept that life is *not* fair and become very resentful of any bad luck that they have. 'Why me?' they ask—never 'Why not me?'. One is reminded of Socrates' wife who is reputed to have said that she could have borne his sentence better if it were not for the injustice of it—and his reply 'Why, my dear, you would not rather I had deserved it?' (Surely she must have been a Libran!)

The positive use of this trait, however, makes the Libran a delightful companion, diplomatic and charming. He is usually a peace lover and will try to reunite those who are quarrelling. Like the Taurean, he enjoys all the good things which life has to offer. Being *positive* and *outgoing* (cardinal), he is well able to exert himself to obtain what he wants, but he also thoroughly enjoys being lazy. He relaxes and thrives in good company and appreciates good food and wine and beauty in all its forms. In contrast, he can become nervous and even ill if he is forced to live or work in dismal surroundings or with uncongenial or quarrelsome people. The Libran is a gentle person who likes everything to be nice.

Being able to 'balance' or 'weigh' (as in a pair of scales) both sides of a question is a very Libran trait, but by the same token this means that the native often has great difficulty in making up his mind. If the pros and cons seem well balanced he may even 'sit on the fence' (surely a 'balancing' act?) forever.

The polarity to Aries is shown in the contrasting attitudes to partnership. To the Libran, his 'other half' is a necessity of life, while the Arian remains primarily concerned with himself.

Mentally, as one would expect with an air sign, the Libran is intelligent and clear thinking. Although this enables him to judge fairly, the difficulty in making up his mind may sometimes mean that his opinions are adopted from the more dominant partner. He is financially shrewd and often makes a successful business man.

Emotionally, he is more Venusian than the Taurean. The necessity of finding a partner makes him tend to rush into love affairs—being 'in love with love' is a common state for the Libran. His charm and thoughtfulness together with warm affection and a desire to please make him an irresistible lover and friend. As he is quick to 'weigh up' faults, however, he is liable to fall out of love just as quickly.

Psychologically, his difficulties stem from the obsession with fairness (balance) and he needs to cultivate a more philosophical attitude to the disappointments of life.

Spiritually, he progresses by the realization of his own self-sufficiency, combined with a 'reaching out' to all others and not just to the one partner, on whom he is inclined to depend.

Health. The kidneys and lumbar region are 'ruled' by Libra. Normally, health is good, due to the Libran's good sense in keeping to well-balanced food and activities, but there is a tendency to trouble in this area, and to headaches (Aries polarity).

Physically. Librans have regular features and a pleasant expression. They are said to be the most beautiful of all the zodiacal types (Venus rulership).

Suitable careers are to be found in all the beauty and luxury trades such as artist, hairdresser, beautician, antique dealer, jeweller; also in 'go-between' situations such as diplomat, receptionist, auctioneer, valuer, solicitor.

The glyph ≏ for Libra is the sign of the balance, reminiscent of the old 'milkmaid's yoke' which went over the shoulders and balanced a pail on each side.

Words associated with Libra: partnership, tact, charm, relaxation, affection, beauty, art, compromise, diplomacy, laziness, justice.

The above description will apply substantially to all who have Sun, Moon, Ascendant or Venus in Libra. Other planets will manifest according to their own natures but with *harmony* and *diplomacy.*

Scorpio (The Scorpion and Eagle) ♏

The Sun is in this sign from 24 October to 22 November.

Being a member of the *water* triplicity, Scorpio has *emotional* and *intuitive* elements and is *negative* (introspective); *fixed* quadruplicity adds the quality of caution, indicating that the emotions are used in practical ways.

Modern astrologers give the rulership of this sign to Pluto, the most recently discovered of the planets, which appears to have a *regenerating* and *refining* influence. The older rulership was given to Mars, because the Scorpio native was recognized as being passionate and intense, but the correlation with Pluto appears to be more appropriate, as these people often demonstrate the urge to 'get rid of' hampering conditions to make way for new life (regeneration). There seems to be a continual process of refining—being tried in the fire of intensity, and emerging 'regenerated'. Scorpios often make many changes of direction as they go through life—usually to the great surprise of other people, as they keep quiet about their affairs, so that they have come to be regarded as secretive. I believe that this is because their decisions are made intuitively—common sense does not come into it—and because they realize that their 'reasons' would not seem valid to other people they say nothing until their plans come to fruition. They will be equally reticent about other people's secrets and are the safest confidants in the zodiac.

Scorpio people feel deeply (water element) and the very intensity of their feelings lends a passionate drive to all that they undertake. Life, at all levels, is lived to the full—they work, play, make love, study, investigate with a single-mindedness which deserves to get results—and often does. No wonder that other people find them fascinating.

It is easy to see that such intensity, wrongly directed, can cause havoc. These traits will do much more harm, if ill directed, than those of Gemini, for instance, who has much enthusiasm, but little passion. Consequently, Scorpio has often been described in the past as though it were the 'worst sign' of the Zodiac. In fact, though passion wrongly used can result in the criminal and violent type (the scorpion with the sting) the aspiring Scorpio native spends a great deal of time and effort in work and causes which he considers worth while, endeavouring with all his resources (and they are many) to 'reach for the heights' (the eagle) in whatever he undertakes.

The polarity with Taurus is shown in the native's attitude to his own feelings. In Taurus, they were on a very personal level, concerned with 'my belongings'. Scorpio's deep and passionate feelings are directed to other people (see *Careers,* in particular). Natives of both signs tend to jealousy.

Mentally, Scorpios have good analytical minds and a great desire to get to the bottom of problems, but they tend to solve them by intuition ('I feel' rather than 'I think'), usually with success. The mind is penetrating and sharp, and they use telling words and phrases. Their streak of ruthlessness can be discerned in the cutting, sarcastic wit with which they can quell an opponent, when necessary (the sting in the scorpion's tail).

Emotionally, the Scorpio native is a loyal friend and a passionate lover. He needs to find release in sexual activity but, at the same time, his feelings must be deeply engaged. The beautiful emotional and 'hidden' meaning of love appeals to him and he will be faithful to his chosen partner. With both friends and lovers he can become vindictive, jealous and quarrelsome if his feelings are injured.

Psychologically, the necessity to penetrate and explore can lead to dangerous experiments 'to find out'. The native should be aware of the dangers and bring his penetrating mind to bear on the problem. This tendency can be channelled to suitable careers where the results may be worth the risk. He should also be aware of the fascination which the purely sensory holds for him (Taurean polarity).

Spiritually, he progresses by means of the 'refining' process, accepting that some things can never be known and respecting the eternal secrets. He needs to cultivate peace.

Health. The generative organs are ruled by Scorpio. Illnesses tend to be those involving the genitals, bladder, throat and nasal passages. Rest and especially *mental* relaxation are necessary to keep the native in good health.

Physically, the Scorpio native often has heavy features and the eyes are often striking. A full lower lip is common. Like the other water signs he tends to become overweight easily.

Suitable careers. Anything which is worth doing for its own sake and which requires all his energies will appeal to the Scorpion. Probing into 'hidden things' and 'bringing them to light', such as detective work and analysis, is very Plutonian. All matters of birth, life and death interest him, probably because of the mystery which surrounds such 'deep' subjects. Scorpios are found in careers which *actively* help others, such as surgeon, spiritual healer, psychiatrist, psychologist, and in work dealing with the public welfare—policeman, detective, undertaker, research worker, analytical chemist.

The glyph ♏ for Scorpio is the serpent coil with the addition of the masculine sign (see Virgo). It is worth noting that, traditionally, Virgo and Scorpio were combined in one sign. They appear to have in common the analytical mind and the urge to work for others.

Words associated with Scorpio: regeneration, passion, research, creation, birth, death, sex, secretiveness.

The description of Scorpio will apply substantially to all who have Sun, Moon, Ascendant, Pluto (and probably Mars) in Scorpio. Other planets will function in Scorpio with *passion* and *intensity*.

The Sun is in this sign from 23 November to 22 December.

Sagittarius ♐
(The Archer)

Sagittarius shows the *fire* element combined with the *mutable* quality, giving *energy, enthusiasm* and *adaptability*. It is a *positive* sign and the ruling planet is Jupiter, expressing *expansion* and *maturity*.

There is no doubt about the rulership in the case of the Sagittarian. Jupiter's influence is shown in the optimistic, relaxed and 'free' attitude which he takes to life. Freedom is very important to him (that is, when he thinks about it—usually he just takes it for granted). It is his and it rarely occurs to him that anyone might take it from him. 'Happy-go-lucky' is a good description of him—as long as no one attempts to fence him in. He gets distressed quickly in confining circumstances, should these arise, but they very rarely do as he is expert at avoiding anything (and anyone) which may tie him down. For the same reason, he is very much an open air person and enjoys long walks and other open air sports—he likes to feel that the freedom of the wide countryside is his, together with the freedom of the wide-ranging mind.

He is tolerant and expansive by nature—'Live and let live' might be his motto—and, in true Jupiterian fashion, he takes a wide view of most projects and cannot be bothered with details. This can sometimes make him superficial and careless, but do not let his easy-going attitude deceive you. He has all the 'go' of the fire element and he has the great urge to explore, both physically and mentally. His greatest enemy is boredom and he constantly sets himself new tasks to accomplish (targets for 'the Archer' to aim at). The wide-ranging mind means that he very often studies over a wide field on a superficial level, but if he finds something which really interests him he is capable of deep study and can become absorbed in it. He is capable of planning on a vast scale (very like Leo, another fire sign) but will not concentrate on detail. Some of his ideas will be too wildly extravagant to come to fruition, but given a good 'back-up' team, he will make a great and enthusiastic leader for an ambitious project. A challenge, whether mental or physical, will stimulate him. This is one reason why he is often a successful sportsman.

The polarity with Gemini is expressed in his adaptability and the wide range of his interests. Both share a dislike of being fenced in. Like Gemini, also, he takes a superficial interest in many things.

Mentally, he is capable of deep and profound study on subjects which really interest him. His mind is versatile and penetrating. His hunches have a habit of turning out right. His optimism and far-seeing mentality enable him to carry out large projects when he has trained himself to deal with one problem at a time, otherwise the necessity of coping with details may mean that they never get off the ground. He is often a very good linguist.

Emotionally, he is as ardent as one would expect of a fire sign. On a friendship level he makes a jovial 'hail-fellow-well-met' companion. His tolerant and expansive attitude makes him welcome a wide variety of friends. On both levels, however, the threat to personal freedom will be dodged as soon as it is sensed. Married Sagittarians need partners who understand this and will not make them feel tied. Lots of them never marry. The old saying used to be 'If you don't catch them young you won't catch them at all.' A partnership, to a Sagittarian is a marriage of true minds—he needs a partner who will stimulate his own intellect.

Psychologically, the Sagittarian's difficulties often stem from impracticality. There is a necessity for the large vision but they often lack the power to achieve it through diffusing their energies, or through being too grandiose in their ideas.

Spiritually, they have great resources. They are philosophers and they recognize the value of detachment from worldly cares. They progress by learning to give others the freedom which they take as a right for themselves, and in general to care about other people. (Tolerance is not the same as caring—in many ways it is the direct opposite—'You do not matter to me, therefore it is easy to tolerate you'.)

Health. The hips, thighs and liver come under the rulership of Sagittarius. Illnesses are likely to affect these parts. Tiredness is usually mental, not physical, and is often caused by boredom. Sagittarians need plenty of exercise in the air to keep healthy, especially using the hips and thighs, such as walking, swimming, horse-riding. 'Liverishness' is very Jupiterian and can be caused by too rich a diet.

Physically, the Sagittarian body is tall and rangy. There is often a high forehead and a slightly receding chin, giving a rather 'horsy' look to the face. (This is particularly true of those with Ascendant in Sagittarius.) H.R.H. Princess Anne has a typical Sagittarian look (and the typical love of horses), but the sign is not prominent in her chart, which shows how careful one should be in attempting to judge zodiacal signs from personal appearance.

Suitable careers are found in all outdoor work, especially if connected with animals—horses in particular; also in all forms of sport and exploration and in the intellectual professions such as teacher, writer, don, lawyer, priest, philosopher and translator of foreign languages.

The glyph ↑ for Sagittarius is the arrow of the Archer. Mythology often depicted him as a man on horseback (or as the Centaur, a man with the body of a horse) thus correlating with the Sagittarian love of horses and of long journeys. Gardeners will also know of *Sagita,* the arrow-headed plant.

Words associated with Sagitarrius: tolerance, philosophy, religion, travel, space, freedom, ideals, morals, optimism, justice, exaggeration, maturity, and all the Jupiterian words.

This description will apply substantially to all who have Sun, Ascendant, Moon and Jupiter in Sagittarius. Other planets will express *themselves* with *freedom* and *tolerance.*

The Sun is in this sign from 23 December to 19 January.

Capricorn ♑
(The Goat)

The *earth* element which is *static, practical* and *negative* combines here with the *cardinal* quality of *activity*. The rulership of Saturn indicates *limitation, discipline* and *responsibility*. This unlikely mixture is adequately represented by the character of the Capricornian. He welcomes discipline and responsibility, realizing that they are necessary if anything is to be achieved. This attitude shows his practicality and that he has 'both feet on the ground' (earth). But he *is* interested in achievement and the cardinal quality of *activity* is used in enabling him to realize his ambitions. He has a constant, active drive to reach the top of his profession, but his way is by continual effort, patience and sheer 'stickability'.

The Saturn rulership often gives 'an old head on young shoulders', and even as children Capricornians get on well with older people (sometimes better than with their contemporaries). They seem to have their own in-built sense of timing. They will never be hurried, in fact they will not even move, if they think the time is not right. 'Slow and steady' is their motto, so that they tend to reach their goal late in life, but every step has been consolidated (earth).

Like all the earth signs, the Capricornian is constructive and can make detailed plans, and once his mind is made up he will not change it. He has a dry sense of humour and can act the giddy goat if the fit takes him.

It is easy, and fatal, for his opponents to underestimate him. He is not showy, 'pushy' or aggressive, but his one attribute that beats everyone else is that he will never give up. Like the mountain goat, he doesn't rush up the steep inclines, but he will plod on, sure-footed, until he reaches the top. His perseverance is formidable.

The polarity with Cancer is shown in the need for security, which to the Cancerian means home life and to the Capricornian the security which is obtained by a position of stability in the business world. Both are great worriers, and both are fond of children.

Mentally, the Capricornian is slow to learn, think and act, but will do all three thoroughly and deliberately. Like the Taurean (another earth sign), he retains what is acquired, and although it may seem unlikely in early school days he will benefit from further education, which he will value. He has the patience and discipline to acquire knowledge and apply it.

Emotionally, he tends to be cool, but will be a faithful husband and a good parent. He will see his main role in the family as being that of a good provider. There is a tendency in Capricornians to bottle up their emotions, which can lead to nervous troubles later in life.

Psychologically, the driving ambition and the necessity to achieve can cause difficulties if the Capricornian does not recognize his limitations in the inability to think and act *quickly.* In some professions this precludes the possibility of reaching the top. If this happens, Capricornians can become very disappointed and depressed. In such a case, they would do well to accept the situation and seek for fulfilment on a more domestic level.

Spiritually, they need to relate more to other people, and to accept their limitations as an aid to growth.

Health. Like Saturn, Capricorn 'rules' the skin and bones—that is, the skeletal system, especially the knees. Joints tend to be weak. Skin troubles are likely, also diseases associated with cold and old age, such as rheumatism. Capricornians need to make a conscious effort to stop worrying about insoluble problems and trivial matters, otherwise food is not digested properly and digestive troubles are caused (Cancer polarity). It is important that emotions should be released (hobbies can be used for this purpose), otherwise this adds to nervous tension.

Physically, the Capricornian often looks saturnine. He tends to be dark-eyed and dark-haired. A long, bony face is characteristic, often with worry lines on the forehead. He walks and talks slowly and deliberately.

Suitable careers will be in practical, routine or organizing work, such as government official, administrator, etc., or those in the public eye, such as politician, head teacher, orator, also as an osteopath (see *Health*), mathematician, scientist, engineer and builder. The Capricornian's ambition is for *power* not glory, and he does not mind being 'the power behind the throne'.

The glyph ♑ for Capricorn looks a little like the goat's horn with the tail of the fish (the mythology is that of a goat-fish or sea-goat). It is perhaps more easily remembered as the horns plus the 'S' for Saturn (in script form).

Words associated with Capricorn: aspiring, responsible, prudent, cold, self-contained, perservering, methodical, modest, exacting, plodding, reliable and all Saturnian words.

This description will apply substantially to all those who have Ascendant, Sun, Moon or Saturn in Capricorn. Other planets will express *themselves* in Capricorn with *prudence* and *aspiration*.

Aquarius (The Water-Bearer) ♒

The Sun is in this sign from 20 January to 19 February.

The *air* element is combined with the *fixed* quality, to give one of the most complex characters in the zodiac. Could anything sound more unlikely than fixed air? The ruler is Uranus adding to the unusual combination the Uranian desire for *change* and *personal freedom,* with the element which is *communicative, intellectual* and *positive* and the quality of *caution.* Let us see how this works out in the Aquarian character.

On first acquaintance, the Aquarian appears to be a very friendly character, gregarious and humanitarian in his outlook and this impression is a valid one. However, as the friendship grows he shows a reluctance to become intimate with anyone and it is possible to know an Aquarian closely (even to be married to him) and to come to the conclusion that you do not know him at all. Like all the air signs, his emotions are cool—but there is more to it than that.

He is afraid of having his privacy invaded, for *the* most important thing to him is his personal freedom. Unlike the Sagittarian, he is constantly on the alert against anything or anyone who threatens it. Naturally, with his humanitarian tendencies, he believes strongly that everyone should be free and he is prepared to fight for his belief. However, his *caution* often stops him from becoming a rebel in an active way and his revolutionary tendencies will show mostly in the exchange of *ideas* (air).

These traits seem to mirror very accurately the characteristics of this Aquarian age. The motto of the present generation seems to be 'Brotherhood—with personal freedom'. Everyone free to 'do his own thing', yet everyone working together in the cause of justice and humanity. Like the Aquarian mixture of 'fixed air', it sounds an impossible combination and is the key to the complexity of the Aquarian Age (and of the Aquarian character).

Aquarians are what Americans call 'clubbable'. They are often to be found in organizations, especially those with humanitarian aims, and they will be prepared to work voluntarily for such bodies, and in general, they are usually willing to help those in need.

The polarity with Leo is shown in the *fixity* of the native. Both are dominating characters, holding steadfastly to their own opinions, even though the Aquarian's aims are 'free as air' and intended to embrace all humanity.

The friendliness of Aquarius is more apparent than deep—with Leo it is usually very real and warm (though Leos, also, will often call everyone 'darling' without meaning very much, in a typical 'actress' fashion).

Mentally, the Aquarian is intelligent, original and inventive. He is a free-thinker, often years ahead of his time, and it does not worry him at all that he may be the only one in step. Tolerance may be shown, but it could well be to cover up the fact that he is indifferent to the opinions of others, so, again, it may be more apparent than real. There is often genuine intuition, but combined with his other traits, it may manifest, at times, as sheer crankiness.

Emotionally, the coolness of *air* and the deep necessity for freedom does not make close relationships easy. Although they are loyal and faithful to their partners, feelings are only expressed with difficulty, if at all. Aquarians need partners who are equally cool and who will not make them feel confined within the marriage bond.

Psychologically, their difficulties arise when they are forced to accept limitations, as these are incompatible with freedom. They need to learn how to be free within confining conditions. Many of them do recognize and accept the need for *discipline,* which reminds us that the old rulership of this sign was given to Saturn.

Spiritually, they progress by extending to others equal rights to the freedom which they find so important for themselves. The true achievement of brotherhood is their goal, and this implies a caring attitude which does not come naturally to the cool, airy Aquarian.

Health. The ankles and the circulatory system are ruled by Aquarius. (Circulation is another *communication* system, like the nervous system of Gemini —correlation with *air*.) Sprains and fractures of shin and ankle are possible sources of trouble, also circulatory illnesses, e.g. hardening of the arteries. (Leo polarity with the heart, which is dependent for its functioning on the blood circulation.)

Physically, the Aquarian is usually good-looking, having regular features, good facial bone structure and a rather long face.

Suitable careers for Aquarians are those which require inventiveness and originality, also those dealing with scientific or unusual subjects such as inventor, astronaut, astrologer, astronomer, lecturer, scientist, research worker, writer, orator; also in work for others, such as charity worker, scientific adviser to developing countries, etc. Careers in broadcasting and television often appeal. As with all the air subjects, careers which give the maximum amount of freedom are best.

The glyph ≈ for Aquarius resembles waves. As this is not a water sign, it is, perhaps, better to think of them as radio waves (something transmitted by *air*).

45

Words associated with Aquarius: freedom, originality, inventiveness, intuition, revolution, disruption, reform, waves, societies and all Uranian words.

This description will apply substantially to all who have Ascendant, Sun, Moon or Uranus in Aquarius. Other planets will express *themselves* in Aquarius with *independence* and *unconventionality.*

♓ *Pisces (The Fishes)*

The Sun is in this sign from 20 February to 21 March.

The combination of *water* element with *mutable* quality makes the Piscean an uncomplicated character. It seems quite reasonable for water to be *adaptable,* as it takes the shape of any container into which it is poured. Neptune is the ruler, bringing *intuition* and *nebulousness* to the *sensitive, emotional* and *negative* element and the *adaptable* quality.

Such a mixture results in a character which is supersensitive and impressionable, influenced by other people and also by its own inner consciousness. The old rulership of this sign was given to Jupiter, and it is true that most Pisceans are naturally optimistic and happy—and they want to stay that way. Furthermore, as they are so sensitive, anything in the way of trouble affects them more than most people, so like their sign, the fishes, they glide away out of difficulties wherever possible.

Many are good philosophers and religion (not necessarily orthodox) means a great deal to them. Like the Sagittarian, they realize the value of detachment from this life. All this is very Jupiterian, but there can be no doubt that the Piscean is truly Father Neptune's child. Like the sea, he can be calm and tranquil one minute and assailed by hidden tempests the next. His sensitivity has picked up a vibration of trouble, as water conducts electricity, long before most people have any hint of it. This makes him a prey to unknown apprehensions—no wonder, then, that he seeks to escape when life gets a bit too much for him. Many Pisceans do this by going into a daydream world, by getting lost in a book or piece of music or by going into a retreat. Some will resort to drink or drugs for this purpose, but it is interesting that many more of them, with their strong sense of intuition, seem to have a built-in warning system about this danger and will not touch either. This sense should not be ignored, since they are particularly susceptible to drug-poisoning.

In trying to avoid all discomforts, most Pisceans treat them as though they did not exist for as long as possible, and so self-deception is a common failing (and even deliberate deception of others, if it will make life more pleasant for them). They like everyone to be happy, and are quite prepared to help others who are in trouble. Their kind and gentle nature, easily moved to tears, makes them react positively to anyone who needs their sympathy. Consequently, they are never short of friends and are usually well-loved. It would be a tragedy for the warm-hearted Piscean if this were not so—he can imagine nothing worse than being unloved.

The polarity with Virgo is shown in the necessity to help others, and a life of service is often chosen by both. Both are adaptable and both suffer from nervous and digestive troubles, caused by worrying.

Mentally, the Piscean tends to adapt to others to the extent that he adopts their ideas and changes his mind according to his company. He is intelligent, however, and highly intuitive. He feels, rather than thinks, that something is right or wrong. He has plenty of ideas and inspiration, but these tend to be *nebulous* (or lack shape—*water*) unless there are more practical qualities shown elsewhere in the birth chart. When the inspiration can be harnessed, the world of make-believe is expressed in the works of the poet, writer or actor.

Emotionally, the native is a good lover and a true romantic. There is a tendency to fall in love with love because he may see the girl of his dreams instead of the one he has actually got. He can be over-sentimental, but he will make a caring lover—always putting the loved-one first. His warmth and his genuine desire to make others happy also ensures that he has plenty of friends.

Psychologically, the Piscean has a great need for privacy and becomes emotionally exhausted and drained by too much contact with others. Sometimes the harshness of the world can be altogether too much for him. He needs to cultivate detachment.

Spiritually he has great resources (old rulership of Jupiter). Although others may see his wish to escape from the world as sheer cowardice, it appears to be a much more subtle thing. The Piscean attitude appears to have been correctly interpreted by W. S. Landor—'I strove with none, for none was worth my strife.' His way of progress is by getting involved—by giving service which forgets self, without letting the world destroy this inner peace. This water sign, more than either of the others, shows the hidden depths and unfathomable nature of the sea; so often described as 'the unknown element'.

Health. The feet are under the rulership of Pisces, and also the pituitary gland, which controls the rhythmic activities of the body. Illnesses are likely to be caused by nervous stress and there is often a strong allergy to drugs (also to fish or water which are not absolutely fresh).

Physically, the Piscean, like all the water signs, tends to be well-rounded. The face is sensitive, eyes prominent, often beautiful, and the lips are full. Even overweight Pisceans are light on their feet—like a dancer.

Suitable careers, are found in all the arts, especially as dancer (rhythm), actor, poet, writer; those where intuition is used such as medium, psychic artist, therapist; those where others are cared for such as nurse, doctor, priest, and all professions connected with the sea.

The glyph for Pisces is ♓ . This represents the two fishes swimming in opposite directions, but bound together.

Words associated with Pisces: mysticism, intuition, sensitivity, abstracts, rhythm, fluidity, liquids, escape, pretence, sleep, dreams, unworldliness, acting, meditation, inspiration and all the Neptunian words.

The above description will apply substantially to all those who have Ascendant, Sun, Moon or Neptune in Pisces. Other planets express *themselves* in this sign with *intuition* and *adaptability*.

We have now reached the end of the descriptions of the zodiacal signs. The subject is inexhaustible and the student is advised to read as widely as possible. The planets are said to be 'exalted' in some of the signs. This means that, while they are not the rulers, they work well in that sign. Similarly, they are said to be 'in detriment' if they are in the opposite sign to the one which they rule, and in 'fall' when in the opposite sign to the one in which they are exalted. A summary follows, but modern astrologers do not consider 'detriment' and 'fall' to be important.

The Sun ☉	rules	Leo ♌
	is exalted in	Aries ♈
	is in detriment in	Aquarius ♒
	is in fall in	Libra ♎

The Moon ☽	rules	Cancer ♋
	is exalted in	Taurus ♉
	is in detriment in	Capricorn ♑
	is in fall in	Scorpio ♏

Mercury ☿	rules	Gemini and Virgo ♊ ♍
	is exalted in	Virgo ♍
	is in detriment in	Sagittarius ♐
	is in fall in	Pisces ♓

Venus ♀	rules	Taurus and Libra ♉ ♎
	is exalted in	Pisces ♓
	is in detriment in	Aries ♈
	is in fall in	Virgo ♍

Mars ♂	rules	Aries ♈
	is exalted in	Capricorn ♑
	is in detriment in	Libra ♎
	is in fall in	Cancer ♋

Jupiter ♃	rules	Sagittarius ♐
	is exalted in	Cancer ♋
	is in detriment in	Gemini ♊
	is in fall in	Capricorn ♑

Saturn ♄	rules	Capricorn ♑
	is exalted in	Libra ♎
	is in detriment in	Cancer ♋
	is in fall in	Aries ♈

Uranus ♅	rules	Aquarius ♒
	is exalted in	Scorpio ♏
	is in detriment in	Leo ♌
	is in fall in	Aries ♈

Neptune	rules	Pisces ♓
♆	is exalted in	Leo ♌
	is in detriment in	Virgo ♍
	is in fall in	Aquarius ♒
Pluto	rules	Scorpio ♏
♇	is in detriment in	Taurus ♉

Exaltation and fall have not been determined for Pluto, and those for Neptune are of recent origin.

Writers of astrological books have often suggested well known people as representative of a certain zodiacal sign. Unfortunately, these have a habit of dating. It is suggested, as an *aide-memoire,* that the student should consider the following 'cast' for a grand variety show, and, perhaps, devise an alternative cast for himself.

The Variety Show

Mr & Mrs Aries	Knife-throwing act (danger, courage, aim).
Miss Taurus	Singer.
Mr Taurus	Backer. (This must be a good show, or he would not risk the money!)
Mr Gemini and Mr Virgo	Cross-talk Comedians. (Virgo is the 'straight man' or 'feed'.)
Mr Cancer	Memory Man (his wife is in charge of the catering).
Miss Leo	Dramatic actress.
Mr Leo	Impressario. (What else?)
Miss Libra	Trapeze artist.
Mr Libra	Juggler. (Both using 'balance'.)
Mr Scorpio	Hypnotist.
The Sagittarians	Equestrian troupe.
Mr Capricorn	The administrator.
Mr Aquarius	The electrician and special effects man.
Miss Pisces	The dancer.
Mr Pisces	Thought reader.

EXERCISES

Note: Before attempting the exercises, learn the symbols and the order in which the signs follow each other.

1. Write your own description of the roles of the Sun and Moon in the birth chart.
2. Do the same for the other planets, in the usual order (i.e. from Mercury, the nearest to the Sun, as given in Chapter 1).
3. Which two planets would you most like to have prominent in your own birth chart? Give your reasons.
4. Copy the diagram on page 26 (Figure 1) and add the approximate dates when the Sun is in each sign.
5. Imagine that you can choose your own Sun sign and Moon sign. Which combination appeals to you most? Give reasons in detail.
6. Taking your own Sun sign and Moon sign as in Exercise 5, say what you think would be the effect of reversing them.
7. If your own Sun sign and Moon sign are as chosen by you for Exercise 5, what would you choose as the Sun sign and Moon sign for a) a marriage partner, b) a business partner? Which of the planets would also be important in each case?
8. How would the following planets work in the zodiacal signs given:
   a) Jupiter in Taurus.
   b) Mars in Libra.
   c) Saturn in Scorpio.

CHAPTER 3

THE HOUSES AND
THE ASPECTS

If you look at the completed birth charts shown in this book, you will recognize the symbols for the planets and the zodiacal signs, and you will remember that we used Oken's description of the planets as the 'what' and the signs as the 'how' of astrology. The final category is the 'where'—in other words, the part of the life which is affected by the planet in the sign. This is shown by the actual position on the birth chart, which is divided into twelve segments or *houses*.

In this book, most of the birth charts are drawn by the method known as *equal house,* which gives each segment an equal number of degrees. There are 360 degrees in a complete circle, so each segment contains 30 degrees. This is the same number of degrees as are occupied by each zodiacal sign, *but the two do not necessarily coincide.* It is possible for a house to start at any degree of a zodiacal sign, for reasons of astronomy which are explained later in the book.

The houses are numbered *anti-clockwise* from the Ascendant, which is usually shown on the left-hand side of the chart, as in Figure 2. The lines dividing the houses are known as *cusps.* (This word is also used for the division between two signs.)

Do not allow yourself to become confused with the mechanics of the erection of the birth chart. This will be explained later. For the moment we only need to know the meanings of the different houses.

When we look at a birth chart, we are looking at a map of the heavens, so that, on paper, it appears to be upside down. We are used to seeing maps where the top indicates north, but the top of the birth chart (somewhere near the Midheaven) is south. This, of course, is where you would expect to see the Sun at midday. Similarly, the east (Ascendant) is on the left.

The signs of the zodiac follow each other in order, but *anti-clockwise,* as do the houses.

The Appearance of the Birth Chart

51

First House   This house begins at the Ascendant and continues for 30 degrees (30°), so that if the Ascendant happens to be 14° Taurus, the first house will occupy all the degrees from 14° Taurus to 13° Gemini. As you would expect of the first house, it is the one which represents the personality. Any planet in this house will affect the native very personally. The *Ascendant* itself has often been described as the persona or the face we show to the world. This may be very different from the basic personality as shown by the Sun. The physical characteristics of a person are often more akin to the ascending sign than the Sun sign. The vitality and temperament are also shown by this house, and any planet which it contains will be considered 'strong' when assessing the birth chart as a whole. If it is within 8° of the Ascendant, it is known as a 'rising' planet and will be a dominating influence in the psychology of the native.

Although *any* sign of the zodiac may be on the cusp of the first house, it may help to to remember the characteristics of this house if you think of it as being the natural house of Aries (first house and first sign of the zodiac) and of its ruling planet Mars—so that the *vitality* and *personal drive* of the native is emphasized here. *Example:* Jupiter in the first house would represent a relaxed and optimistic *personality*.

Second House   Being the 'natural' house of Taurus (the second sign of the zodiac) and its ruling planet, Venus, the second house represents possessions, security, finance—all the things which 'earth' the native. Activities connected with accumulating possessions, business, and productiveness, are all 'ruled' by this house. *Example:* Mars in the second house would indicate *activity* and *energy* devoted to these pursuits.

Third House   This is the house of the immediate environment—short journeys, neighbours, near relatives, communications. The natural house of Gemini also emphasizes the mentality, speech, education and the nervous system. *Example:* The Sun in this house would indicate that the *basic* interests are in this area, whatever the zodiacal sign on the cusp of the house.

Fourth House   This house represents the home base, also the parents and the private life. It is the natural house of Cancer and the Moon. Planets here show the need to make a secure base and then to protect it. If this part of the birth chart has a preponderance of planets, the native prefers a private, rather than a public, life. *Example:* Saturn in the fourth house indicates that feelings of *responsibility* and *stability* are present in this area of the life.

Fifth House   The house of creativity (self-expression), parenthood and enjoyment in outgoing ways, especially activities and sports. The natural house of Leo and the Sun shows the ability to enjoy life and to fulfil the potential of the native. *Example:* Neptune in this house suggests that *intuition* and a feeling for rhythm is brought to these pursuits which might result in the creation of poetry or music.

This house represents work, service to others, discipline, authority and health **Sixth House** matters. It is the natural house of Virgo and Mercury. Planets in this house should be studied to indicate attitudes to work and health in particular. *Example:* The Moon in the sixth house suggests *fluctuation* in the amount of energy or enthusiasm brought to the pursuits indicated by the house.

The first six houses have all been related directly to the person. The last six relate to the attitude to others. In a sense, they 'pair off' with their opposite numbers, just as the signs of the zodiac did, expressing polarity.

As the natural house of Libra and the planet Venus, this house refers to partner- **Seventh House** ships and close relationships. The sign on the cusp of this house should be considered when you are assessing the emotional make-up of the native. It often indicates the type of marriage partner, as well as the attitude to other relation- ships. Planets here are likely to show that partnership is very important to the native. *Example:* Uranus here would suggest *upheavals* in relation with others and a necessity for the native to maintain a feeling of *personal freedom* within a relationship.

As the second house was the house of possessions, so the eighth house indicates **Eighth House** money from legacies and also dealing with the money of others. This indicates financial ability, including that required by business, the Stock Market, Insurance, etc. It also deals with the giving of money by legacies. It has connotations with the sign of Scorpio and the planet Pluto. It therefore refers to matters of life and death on a profound level (showing the intensity of Scorpio) and has a connection with occult matters. It also has to do with feelings shared with others. *Example:* The planet, Jupiter, in this house would show the possibility of *financial* success and also the receipt of money from others.

The third house dealt with the mental state of the native and also with short **Ninth House** distance travel. The ninth house indicates further education and the possibility of study in depth, very often of profound subjects. Long distance travel is indicated here and also the possibility of living abroad and of being a good linguist and having to deal with foreigners. Being the natural house of Sagittarius and the planet Jupiter, it has to deal with philosophical concepts. Planets here will show interest in such matters. *Example:* The planet Jupiter, at home in its own house, will show that the native will be able to expand his mind and experience by means of one or more of the matters which come under the ninth house.

Tenth House   As the fourth house dealt with matters of the home, so the tenth house deals with matters of the public life and career. The sign on the cusp will show the type of ambition and responsibilities which will be undertaken by the native. Social and public standing are also shown by this house. This is the natural house of the Midheaven, although it does not always contain it. It is also the natural house of Capricorn and the planet Saturn. Planets here will show that the native tends to be a person who is interested in his standing in the world rather than a private person as shown by the fourth house. *Example:* The Sun here will indicate one who is *basically* concerned with all these matters—a career man whose status is important to him.

Eleventh House   As the fifth house was the house of pleasure of all types, so the eleventh house is the house of pleasures which include groups of friends or acquaintances. It links with clubs and societies and intellectual pleasures. Often there are humanitarian objectives as would be expected with Aquarius being the natural sign and Uranus being the natural planet ruling this house. *Example:* Venus here would indicate great attraction to this way of life and easy *relationships* within a group.

Twelfth House   This used to be called 'the house of one's own undoing', since it links with escapism and conditions in which the native is 'enclosed', such as hospitals and institutions. It is the natural house of Pisces and Neptune and it is now better understood as indicating withdrawal in the mental sense. It indicates a need for privacy at times for refreshment and renewal. It also has links with self-sacrifice and service to others. *Example:* Mercury here would indicate that mental pursuits need to be followed in seclusion. (This position might appear in the chart of a person who found it helpful to meditate.)

THE ASPECTS

Apart from considering all the planets and how they function in the various zodiacal signs and houses, the practising astrologer takes another important factor into consideration when interpreting a birth chart. This is the interaction of the planets on each other. As we shall see, some will be working in harmony, while others appear to be working against each other. We judge these by measuring the distances between them.

The subject now begins to look technical, but you will find it quite easy if you take one step at a time. Anyone who can do simple addition and subtraction can set up a birth chart and measure the angles between planets.

You will learn to set up the chart in the next chapter, but to complete the interpretation section here is the list of the most commonly used aspects between planets, together with the interpretation of them.

The Conjunction
♂

As its name implies, this occurs when two planets are close together. Most astrologers consider that there is a conjunction if planets are within 8° of each other. (This is referred to as an 'orb' of 8°.) Very often, planets that are so close together will be in the same sign and house, so it is obvious that both planets will be expressing *themselves* in the manner of that sign and house and will, therefore, have a lot in common. For instance, the Sun and Mercury in Cancer in the sixth house would indicate that both the basic personality (Sun) and the mentality (Mercury) would be expressed *protectively* (Cancer) in work conditions (sixth house). Note that Mercury can never be more than 28° from the Sun.

Even when the planets do not share the same sign and house, they will work together if they are 'conjunct', i.e. forming a conjunction by being within 8° of each other (but see *Disassociated Aspects* below).

The Opposition
♀

Here the two planets are opposing each other across the chart. An exact opposition occurs when they are 180° apart, but again an orb of 8° is allowed. This used to be considered a difficult aspect, but it makes for a good balance if the native learns to use it well. Unless an opposition occurs between one planet at the end of a sign and one at the beginning of a sign, it usually happens that planets in opposition are both in a positive sign or both in a negative sign and, therefore, they have that in common.

The Trine
△

To form an exact trine aspect, two planets will be 120° apart. As the zodiacal signs are each of 30°, this means they are four signs apart. Consequently, they will be of the same triplicity—both in fire signs, or both in earth signs, etc. This gives them characteristics in common, so that they work well together. The usual orb allowed is 6°, so that if they were 114° to 126° apart they would still be said to be *in trine*.

The Sextile
✻

This occurs when two planets are 60° apart. Because this is a smaller and weaker aspect than the trine, an orb of only 4° is allowed. This is also a harmonious aspect and the planets will usually be both positive or both negative. In addition, though not being the same triplicity, they will be in compatible ones. *Fire* and *air* signs work well together and *earth* and *water* signs are equally in harmony. (A good way to remember this is that air stimulates fire to burn, whereas earth and water douse it. Similarly, fire and air will both dry up the earth, while water will make it fertile.)

55

The Square Two planets at a distance of 90° from each other are said to be *in square aspect.*
This aspect is as important as the trine and an orb of 6° is allowed. In this case,
the planets will be separated by three signs of the zodiac and they will not be in
harmony. For example, a planet in Leo would form a square with a planet in
Scorpio (a fire sign and a water sign) which is not compatible. A planet in Leo
could also form a square with one in Taurus, an earth sign and a fire sign, so,
again, not compatible. This explains why signs in the same quadruplicity do not
work well together, as they are always incompatible. Where a planet forms squares
to two planets which are in opposition, this is called a T-square.

These are the main aspects, but many astrologers use others, although
recognizing that they will not have such a strong influence in the birth chart. We
should consider some of these, for all of which an orb of only 2° is used.

The Quincunx Here the planets are 150° apart. The signs concerned will have no characteristics
in common, and, therefore, this aspect is one of strain. For example, a planet in
Aries would be in quincunx aspect to one in Virgo. Aries is positive, fire and
cardinal. Virgo is negative, earth and mutable. In some birth charts this aspect
will be more difficult for the native to live with than the square, especially if the
aspect is exact. Do not forget that only an orb of 2° is allowed in judging whether
planets are quincunx.

The Semi-Square This is half a square, or 45°, as its name implies. Like the square, it is a difficult
aspect, but its influence is much weaker.

**The
Sesquiquadrate** This is a square plus half a square or 135°. The interpretation is as for the semi-
square.

The Semi-Sextile Two planets exactly 30° apart are semi-sextile. Like the quincunx, they will have
nothing in common, but the influence is usually quite weak.

The student should know of two other aspects, the *quintile* (Q), 72° apart,
and the *bi-quintile* (BQ), 144° apart. These are little used in modern astrology,
but are both said to be helpful. Some astrologers regard them as more important
on spiritual and esoteric levels.

56

SUMMARY OF ASPECTS

Neutral Aspects*

	Exact aspect (° apart)	Orb allowed (°)
The conjunction	0	8
The opposition	180	8

'Easy' Aspects

	Exact aspect (° apart)	Orb allowed (°)
The trine	120	6
The sextile	60	4

'Difficult' Aspects

	Exact aspect (° apart)	Orb allowed (°)
The square	90	6
The quincunx	150	2
The semi-square	45	2
The sesquiquadrate	135	2
The semi-sextile	30	2

Because of the amount of orb allowed, it sometimes happens that an aspect is formed between two planets where one is very near the end of a zodiacal sign and the other is very near the beginning of a sign. This has the effect of weakening the power of the aspect.

Example: A trine aspect would normally mean that both planets were in the same triplicity, but in the case of a disassociated sign this would no longer be true and there would be a consequent loss of the characteristics which the two planets would have had in common. For instance, a Gemini-Libra trine, with two air signs involved, would be stronger than a trine between Gemini and Scorpio (which are two signs with nothing in common). See also Figure 4, where the Moon at 2° Taurus is in trine to Mars at 29° Leo.

Disassociated Aspects

A birth chart represents the psychology of the native as at the time of birth, but it also represents the potential. If the native develops all the many facets of his character, what may he become? Most birth charts are bursting with potential, much of which is never realized. It is the astrologer's role to reveal this and to show the native how to work with it (instead of against it, as many people do).

The 'easy' aspects are pleasant to see in a chart, but they are not the ones which develop character. It is by overcoming our difficulties that we learn, and so a preponderance of 'difficult' aspects in a chart should not be interpreted as 'doom and gloom'. Indeed, they represent a challenge which, if accepted, can make for a full and exciting life—the 'life more abundant' of which Christ spoke.

Consider the birth chart of Albrecht Schweitzer (Figure 3), whose chart shows

'Easy' and 'Difficult' Aspects in Interpretation

*i.e. dependent on the planets involved.

the pattern known as the *Grand Cross,* which is full of squares and oppositions. This brilliant man, whose work in his hospital at Lambaréné must have been both arduous and sad (not to say frustrating, especially in the early pioneering days), has had a difficult but a self-chosen life of sacrifice and endurance. No doubt his work has been his reward, and what has been his spiritual gain only he will know.

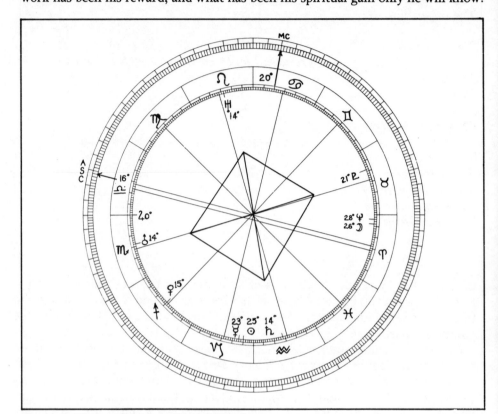

Figure 3. Chart to Illustrate 'Grand Cross'.

The 'easy' aspects are well represented in the chart (Figure 4) showing the pattern known as the *Grand Trine.* This is formed when three planets are each in trine aspect to the other two, forming the triangle in signs of the same quadruplicity. It has sometimes been suggested that too many 'easy' aspects make the native too inclined to sit back and take things easy, and, certainly, in a chart where there is little strength of character, the native may be someone who feels that 'all the world owes me a living'.

More often, as in the chart illustrated, the trines show an ease of working in a certain area of the life, leaving the 'difficult' aspects to battle with. In this case, the chart is that of a spiritual healer, whose Grand Trine is in the water triplicity, indicating the ease with which he handles emotion and intuition—the chart of a 'sensitive' in fact. This chart has not a great deal in the way of 'difficult' aspects and it seems likely that someone doing this type of work would not need to have too many personal problems.

A Grand Trine in fire signs would indicate someone who had no difficulty in using initiative and in taking energetic actions, but the same chart might show

58

much more difficulty in coping with the emotional life. In every case, the chart must be considered as a whole.

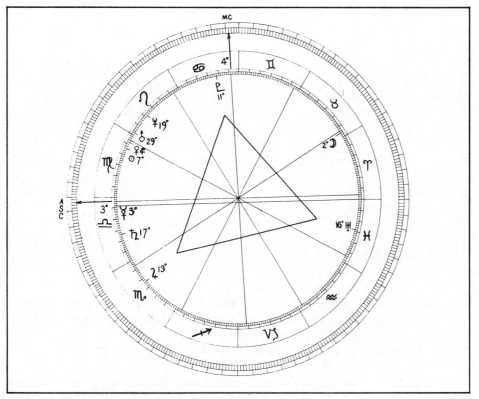

Figure 4. Chart to Illustrate 'Grand Trine'.

Chart Patterns

In recent years, theories have been put forward as to the interpretation of various patterns in the chart. Some of these seem rather far-fetched and have yet to be proved satisfactory while others seem to be self-evident. For instance, it is obvious that planets scattered all round the chart will indicate someone with wide interests, while a chart showing all the planets concentrated in one sector will indicate that the native is mainly concerned with a narrow area of life—that indicated by the houses occupied.

Similarly, planets concentrated around the southern hemisphere (the top of the birth chart, remember) suggest that the life will be lived mainly in public, that is, that the native is concerned with the affairs of the world and his status in it. A 'private' person who is more concerned with home life will have most planets in the north, concentrated around the fourth house and adjoining houses. Planets on the left (east) indicate someone whose life is firmly in his own hands—if you remember the meaning of the first and second houses you can see that this is bound to be so. Planets concentrated in the west signify that the native's life is largely in the hands of others—sixth, seventh and eighth houses. This does not necessarily mean that he will allow others to rule him, but, more likely, that he will be a servant of the public.

Where there is only one planet on one side of the chart, this planet will play a

59

dominant part in the life, while lots of opposing planets indicate a personality with two opposing sides to the nature (almost as though there were actually two different personalities). Such people often approve of one side of their nature and try to conceal or crush the other side of their personality. They need to appreciate that both are valid parts of them and time should be made in their lives for both to be expressed.

While you are still learning the rudiments of interpretation, you need not pay too much attention to chart patterns. With experience, however, you will find that they can give deep psychological insights into the personality of the native.

How to Synthesize By now you will realize that a single birth chart can provide you with a mass of information, much of it contradictory—not surprisingly, since many of us *are* a bundle of contradictions—and you will wonder how to make a cohesive whole from all the many pieces.

My method has always been to make notes, in order, as follows.

1. The ascending sign.
2. The Sun in the zodiacal sign and house.
3. The Moon in its sign and house.
4. Continue with each planet in turn, noting any that are particularly 'strong' because they are in their own sign, or the ruler of the Ascendant.
5. The position of the Midheaven (MC).
6. Major aspects between the planets in order (see Chapter 4).

You will most certainly find that traits which are dominant in the native will be repeated by reference to signs, houses and aspects.

A full interpretation is given in Chapter 5, using a birth chart which we will now set up.

EXERCISES

1. Give a brief interpretation of the following aspects:
   (a) Moon in Taurus in second house square to Mercury in Leo in fifth house.
   (b) Sun in Pisces in third house trine to Neptune in Cancer in seventh house.
   (c) Venus in Libra in fourth house in opposition to Mars in Aries in tenth house.
2. Which is the strongest combination given in Exercise 1? Give your reasons.
3. Explain why it is not possible for the planets' positions given in Exercise 1 to be in the same birth chart.
4. Combine your knowledge of the various components of the birth chart, in terms of interpretation, by attempting to interpret the chart on page 59 showing the Grand Trine in Water. You already have some clue to the nature of this native, but remember this is only one facet of the personality. Do this exercise in as much detail as possible. Show in the margin the astrological reason for your statements (as shown in the interpretation of the chart in Appendix II).

CHAPTER 4

PREPARATION FOR CASTING A BIRTH CHART

So far we have concentrated on the various factors to be interpreted in the birth chart. Now we come to the technical work necessary to set up (or cast) the chart. Do not let the word 'technical' frighten you. By taking one step at a time and by re-reading and checking on each section before passing on to the next page, you should have no difficulties.

Now, we get to know of the tools of the trade, which are as follows:

An understanding of basic astronomy, concerned only with the part called the solar system.

An ephemeris, which is, among other things, a table showing the position of each planet at a certain time (usually noon or midnight, Greenwich Mean Time) on each day of the year.

Some printed chart forms, or writing materials, ruler and a pair of compasses so that you can make the forms yourself.

In order to make the explanations as clear as possible, we will work throughout this section on one birth chart.

Our subject is a young woman for whom we have the following birth data: born 11.50 p.m. in London, England on 2 June 1949. This immediately tells us that we will need an ephemeris for the year 1949, so first we will get to know the ephemeris.

There are several different types of ephemerides (plural of ephemeris and pronounced *ee-fém-er-id-eeze*), most of which contains tables for many years. When you become proficient at using them, you may want to invest in one of these books, but, for the beginner there is undoubtedly no clearer one than that published yearly by W. Foulsham & Co., and known as *Raphael's Astronomical Ephemeris.*

An Introduction to the Ephemeris

To work on our birth chart we shall require the one for the year 1949 and it is from this that the relevant pages have been reproduced in this book.

Because you will certainly want to work on your own birth chart and to buy the ephemeris for that year, you should know of slight changes which have appeared in the editions of *Raphael's Ephemeris* over the years.

(1) Until 1960, this ephemeris gives the planets positions as at noon, Greenwich Mean Time. From and including 1960, they are given in ephemeris time. The beginner can disregard the difference, which is less than 1 minute of time.

(2) The planetary symbols are as given in this book, with the addition of ⊕ for Earth.

(3) The planet Uranus is always called Herschel.

(4) The position of Pluto is not given before 1934, as it was only discovered in 1930. From 1934 to 1938, its position on the first day of the month is given at the bottom of the page for each month. From 1940, it is given in a separate table of its own, at the bottom of page 39.

(5) British Summer Time is given from 1925 to 1961 and for some later years, but is not always accurate due to alterations made after the printing of the ephemeris. A full table of British Summer Time (and Double British Summer Time) is given as an appendix to this book. It is suggested that you should note the correct times on each ephemeris as you collect them.

(6) *Raphael's Ephemeris* for 1939 contained some changes which were not repeated in subsequent ephemerides. These are as follows:

The symbol for Pluto (usually ♇) is printed ♂
The position of Pluto is given for alternate days at the top of the left-hand page for each month.

Other variations will not affect you at this stage of your study. A full list is available in a book called *How to Read the Ephemeris* by Jeff Mayo, D.F.Astrol.S., published by L. N. Fowler & Co. Ltd.

On first glance, the ephemeris looks quite frightening, especially to those who are not scientifically or mathematically minded, but only a few of the pages are used in setting up a birth chart. Most of the symbols will be familiar to you already.

The ephemeris is a book of astronomical tables. Two pages from *Raphael's Ephemeris* are reproduced in Appendix V. The information that we shall require is printed below the black line (we shall come back to the top of the pages later).

The columns below the black line, on the left-hand page, are headed as follows:

1.   *DM* equals day of the month.
2.   *DW* equals day of the week.
3.   *Sidereal time.* This is the star time (explained in Chapter 6) and is given for noon G.M.T.
4.   ☉ *Long* equals Sun's longtitude (The Sun's position in the heavens as seen from Greenwich).
5.   ☉ *Dec.* equals Sun's declination (you can ignore the declination columns for the moment).

6.   ☽ *Long.* equals Moon's longtitude.
7.   ☽ *Lat.* equals Moon's latitude. (This can also be ignored at this stage.)
8.   ☽ *Dec.* equals Moon's declination.
9/10. *Midnight.* These two columns give the Moon's longtitude and declination at midnight.

The right-hand page repeats the day of the month, followed by the longtitudes of the planets. Note that the planets are given in *reverse* order, i.e. Neptune, the furthest from the Sun (except Pluto), is given first, working out towards Mercury. You are advised to start with Mercury and work inwards when inserting the planets into the birth chart. (You can ignore the columns headed 'Lunar Aspects'.)

Note, also, that in every case the zodiacal sign is given on the first day of the month and is not repeated until there is a change of sign. If you are working across the page at any date other than the first of the month you simply glance further up the column to see the zodiacal sign. Do not use the first day's line automatically as the sign may have changed between then and the date on which you are working.

Pluto's position has been reproduced on page 206 and this is given for every ten days. As it is so far away from the Sun it is very slow moving and the information given is accurate enough for all practical purposes.

Finally, we shall be using the tables of houses for London (Lat. 51° 32' north) which are reproduced in Appendix V. *Raphael's Ephemeris* also gives tables of houses for Liverpool (Lat. 53° 25' north) and New York (Lat. 40° 43' north). For other latitudes a separate table of houses is available, but the table for London is valid for *any* place on the same latitude as London and similarly with the other tables.

These tables are to enable us to find the Ascendant and MC according to the birth time and place and they are valid for *any* year.

Other information given in the ephemeris will be explained as it is needed.

There are many solar systems in the known universe, but we are concerned here with the one which contains the Sun around which our own planet, Earth, revolves.

The Earth in the Solar System

From Earth, it appears to us that the Sun and all the planets revolve around *us,* and we see them against the changing background of the sky, which we have divided into twelve segments and to each of which we have allotted a name—one of the zodiacal signs.

Most western astrologers use the *tropical zodiac;* that is, they work with the planets' positions *as they appear in these twelve segments of sky.* Eastern astrologers tend to use the *sidereal zodiac*—the position of the planets as seen against the constellations of stars. We shall use the *tropical zodiac* throughout this book and it is important to remember that it is really the Earth and the other planets that are revolving round the Sun (see Figure 10, Chapter 6).

It would be comparatively simple if the Earth's only motion was that of the revolution round the Sun, which is completed in approximately 365¼ days; but the Earth is also rotating on its own axis, and performing a complete rotation approximately every twenty-four hours.

63

In setting up the birth chart, each of these movements need to be taken into consideration, and it is suggested that the serious student should read through the chapter on astronomy (Chapter 6) at this point. Those who are quite happy to set up the birth chart by rule of thumb need only be aware of the following facts.

The path which the Sun *appears* to follow through the heavens is known as the *ecliptic.* Since the planets are also moving round the Sun, they also *appear* to us from Earth against the background of the ecliptic and in a band of about 8° on either side of it. (This is known as the background of the Zodiac.) We can plot the positions of the planets by measuring eastwards along the ecliptic from 0° Aries, and this measurement is called *celestial longtitude.* This is the information which is given in the column headed LONG. in the ephemeris. The position is given in degrees, minutes and seconds (° ′ ″). There are 60″ (seconds) in a minute, 60′ (minutes) in a degree and 360° (degrees) in every circle.

As the Earth completes a rotation on its own axis in approximately twenty-four hours, it turns through 360° in this time, which is 1° in four minutes. This explains the first important adjustment which has to be done in setting up a birth chart, so remember that *one degree equals four minutes of earth time.*

However, twenty-four hours is only an approximate time for the Earth's rotation. In fact, it is nearly four minutes less, and a second adjustment has to be made for this. Four minutes in twenty-four hours is equivalent to ten seconds in one hour, so for each hour away from noon (if using an ephemeris for noon) we make an adjustment of ten seconds. This is known as *acceleration* or the *acceleration on the interval.*

With this information we can begin to set up the birth chart for our subject.

Drawing the Birth Chart

For practice purposes, it is quite adequate to draw up your own chart forms, although there are plenty of printed ones available (see stockists, in Appendix IV). You need to draw two circles, one inside the other, and then divide the circumference into twelve equal segments of 30° each. In order to do this, all you need is a pair of compasses and a protractor. While you are still a beginner, I suggest you draw as large a chart as the sheet of paper will allow. This will make it easy for you to further mark off the circumference in 5° segments, which is a great help in pinpointing the planets' positions. If you buy the printed chart forms they will be further marked in 1° sections (see chart on page 37). All charts in this book are so divided.

Presentation of the Chart

It is always a pleasure to see a chart presented clearly and neatly, but for a beginner there is the added bonus that there is far less chance of making a mistake if everything is clear at a glance. Get into the habit of using big charts, and note the following details:

1. If you enter each planet in an upright position you will not need to twist the chart form round to study it.
2. If you first list the planets' positions on a separate piece of paper, you will see at once if there are more than one in the same sign or house so that you can make sure you are leaving room for them all when entering them on the form.

3. When you have listed your planets' positions, it is a good idea to mark on the circumference of the circle exactly where each one will be. This may conveniently be done by slightly extending the line marking the degree, towards the centre of the circle.
4. Enter the degrees and minutes beside each planet (as shown in the diagrams throughout this book).

If you intend to become an astrological consultant it is even more important that your work should be neat and clear. You will probably want to lecture on charts from time to time and your fellow astrologers will expect to be able to interpret your charts at first glance. Get into the habit, *from the beginning,* even if you are practising on paper, of making your work a pleasure to see. You will be pleasantly surprised to realize how much easier it appears when it is all set out clearly.

SETTING UP THE BIRTH CHART

We will now take each stage in setting up a birth chart for our subject, who we will call Carol. Her birth data, you will remember is: born 11.50 p.m. in London, England, on 2 June 1949.

Stage I: Converting to Greenwich Mean Time

We shall be working with an ephemeris based on noon, Greenwich Mean Time (G.M.T.), and in order to convert the *time of birth* given by the native to Greenwich Mean Time we shall need to know the following:

1. The latitude and longitude of the *place* of birth.
2. Whether the *time* of birth has been given in Greenwich Mean Time, Eastern Standard Time, British Summer Time or any other local time.

The latitude and longitude you will be able to get from an atlas, or more accurately, from a gazetteer. *(Phillips World Atlas* is recommended as it gives the latitude and longitude for all the principle towns in the world very clearly, in alphabetical order, in the index.)

The other information you will need to get, initially, from the native, and you must then adjust this time to Greenwich Mean Time (see Appendix I). More information will be given later when we set up a chart for the southern hemisphere.

There is no difficulty with the chart we are doing for Carol as London is on the Greenwich Meridian Line, which is 0° longitude. Being English, she will have given her time of birth as Greenwich Mean Time, adjusted (if applicable) to British Summer Time (or Daylight Saving Time as it used to be called).

On the printed birth chart forms, there is usually a section which enables this information to be summarized. If you are drawing the forms yourself, you should do a similar summary (as shown in Figure 5).

You will see from the B.S.T. table in Appendix I that we have to subtract one hour from the time given to allow for British Summer Time and this gives us the

G.M.T. of 10.50 p.m. This also means that her birth date is still 2 June 1949. This is important as the adjustments which need to be made to some birth times to bring them to G.M.T. can result in *a change of birth date* to the day before or the day after the one actually given by the native. It is, therefore, necessary to note the revised birth date after you have finished this part of the calculation.

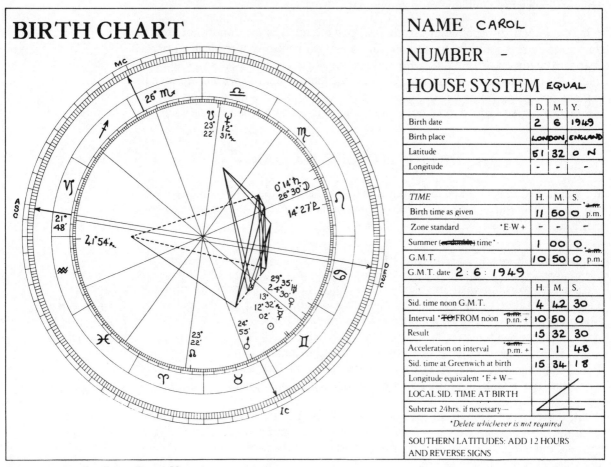

BIRTH CHART

NAME	CAROL		
NUMBER	-		
HOUSE SYSTEM	EQUAL		

	D.	M.	Y.
Birth date	2	6	1949
Birth place	LONDON	ENGLAND	
Latitude	51	32	0 N
Longitude	-	-	-

TIME	H.	M.	S.
Birth time as given	11	50	0 p.m.
Zone standard *E·W +	-	-	-
Summer (double) time *	1	00	0 a.m.
G.M.T.	10	50	0 p.m.
G.M.T. date 2 : 6 : 1949			

	H.	M.	S.
Sid. time noon G.M.T.	4	42	30
Interval *TO/FROM noon p.m. +	10	50	0
Result	15	32	30
Acceleration on interval a.m. / p.m. +	-	1	48
Sid. time at Greenwich at birth	15	34	18
Longitude equivalent *E + W −			
LOCAL SID. TIME AT BIRTH			
Subtract 24hrs. if necessary —			
*Delete whichever is not required			

SOUTHERN LATITUDES: ADD 12 HOURS AND REVERSE SIGNS

Figure 5. Carol's Chart (Equal House).

Stage II: Finding the Sidereal (Star) Time

We now need to find out the exact sidereal time *at the place of birth.* (An explanation of sidereal time is given in Chapter 6.)

You will see from the pages of the ephemeris which are reproduced on page 201 that the third column gives the sidereal time for 2 June as 4 hours 42 minutes 30 seconds, but this, of course, is for noon G.M.T. Now we have already discovered that Carol's G.M.T. of birth is 10.50 p.m., so we must *add* 10 hours 50 minutes to the noon G.M.T. sidereal time. This results in a sidereal time of 15 hours 32 minutes 30 seconds. (If Carol's G.M.T. birth time had been *10.50 a.m.* we would have *deducted* 1 hour 10 minutes, i.e. the amount of time *before* noon.)

We now *add* (because it is a p.m. birth) 10 seconds for every hour after noon, i.e. $10 \times 10^{5}/_{6} = 108$ seconds (to the nearest second), or 1 minute 48 seconds.

This gives a sidereal time at Greenwich of 15 hours 34 minutes 18 seconds.

If Carol had not been born near the Greenwich Meridian Line, we would also need to adjust for longitude, at the rate of four minutes to one degree (adding for an east longitude and subtracting for west longitude).

Our whole computation is summarized in Figure 5 (page 66) in the way in which it is usually tabulated on printed chart forms.

We now turn to the table of houses for London (page 204). The first column is headed 'Sidereal Time' and we look for the nearest time to the local sidereal time which we have arrived at for Carol (15 hours 34 minutes 8 seconds). You will see that three sets of sidereal time are given on each page, followed by columns indicating tenth house, eleventh house, twelfth house, Ascendant, second house and third house. We are not interested in the 'house' columns at the moment, as they are not valid for the equal house system which we are using, but we *do* want to know the Ascendant and the MC. The MC position will be the same as the degree and sign given for the tenth house.

On the right-hand page, towards the middle, a sidereal time of 15 hours 34 minutes and 41 seconds is given. This is as near to Carol's time as makes no difference. The next column to it, headed 10 (for tenth house) shows the sign for Scorpio (♏) immediately below the 10, and opposite the sidereal time of 15 hours 34 minutes 41 seconds it shows 26 degrees; so Carol's MC will be 26° Scorpio (♏).

Ignoring columns headed 11 and 12, we come to the Ascendant. Here the sign for Sagittarius is shown at the top of the column, but if we follow this column down, we shall see that the sign changes to Capricorn before we get to the sidereal time of 15 hours 34 minutes 41 seconds. At that point 21 degrees 48 minutes is shown, so Carol's *Ascendant* is *21° 48′ Capricorn* (♑).

We can now divide our blank birth chart form into houses beginning with the Ascendant on the left-hand (eastern) side. For ease and neatness, we want to keep the Ascendant as nearly due east as possible, so, since the Ascendant is nearly 22° (i.e. nearing the end of the sign, which, of course, contains thirty degrees), we will put it in the sector slightly above, as shown in Figure 5.

Mark the point of the Ascendant at where you judge 21° 48′ would come. If you are using a printed birth chart form, you will be able to actually count 21° and 22° and place your mark between them.

Because this is the equal house system, you can now mark all the sectors at 21° 48′. Label each sector with the glyphs of the signs *anti-clockwise,* following on from Capricorn, in the usual order—i.e. Aquarius, Pisces, then starting at Aries again.

Draw a line between 21° 48′ Capricorn and 21° 48′ Cancer. This is the Ascendant/Descendant line and it is suggested that you use a double line to distinguish it. Now draw a line from 21° 48′ Aquarius to 21° 48′ Leo, and so on all round the chart. You will then have twelve equal sectors (or houses). The one from the Ascendant to 21° 48′ Aquarius is the first house, and so on, *anti-clockwise* all round the chart, so that the twelfth and last house is the one above the Ascendant. Finally, mark in the MC at 26° ♏ , as shown on the birth chart (Figure 5).

We are now ready to make a list of the planets' positions prior to inserting them in the chart. You will remember that the page of the ephemeris for June gives us the *noon G.M.T.* positions, but in order to complete Carol's chart we need the positions for 10.50 p.m. G.M.T. This means that we have some simple calculations to do.

Except for examination purposes, the nearest degree is usually accurate enough, since very few people give their birthtime to the exact minute, and it is often possible to make an adjustment mentally to get the nearest degree.

In order to adjust for any time other than noon G.M.T., we need to know how much each planet moves in one day. This is very simply found by deducting the difference between the noon position of the birth date and the following day, for a p.m. birth time, or the birth date and the previous day for an a.m. birth time. We can then adjust for part of the day.

Example: Let us suppose that our subject was born at 6 p.m. on 11 June 1949. We can see from the table on page 200 that the Sun had a longitude of 20° 12′ 46″ Gemini at noon on 11 June, and that it had moved to 21° 10′ 5″ Gemini by noon on 12 June. To find the Sun's daily motion we subtract the 11 June figure from the 12 June figure, as follows:

Sun on 12 June	21° 10′ 5″
Sun on 11 June	20° 12′ 46″
	57′ 19″ (57 minutes 19 seconds)

If this seems confusing to you, just remember that there are 60 seconds in a minute and 60 minutes in a degree, so that, as in normal subtraction, you 'borrow' 1 minute in order to take 46 seconds away from 5 seconds, which then becomes 65 seconds, and similarly with the minutes.

Now that you have the measure of the Sun's daily motion from noon to the following noon (i.e. 24 hours) it is easy to see that the birth time of 6 p.m. will measure noon of the birth date plus one-quarter (6 hours out of 24) of the daily motion, so the Sun's position at the birth time of 6 p.m. will be:

Sun on 11 June	21° 10′ 5″ Gemini
¼ of 57° 19′	14′ 20″ (to the nearest second)
	21° 24′ 25″ Gemini

This would be entered in the birth chart as 21° 24′ ♊ , as seconds are usually disregarded, or rounded up to the nearest minute.

Similarly, you will be able to see that a birth time of midnight G.M.T. would need half of the daily motion of each planet added to the birthday noon date, and that an 8 p.m. G.M.T. birth time would need one-third of the daily motion added to the birth date. A 6 *a.m.* birth time would need to have three-quarters of the daily motion added to the noon date of the *previous day* (or, if you prefer, one-quarter *deducted* from the birthday noon date, but always do it the same way, or you will get confused).

However, Carol has a G.M.T. birth time of 10.50 p.m. and, although you may very well decide that, if the nearest degree is accurate enough, you could work out the position in your head, it is not so easy when we come to the Moon's position, as the Moon moves so rapidly. Therefore, we will learn how to do it accurately and to examination standard. If you have grasped the principle of the foregoing example, you will have no trouble with the calculations which follow.

People who are used to handling slide rules or some of the more sophisticated pocket calculators will be able to work out the positions with these. For those who are not, *Raphael's Ephemeris* has a table of proportional logarithms on its last page and this table is reproduced on page 200.

The figures along the top line from 0 to 15 can refer to either hours or degrees. The figures down the side in the first and last columns from 0 to 59 refer to minutes. As there are 60 minutes in a degree and also 60 minutes in a hour, these logarithm tables can be used for both time measurements and space measurements. You find the logarithm of the appropriate time by following the column downward of hours and the column across of minutes and taking the figure at which they intercept. *Example:* the logarithm of 1 hour 4 minutes is 1.3522.

Explanation of the Logarithm Table

Although it is important that you should understand how these are calculated, *Raphael's Ephemeris* does list those for the Sun, Moon, Mercury, Venus and Mars. As the other planets are relatively slow moving they can be seen at a glance. In order that you should become thoroughly conversant with the procedure we will work through each of the planets for Carol's birth date and time.

Daily Motions of the Planets

You will realize that the time from noon to 10.50 p.m. is relevant for all the planets, so we will need to add the logarithm (log) of the time from noon—10 hours 50 minutes—to the logarithm of the daily motion of each planet. By following the column downwards headed 10 and the column across numbered 50, we get:

Planet Positions for Carol's Birth Chart

Log of 10 hrs 50 mins = .3454

The positions are now worked out as follows:

The Sun

Noon position on 2 June	11° 36′ 17″ Gemini
Noon position on 3 June	12° 33′ 45″ Gemini
Daily motion	57′ 28″

Disregarding seconds,

Log of 57 mins	1.4025
Add log of 10 hrs 50 mins	.3454
Sun's motion to 10.50 p.m.	1.7479 log

Now look for this log in the chart and you will see that the nearest figure (1.7434) comes in the first column headed 0 and with 26 minutes beside it. This figure of 0° 26′ is added to the noon positions on 2 June.

$$
\begin{array}{lr}
 & 11°\ 36'\ \text{Gemini} \\
 & 0°\ 26' \\
\hline
\textit{Sun's position at 10.50 p.m.} & 12°\ 02'\ \text{Gemini}
\end{array}
$$

Note. The figure of 26 minutes is called the anti-log and this expression will be used in future.

The Moon At noon on 2 June the Moon's longitude is 20° 13′ 21″ Leo and on 3 June it has moved to 4° 8′ 20″ Virgo. Remembering that each zodiacal sign contains 30 degrees, the full computation will be as follows:

To get to the end of Leo (30°) the Moon will have moved:

$$
\begin{array}{ll}
 & 30° \\
\textit{Minus} & 20°\ 13'\ 21''\ \text{(noon position on 2 June)} \\
\hline
 & 9°\ 46'\ 39'' \\
\textit{Add} & 4°\ \ 8'\ 20''\ \text{Virgo (noon position on 3 June)} \\
\hline
 & 13°\ 54'\ 59''\ \text{(13° 55′ to nearest minute)}
\end{array}
$$

Moon's daily motion = 13° 54′ 59″

Once you have grasped the principle, you can write it thus:

$$
\begin{array}{ll}
 & 4°\ \ 8'\ 20''\ \text{Virgo} \\
\textit{Minus} & 20°\ 13'\ 21''\ \text{Leo} \\
\hline
 & 13°\ 54'\ 59''
\end{array}
$$

Using the table of logs:

Moon's daily motion	13° 55′ = log .2367
Add log of 10 hrs 50 mins	.3454
	.5821

Anti-log	6° 17′ (5820 nearest log)

Noon position on 2 June	20° 13′ 21″	♌
Add 10 hrs 50 mins	6° 17′	
Moon's position at birth	26° 30′	♌

Relative to the speed of the Moon, the planets move very slowly and the positions   ***The Planets***
can often be worked out mentally. We will work out the positions for Mercury and
Venus by logs, so that the procedure for accurate work is thoroughly understood.

If you follow the right-hand page of the ephemeris (page 201) you will see that
the column for Mercury's longitude on 2 June appears as 13 ℞ 47. The ℞
indicates that the planet is *retrograde,* i.e. it appears to us, from Earth, to be
moving backwards. This means that we must *subtract* the 3 June noon position
from the 2 June position (instead of the other way round) and we must also
subtract the anti-log from the 2 June noon position.

The computation is as follows:

Noon position on 2 June	13° 47′ Gemini
Less noon position on 3 June	13° 13′
☿ *'s daily motion*	34′
Log of 34′	1.6269
Log of 10.50 p.m.	.3454
	1.9723
Nearest anti-log	1.9823 = 15′
Noon position on 2 June	13° 47′ Gemini
Subtract (retrograde)	15′
☿ *'s position at birth*	13° 32′ Gemini

Venus is not retrograding, so the position is worked out in the usual way.

Noon position on 3 June	25° 10′ Gemini
Noon position on 2 June	23° 57′
♀ *'s daily motion*	1° 13′
Log	1.2950
Add log of 10 hrs 50 mins	.3454
	1.6404
Nearest anti-log	1.6398 = 33′
Noon position on 2 June	23° 57′ Gemini
Add 10.50 p.m. anti-log	33′
♀ *'s position at birth*	24° 30′ Gemini

To complete the planets' positions at the time of birth, try to work with the
logarithm table yourself for Mars and Jupiter. The other planets' positions can be
calculated mentally. You should arrive at the positions as shown in the completed
birth chart in Figure 5.

For Pluto you will see by the table in Appendix V that the position on 31 May was
14° 25′ Leo and on 10 June it was 14° 35′ Leo. Thus, it is moving 10 minutes in

71

10 days. You will easily calculate that on 2 June it was at 14° 27' ♌ and, although this is the noon position, it will still be correct for the birth time to the nearest minute.

If you have listed the planets' position's *before* inserting them into the chart, as suggested, you will see that Gemini is a crowded sign, containing four planets. In particular, the Sun and Mercury are less than two degrees apart. As long as the actual positions are marked correctly you need not crowd the symbols and figures too closely together. Where there are three or more planets within a few degrees it is sometimes necessary to put the symbols almost side-by-side, but when possible you should try to keep them near the circumference as shown.

Before analysing the completed birth chart for Carol in detail, it is suggested that you do the exercises on computation given at the end of this chapter. Once you have been able to complete these you will have mastered the basic computations necessary to set up a birth chart. You will learn later how to set up charts for any place in the world, but the basics do not change, so you are well on your way to becoming an astrologer.

Preparing for Analysis

The printed birth chart forms list several important factors which need to be taken into consideration when analysing the chart. If you are not using these forms you should list these factors on a separate sheet of paper. They are as follows:

1. *The ruling planet.* This is the planet which 'rules' the Ascendant (*not* the Sun). In the case of Carol, the Ascendant is Capricorn, so the ruling planet will be Saturn.

2. *Ruler's house.* This is the house in which the ruler of the Ascendant falls, and in Carol's case this is the eighth house.

3. *Rising planet.* Any planet within 8° of the Ascendant is a rising planet, so there may be more than one. In this case, only Jupiter is near the Ascendant and it is 10° away, so this space would be left blank on a printed chart form.

4. *Positive and negative.* For this information we count how many planets are in positive signs and how many are in negative signs. (Planets include the Lights, of course.)

5. *Triplicities.* The planets are analysed according to whether they are in fire, earth, air or water signs.

6. *Quadruplicities.* The planets are analysed according to whether they are in cardinal, fixed or mutable signs.

Factors 4, 5 and 6 can conveniently be analysed by starting with Aries and counting the planets in each sign according to the category. I have been in the habit of heading up columns and putting a stroke under the appropriate column for each planet and then adding up the columns at the end. Instead of the stroke, we will put the planet's symbol for Carol's chart, which will then appear as shown (Figure 6).

So the result is that she has planets in eight positive and two negative signs, two in fire, two in earth, six in air and none in water; one in cardinal, four in fixed and five in mutable signs. She is, therefore, predominantly *positive, air* and *mutable*.

We should also note against the triplicities the Ascendant (earth) and MC (water).

7. *Own sign.* Planets which are in the signs of which they are the rulers will be 'strong' (important in the birth chart) because of their position. Not all chart forms list this, but it is recommended that you make a note of it.

8. *Mutual reception.* This occurs when two planets are in signs which are 'ruled' by each other—e.g. Mars in Cancer, Moon in Aries. In this case, there will be interaction between the planets as though they were conjunct.

Since there is no quick way of finding whether planets are in their own sign or in mutual reception other than by considering each of them in turn, it is convenient to look for both at the same time. If you begin with the planet nearest to Aries and work round each in turn, your reasoning for Carol's planets' places would be something like this:

'Mars is in Taurus—not its own sign. Mars rules Aries, but there is no planet in Aries, so Mars can not be in mutual reception to anything either.

The Sun is in Gemini—not its own sign. Mercury rules Gemini, but Mercury is not in Leo, which the Sun rules, so the Sun is not in mutual reception . . .', and so on.

You should discover that Mercury is 'strong' in its own sign Gemini, and that none of the planets are in mutual reception.

9. *Angularity.* We have seen that a rising planet, i.e. one near the Ascendant, is considered 'strong'. It is also considered to have some significance if it is near any of the angles, i.e. Ascendant, Descendant, MC or IC (opposite point to MC). Here the only planet which qualifies is Mars which is within two degrees of the IC. It seems likely that, far from being 'strong', some planets near the IC are probably rather weak, or their influence is hidden as they are in the 'private life' sector of the chart. (The Moon of course would be 'at home' in the fourth house.)

Traditional astrology designated the first, fourth, seventh and tenth (i.e. cardinal) houses as *angular,* the fixed houses as *succedent* and the mutable houses as *cadent,* and it suggested that the angular houses were the 'strongest' and the cadent houses the 'weakest'. Modern astrologers believe that all the houses carry equal weight and prefer to use the designations of cardinal, fixed and mutable to express the different types of activity shown by these houses. In any case, when using equal house division, the MC/IC may not fall in the traditional 'angular' houses, although they form two of the angles, so we should limit our notes under 'Angularity' to those planets which are within 8° of the angles.

10. *Shaping.* This is a heading which does not appear on printed forms, but you should certainly expand your notes to include anything outstanding in the pattern of the planets places (see Chapter 3).

For Carol's chart, we should note that (1) the planets have a western bias and (2) Jupiter alone dominates the eastern hemisphere and is in the first house. You will remember that the first house is the house of the personality and any planet there will be important by virtue of its position, even though it is not near enough to the Ascendant to be considered a 'rising' planet. (3) Also note that Gemini contains four planets. Three or more in one sign form a Satellitium or Stellium (Figure 7).

POSITIVE	NEGATIVE	FIRE	EARTH	AIR	WATER	CARDINAL	FIXED	MUTABLE
☉ ♇	♂	♇	♂	☉ ♅		♆	♂ ☽	☉ ♅
☿ ☽	♄	☽	♄	☿ ♆			♇ ♃	☿ ♄
♀ ♆				♀ ♃				♀
♅ ♃								

Figure 6. Analysis of Carol's Planets.

Ruling Planet ___ ♄ ___   Positive ___ 8 ___

Ruler's House ___ 8th ___   Negative ___ 2 ___

Rising Planet ___ - ___   Angular ___ ♂ (I.C.) ___

Mutual Reception ___ - ___

Triplicities:—

Fire ___ 2 ___

Earth ___ Asc 2 ___

Air ___ 6 ___

Water ___ MC ___

Quadruplicities:—

Cardinal ___ 1 ___

Fixed ___ 4 ___

Mutable ___ 5 ___

Western bias 4 East (1st House)

☿ own sign

Satellitium in ♊ in 5th/6th

Figure 7. Summary of Carol's Chart.

COMPUTING THE ASPECTS

Already, we have a lot of information to enable us to analyse Carol's psychological make-up. There is another body of information to be gleaned from analysing the aspects between the planets. In order to compute these, we will work through each planet beginning with the Sun and consider its relationship to all the other planets in turn. We will use the layout of the printed chart forms (Figure 8). At this stage we will ignore the quintile and bi-quintile aspects. This means that we are dealing with aspects which are multiples of 5° or 10°. Since the largest orb allowed is 8°, it is sometimes possible to see at a glance that there will be no aspect between two planets.

The first aspect to be considered is that of the Sun to the Moon. The Sun is **The Sun** 12° 2′ ♊ and the Moon is 26° 30′ ♌ . There are, therefore, two full signs (60°) between them (i.e. from 12° 2′ ♊ to 12° 2′ ♌ *plus* 14° 28′).

This is much more than an 8° orb so it is certainly out of aspect for a sextile. Adding the 14° 28′ on we get a total of 74° 28′ between them, and this is 15° 32′ away from being a square (90°), so there is no aspect between the Sun and the Moon. In fact, we can see that an exact square would be 12° 2′ ♍ and since the Moon is not even into Virgo, it is obvious at a glance that the Moon will not be in orb for a square aspect.

While you are still learning you may prefer to count the number of degrees between the two planets each time, but once you are more experienced you will be able to rule out the 'out of orb' aspects at a glance.

The Sun is less than 2° away from Mercury, so this forms a conjunction. We can put the glyph for the conjunction into the appropriate square on the chart form, and similarly with any other aspects we find (Figure 8).

Venus is over 12° away from the Sun so there is no aspect between them.

Mars is over 17° away, so, again, there is no aspect.

Jupiter is not quite 2° Aquarius and the Sun is 12° Gemini, so the orb would be 10° (12°-2°) which is 'out of orb' for any aspect.

Saturn is at 0° Virgo, so the orb for any aspect would be 12° (the degree of the Sun) and again this is too large to be considered.

Uranus is 29° 32′ Gemini and this is 17° 30′ more than the Sun. Once again, no aspects.

Neptune is 12° 32′ Libra, so the orb is only 30 minutes. There are four signs between Gemini and Libra, so the aspect is a trine. Trine aspects are easily seen,

PLANET	DEC.		☉	☽	☿	♀	♂	♃	♄	♅	♆	♇
SUN	22° 15′ N	☉		·	☌	·	·	·	·	·	ᴱ△	✳
MOON	16° 41′ N	☽			·	✳	□	·	ᴰ☌	✳	L	·
MERCURY	20° 10′ N	☿				·	·	·	·	·	△	✳
VENUS	23° 58′ N	♀					ᴱV	·	ᴰ✳	☌	·	·
MARS	18° 53′ N	♂						ᴰ△	ᴰ□	·	·	·
JUPITER	20° 05′ S	♃							⊼	ᴰ⊼	·	·
SATURN	12° 58′ N	♄								ᴰ✳	·	·
URANUS	23° 40′ N	♅			P						ᴱL	
NEPTUNE	3° 28′ S	♆										✳
PLUTO	23° 49′ N	♇			P					P		
ASC.		ASC.	·	·	·	·	△	·	·	·	·	
M.C.		M.C.	·	□	·	⊼	ᴱ☍	ᴺ✳	ᴰ□	·	L	·

Figure 8. Aspect Grid for Carol's Chart.

since both signs are in the same triplicity. (As this is an exact aspect, we can note 'E' in the aspect grid above the △ as a reminder.)

Pluto is 14° 37' Leo and the Sun is 12° 02' Gemini. This gives an orb of only 2° so there will certainly be an aspect. If we count the degrees from the Sun to Pluto we can see there are 62° 35' (i.e. from 12° 02' Gemini to 12° 02' Cancer is 30° and another 30° to 12° 02' Leo), so this is a sextile aspect.

The Moon The Moon's position is 26° 30' Leo. The first planet to be considered in order is Mercury, which is 13° 30' Gemini. By simple subtraction we can see that any aspect will need an orb of 13° which is too wide, so there is no aspect.

Venus is at 24° 30' Gemini, which is an orb of only 2° so there will be an aspect between the Moon and Venus. By counting 30° between each sign, we can see that the exact aspect is 62°, so this is a sextile. (In equal house charts you could count the houses instead of the signs as both contain 30 degrees, but this is not recommended as it may confuse you when reading charts set up by other house systems.)

Mars is 24° 55' Taurus, and this gives an orb of less than 2° so we will need to count the signs. There are three full signs from 24° 55' Taurus to 24° 55' Leo, so this will be 90°—a square aspect.

Jupiter is 1° 54' Aquarius and Moon is 26° 30' Leo. Do not make the mistake of thinking that the orb between them is 24° 36' (26° 30'-1° 54'). You must remember that there are only 30° in a sign, and we could, therefore, express the orb as 31° 54'-26° 30', which is an orb of only 5° 24', so there could be an aspect and we must count the signs. In fact, there are five signs between 26° 30' Leo and 26° 30' Capricorn, so this would be a quincunx, but the orb is 5° 24' (i.e. Jupiter is 5° 34' on from 26° 30' Capricorn) and this is *too large an orb for a quincunx* aspect, so there is no aspect between the Moon and Jupiter.

Saturn and Moon are only 3° 40' apart, so it is easy to see that they are conjunct. Note, however, that they are in different signs, so that this is a *dis-associated aspect*. We will make sure that we do not miss this by noting a small 'D' in the corner of the square, above the symbol for the conjunction.

Uranus and the Moon have only a 3° orb, and since Uranus is very near Venus, the aspect will again be a sextile.

The orb between Neptune and Moon is nearly 14°—too big for an aspect you may think, but here there is only one sign and 14° (i.e. 44°) between them, which is within one degree of a semi-square.

Pluto and Moon are in the same sign but there is nearly 12° between them, so there is no aspect.

The Planets Aspects between the planets are measured in the same way and it is suggested that you try to work out the rest for yourself without reference to the key (Figure 8).

Work these out in the same way. You should get the same results as shown in the key. Where there are any differences, read the explanations again in full, until you can see where you have made errors.

Most astrologers use pens of two different colours; for instance, you could use a green pen for the 'easy' aspects and a red pen for the 'difficult' ones.

It is convenient to mark the planets' positions by a dot on the inside of the glyph of each. Then use your pen for the 'easy' aspects to draw straight lines between the dots marking each pair of planets which are in trine or sextile, as already worked out on the aspect grid. Then, using the other colour, draw in the lines marking squares, oppositions and so on. (It is usual to show the opposition as 'difficult', although, like the conjunction, it is really neutral, as much depends on the planets involved.)

This completes all the work to set up the birth chart.

EXERCISES

1. What is the sidereal time for a birth at 10 a.m. E.S.T. at New York on 4 December 1954? What are the Ascendant and MC for this chart? (The table for December 1954 and the table of houses for New York is on page 203. E.S.T. is shown in Appendix I.) *Do not forget to adjust for longitude* (74° W).
2. Working with the logarithm table, find the positions for each of the planets for the New York chart.
3. Draw the New York chart and insert the positions of the planets, taking care to keep the whole presentation as neat and clear as possible.
4. Prepare a grid to work out the aspects between the planets on the New York chart and insert the main aspects. Do not forget the degrees of orb allowed (see page 57).
5. Complete the chart by noting the positive and negative planets, the triplicities and quadruplicities and any additional notes that would be helpful for interpretation.

CHAPTER 5

INTERPRETATION OF THE BIRTH CHART

We shall now attempt a brief interpretation of Carol's birth chart.

There will be a mass of material available and beginners always experience difficulty in organizing it. You may find it helpful to make rough notes on each of the planets by sign and house position (not forgetting to include the Ascendant and MC), and then write notes on the aspects and anything else which is important (such as shaping). You can make a brief summary under headings, such as (1) basic personality (2) mental ability (3) attitude to personal relationships, etc. Such a summary should also include health, career and, of course, any particular problem which the client wishes you to consider. For examination purposes, you will be required to show, in the margin of the text of the interpretation, the astrological data on which you base your statements. (The astrological data is sometimes referred to as the *significator.*)

For Carol's chart your brief notes might well be as follows:

Positive/Air/Mutable. Outgoing, mentally-orientated, adaptable.

Ascendant. Capricorn—Earth. Practical, persevering, ambitious, disciplined.

Sun in Gemini in fifth (house). Personality—adaptable, versatile, lively mind. Communications important. Nervous system emphasized (aspects will show whether good or bad). Cool and detached, needs discipline to stick at one thing. All in house of creativity—emphasizes children.

Moon in Leo in eighth. Impulses and subconscious reactions—instinctively feels proud and queenly. Generous and warm-hearted. Flair for drama. Attracted by the deep matters of life and death. Leo feeling of belonging 'at the top' reinforces Capricorn ambitions.

Mercury in Gemini in fifth. Mentality—planet strong in own house. All as Sun. (?teacher—children, words, mentality).

Venus in Gemini in sixth. Personal relationships—versatile and adaptable—tends to coolness. Important in work conditions. Probably gets on well with colleagues. Happy to be of service to others.

Mars in Taurus in fifth. Energy and initiative 'earthed' in Taurus—may be weak or only used in practical down-to-earth ways, but in creative fields, and/or with children.

Jupiter in Aquarius in first. Relaxation and expansion—strong in first house— *personality* is relaxed and optimistic, but freedom very important. (Planet of drama suggests she could dominate a stage—dramatic actress? Also Moon in Leo indicates drama.)

Saturn in Virgo in eighth. Responsibility—taken in practical ways (earth) and with regard to details—particularly where she feels worth while and serious matters (eighth house) are concerned. Strong—ruler of the Ascendant.

Uranus in Gemini in sixth. Unconventional tendencies and inventiveness shown in versatile activities and work situations.

Neptune in Libra in ninth. Inspiration used in diplomatic ways in study, travel, dealing with foreigners. (Aspects will show whether intuition is to be trusted.)

Pluto in Leo in seventh. Refining influence works *powerfully* (Leo) in connection with partnerships. (Could result in changes of life partner.)

MC in Scorpio in eleventh. Career needs to involve others (eleventh house) and to satisfy urge for discovery. Interest in 'deep' matters and urge to explore them and then use knowledge for benefit of others. (Some type of teaching indicated again— or perhaps an audience.)

Sun ☌ Mercury. Emphasizes importance of the mind—dominant part of the **Aspects** personality (especially in Gemini).

Sun △ Neptune. Rich 'inner' life. Should follow her intuition. Rhythm important. Could be mediumistic. (Poet, dancer, musician?)

Sun ✳ Pluto. Good at discarding outworn conditions.

Moon ✳ Venus. Emotionally capable of handling personal relationships.

Moon ☐ Mars. Fluctuation of energy and initiative. Health (Mars) may have been poor in childhood (Moon). May indicate lazy attitude to taking initiative, in which case Capricorn ambition would become dormant.

Moon ☌ Saturn (disassociated). Subconsciously recognizes need for discipline.

Moon ✳ Uranus. Emotionally capable of coping with changes and unexpected situations—may even find them exciting and challenging.

Mercury △ Neptune. Mind is intuitive—can work well with fantasy material (fiction-writer?). Intuition can be relied on. Not subject to deception.

Mercury ✳ Pluto. Mind easily discards outworn ideas and embraces new ones.

Venus ⊻ Mars. Some difficulty of a sexual nature—weak aspect, not very important. Probably sexual drive not strong.

Venus ✳ Saturn (disassociated). Wide (i.e. almost "out of orb'). Responsibility and practicality used in relationships with others. Discipline in work matters affecting others (Venus in six).

Venus ☌ Uranus. Stimulated by the unusual or unexpected. Likely to form relationships as a result of sudden fascination. Both planets in six—work benefits from combination of artistic and inventive faculties.

79

Mars △ *Jupiter* (disassociated and wide). Able to relax and to initiate, especially mentally (Jupiter in Air). Helps optimistic outlook— will be weakened because of disassociation and wideness.

Mars □ *Saturn* (disassociated). Energy suffers and initiative is not maintained (will weaken Capricorn ambition).

Jupiter ⊼ *Saturn*. May find difficulty in recognizing her limitations (Jupiter wants to *expand*—Saturn *limits*). Some war in the nature at this point. Restless.

Jupiter ⊼ *Uranus* (disassociated). Another indication of restlessness. Not happy with sudden changes. Cannot relax in any unexpected situation.

Saturn ✳ *Uranus* (disassociated). Disciplined and controlled in crises. (*Note:* this is not a contradiction of the last aspect—it is possible to remain cool in an unexpected situation yet still feel very unhappy about it. However, both aspects are disassociated, so will be weakened.)

Neptune ✳ *Pluto*. Intuitive and aspiring. Mediumistic tendencies. (*Note:* these two planets are both slow-moving and remain in aspect for long periods of time, so do not attach too much importance to them.)

Ascendant △ *Mars*. With Ascendant in Capricorn and both in Earth signs, native should have plenty of initiative and perseverance in a very practical way.

MC ☍ *Mars*. Lack of initiative to make a career, or forced to adopt a career which is not liked.

Moon □ *MC*. Emotional feelings, or childhood conditions, do not help career and public life.

As you will see, some of the data is contradictory and some things are emphasized by being repeated with various significators.

Brief Interpretation   The interpretation of this chart was originally done, with the native's permission, as part of a demonstration of astrology and other physiological patterns (graphology, palmistry, etc.). The native was not known to the lecturer, whose interpretation follows. (Most of the audience had some knowledge of astrology.)

'I know that I am looking at the birth chart of a female, aged twenty-seven. The first thing to notice is that she is a Sun-Geminian—and also has Mercury, Venus and Uranus in Gemini. It will not surprise you to hear that her psychological make-up is positive/air/mutable, since Geminians are all of these things. This indicates that she is outgoing, communicative and adaptable—also adept; in other words, as agile with her hands as with her brain.

I expect most of you know something of the Geminian character, and you will know the main difficulty is that 'the world is so full of a number of things', all of them highly interesting to Gemini, that very often nothing gets completed. What joy, then, to see in the chart of such a Geminian native that the Ascendant is in good old reliable, ambitious, practical Capricorn, with Saturn, its ruler, in good old reliable, practical Virgo. So we have that rare species, an airy-fairy creature with both feet on the ground. Bags of versatility, full of ideas, lots of interests—and practicality, ambition and perseverance as well. Here is someone who should be at the top of the tree and it won't be her fault if she is not.

I say 'at the top' deliberately for here is the Moon in Leo, indicating that (if only subconsciously) this lady sees herself as the queen bee, the leader, the one who is a great organizer and whose rightful position is at the top—and all this in the house traditionally associated with business. (Also with fundamental matters of life and death—but I will return to that point.)

So what might be lacking which would prevent a bright-eyed and bushy-tailed Gemini with plenty of Capricorn perseverance and the self-esteem of the Lion from getting to the top? The lucky breaks, perhaps? But no, even this has been added. Jupiter in the first house, rising and leading the other planets by a mile—in fact, a singleton (single planet) in the eastern hemisphere of the chart. The Sun, too, is well aspected by Mercury, Neptune and Pluto and has no difficult aspects, so the lady should have more than her share of good fortune.

There are, in fact, very few difficult aspects in the chart, but one of these is the square from Moon to Mars which suggests that the vitality and initiative may fluctuate, and there is also a square, though disassociated, from Mars to Saturn which, again, suggests depletion, or a brake put on the energies from time to time. These aspects also suggest ill-health in childhood, which may now be largely outgrown. However, I would suggest to my subject that she guard against cold, throat infections and 'liverishness'. Mars in Taurus, as well as the difficult aspects to Jupiter, will suggest that caution is needed in the consumption of rich food and wine, which will tend to upset the liver processes.

Mars in Taurus also suggests that the lady is not at all 'pushy'. I think she will get to the top of that tree, if, indeed, she is not already there, but it will be due to the sheer perseverance of the Capricorn Ascendant and organizing talent of the Leo Moon, harnessing her undoubted Geminian gift for versatility and for learning and communicating, and not at all to any attempt on her part to push herself forward.

In fact, this Mars, with its somewhat mixed aspects, suggests that she may find it difficult to be assertive and even become emotionally upset by anger, so that she tends to 'bottle up' her own anger, even when it is justified. This will also weaken the normal Capricornian ambition and she may feel uninterested in the achievements which should come so easily to her.

One good aspect which Mars makes is the trine to Jupiter (though, again, it is disassociated), but the rising Jupiter combined with Moon and Pluto in Leo and all that Gemini (whose business is words) make me feel that I may be talking about a young actress, or, perhaps a teacher of music and drama. The first house Jupiter suggests an expansive, relaxed personality who could 'hold the stage'. This is accentuated by the fact that Neptune is in exact trine to the Sun and a close trine to Mercury, so dancing, rhythm and movement must be second nature to her.

I said I would come back to the point about the Moon being in the eighth house—traditionally associated with matters of life and death, and traditionally ruled by Scorpio. Now the MC is in Scorpio and this combined with the rising Jupiter, Moon in the eighth house and the Neptune trine Sun and Mercury all suggest that this lady could be mediumistic. I think that she will certainly know that she can trust her instincts and she is not open to deception either by others or by herself. I am sure she must be interested in occult and spiritual matters.

Saturn in Virgo suggests that she will strive over much for perfection, with

81

the square to Mars having the effect of 'damping down' her enthusiasm.

This lady finds no difficulty in throwing off conditions which are preventing her from progress. She is able to exteriorize her inhibitions and discard them. She stays cool under pressure (at least, to outward appearance, although she probably 'lives on her nerves'), and she finds the unexpected exciting and challenging.

She is basically cool-natured, but reacts positively to magnestic people.'

The rest of this lecture concerned the future, which we shall examine later.

The Approach to Clients

This analysis is an example of what can be done by an experienced astrologer after a few hours study of a completed birth chart, but, of course, much has been omitted. Had the native come to the astrologer with a personal problem the approach would have been quite different: the whole personality would have been discussed in a more serious vein and with special attention to the problem area. Of course, astrological terminology should not be used to clients unless they are students of astrology or have a good knowledge of the subject.

In doing work for a client, an astrologer needs to know the reason why the analysis of the birth chart has been requested. Astrology is not a guessing game, and it is degrading the subject to allow people to use it as such. I always explain to would-be clients that I am rather like a doctor who can only help you if he knows your symptoms. Any client who wishes you to do an analysis for them should be prepared to give you some basic details. I do not do work for anyone who is not willing to state their problem in plain language. The way they state it will usually enable you to assess their background, education, etc., but if you are not sure, and it is relevant to the problem, do not hesitate to ask.

While you are learning you should gain as much experience as possible by setting up charts of people known to you, and letting your friends act as guinea-pigs. In doing the analysis do not be influenced by what you think you know of them (very few of us know more than one or two people intimately) but work only from the birth chart. You may get some surprises, but you will also realize that the birth chart does give a recognizable portrait in every case.

Presenting the Birthchart and Analysis

For your own records, to help you to become more proficient and also because your client may come back to you for more information at a later date, it is essential to keep a copy of all your work. An ordinary alphabetical system of clients' names for keeping your own copies is simple and efficient. On the copy you can note the astrological significators (as you will be required to do in examinations) but, of course, these should not appear on the client's copy.

If you use a folder, with the chart stapled on the left-hand side and the analysis stapled in one corner only on the right, you will find it easy to talk to your clients from the chart; or, if you are not interviewing them, the whole folder will be a neat and attractive presentation to send them through the post.

Before you launch into the analysis, there should be a page explaining the nature of astrology and, in particular, it should emphasize that astrologers *do not foretell the future* but only indicate likely trends. We will discuss this in more detail later. This first page should also tell the client that the Ascendant, Sun and Moon signs are all very important and state the zodiacal signs in which these are situated in the client's birth chart.

The following 'Note on Astrology' is the one which I send out to all my clients. They already know that I do not foretell the future, since this is emphasized in the initial leaflet which I send to them listing my services and fees.

'It is believed that the first astrologers were also astronomers. As they studied the movements of the planets they observed that certain happenings on Earth appeared to correlate with these movements. We now understand how the Sun's position affects the seasons on Earth and how the Moon affects the tides, but we still cannot explain why the Full Moon adversely affects the mentally unstable nor why there are more haemorrhages at that time, although doctors are now agreed this is so.

Example 'Note on Astrology'

From the observations over hundreds (perhaps thousands) of years, made in all parts of the world, it appears that a person's character will correlate with the positions of the various planets at the time and place of birth. As he has free will, it is his responsibility how he shapes the character he is born with—a natural leader may become a Field Marshal or the leader of a gang of crooks.

No matter what 'the stars foretell', a man, by his own initiative and willpower, can wring a victory from difficult circumstances, just as, by his own laziness, he can let his best opportunities slip away.

Astrology can help by revealing latent talents and psychological difficulties, by providing parents with guidance in bringing up their children, by helping those in close partnership to understand each other, and, in general, to help people obey the Delphic command 'Man, Know Thyself'.

Note on this chart:
Most people know their Sun sign and believe that it is the most important feature on the birth chart. However, the Ascending sign (the one rising on the eastern horizon at the time and place of birth) is equally important, and so is the Moon sign.

In your birth chart,

The Ascendant is in . . . The Sun is in . . . The Moon is in . . .'

The following are the first few paragraphs of a suggested analysis for Carol, with the astrological significators shown in the margin. She has no knowledge of astrology, so we do not use astrological terms to her.

⊙ Ⅱ You are aware that, at the time of your birth, the Sun was in the sign called
☿ Ⅱ Gemini, and the birth chart indicates that you will be very typical of a Geminian. I should expect you to be lively, interested in a wide variety of things
POS\MUT and very good at communicating your ideas to others. I should think that you
Ⅱ in 5 are able to use both your hands and your brain creatively—perhaps as a teacher

♀ ♅ ♊ of handicrafts. Teaching of some kind would be a natural profession for you, as a Geminian, especially as there are indications that you are fond of children. You
♃ ♒ are rather cool-natured and your personal freedom is very important to you.

Asc. ♑ Many Geminians make the mistake of becoming involved with too many things, and, lacking practicality, they tend to get nothing done. However, there
♄ in ♍ are indications in your birth chart that you are very practical and are able to organize your activities to achieve your objectives. You also have a reliable
☽ in ♌ 'inner voice', which will give you a clear indication of the right direction in
☉ △ Ψ which to move, and will enable you to make changes—often complete breaks
☿ △ Ψ with old conditions—without difficulty. I expect that you are aware that your
Ψ ⚹ ♇ hunches are reliable.

☽ in ♌ Although you are not at all self-assertive, you probably feel that you should
□ ♂ in ♉ be 'at the top' in whatever area of life appeals to you most.

Indications are present for a most successful career, but you may well be
West bias uninterested in this and choose a life of service to other people. This could be in
♀ ♂ ♅ in 6 connection with unusual activities in which your considerable powers of invention might be used.

What to Include in the Analysis This is a general guide to the straightforward type of analysis with which you need to practise. I suggest that you complete this analysis, as part of your training, first making a summary for yourself, something like this, so that you see what you have to include under the different headings.

Basic personality:
Positive/air/mutable. Ascendant—Capricorn. Sun-Gemini. Moon-Leo. Jupiter in first house.
Mentality:
Sun-Gemini. Mercury-Gemini. All aspects to Mercury. Third house (Pisces). Intuition—Neptune. Originality—Uranus. Ninth house (Virgo)—further education—Neptune there.
Relationships:
Moon (childhood). Venus in Gemini. All aspects to Venus. Seventh house (partnerships). Pluto in seventh house. Eleventh house (friends) Sun-Gemini. Fifth house—children. Venus/Mars aspects.
Health and Energy:
Mars (vitality). Sun in Gemini. Sixth house and all planets in sixth. Mercury (nervous system). Capricorn Ascendant. Aspects to Mars. First house (Jupiter).
Relaxations and Aspirations:
Jupiter (in first house). Sun-Gemini. Fifth house (creativity and pleasures). Twelfth house. Pluto (Refining). Moon-Leo.
Work and Career:
Sixth house (work and service) and MC (choice of career). Sun-Gemini. Moon-Leo. Tenth house—career. Saturn—discipline. Jupiter—success. Second and eighth houses for finance and business acumen.
This can be expanded to suit the circumstances.

Do not suppose that you can include every significator in your analysis. It would become over-detailed and, perhaps, rather boring to read. At this stage, you should concentrate on producing a readable and interesting synthesis. As you become more experienced, and as you read more widely, you will become aware of the deep psychological conflicts which are often indicated in the birth chart, and you will be able to give your clients some insight into the areas of their own personality which are hampering them in some way.

For the present, do not lose sight of the fact that what you are interpreting is a *birth* chart. It was relevant for the moment of birth as showing what sort of characteristics the native had brought with him. But clients are no longer children when they consult you and it is likely that these characteristics have been *modified* by them in the course of the years. For this reason, it is wise to avoid saying 'you *are* . . . such and such'. Words like 'tendency to' or 'childhood characteristics' often describe the situation better.

Summary of Preparation for Analysis

1. Interpretation of Ascendant.
2. Interpretation of planets and lights by sign and house.
3. Interpretation of aspects.
4. Interpretation of other factors, e.g. strengths of quadruplicities and triplicities.
5. Make notes under various headings. Examples:
   a) *General characteristics:*
      Consider 'make-up' (e.g. positive/fire/cardinal).
      Ascendant, Sun and Moon, including aspects to them.
      Ascendant ruler and aspects to it.
      Any planets in first house.
      Any planets 'strong' in the chart.
   b) *Mentality:*
      Consider Mercury, including aspects.
      Sun and Ascendant.
      Any planets in third house (communications, education).
      Ninth house for further education, deeper study.
      Planets in Gemini and Virgo.
      Planets in Pisces and twelfth house for intuition and imagination—also Uranus (inventiveness) and Neptune, if strong.
   c) *Personal relationships:*
      Consider Venus, including aspects.
      Sun and Ascendant.
      Moon (emotions).
      Planets in Cancer and fourth house (home and family).
      Planets in Libra and seventh house (partnerships).
      Position of Mars and planets in Scorpio and eighth house for sexual vitality.
      Fifth house for creativity, love and children.
   d) *Health:*
      Sun and Mars for vitality, including aspects.
      Planets in first house.

Mercury for nervous system. Sixth house for health generally. Aspects to any planets in sixth.

Difficult aspects to Moon (emotions).

e) *Career:*

The tenth house and MC, Sun and Ascendant for congenial work. Sixth house and planets in Virgo show ability to work. Capricorn and Saturn for ambition and attitudes to responsibility.

Second house and Taurus for concern with all the practical things which sustain life—money and what it can buy. Eighth house for business flair and ability to deal with other people's finances.

Fifth house for hobbies and Jupiter, by house and sign for relaxation and enjoyment. Ninth house for travel.

This list is by no means exhaustive, but it will provide a good working basis for analysis at this stage of your knowledge of astrology.

EXERCISES

1. Interpret the New York chart which you prepared as an exercise following Chapter 4. You are to assume that the native is three years old and that the analysis has been requested by his mother. His name is Philip.

   Before you begin the written interpretation, make your notes as shown in this chapter. You will find a brief interpretation of the aspects in Appendix III (page177), but do not be afraid to use your own interpretation in the light of the chart as a whole. If you keep in mind the natures of the two planets in aspect you will not make any major errors.

   Philip's mother wants general guidance on his upbringing and his health and on education.

   Before the interpretation, write your own preface, explaining the nature of astrology.

2. Interpret Carol's birth chart in greater detail. Assume that she has no particular problems and merely wants a general indication as to how she should realize her full potential.

CHAPTER 6

THE
ESSENTIAL ASTRONOMY

Man is a creature who feels, thinks, loves, invents, grows, communicates, creates, aspires, learns—and that is just for starters! In order to do all these things, he is capable of great ranges of expression which may be free, disciplined, expansive, energetic, uplifting, fluctuating, persistent—and so on. The complexity of such a creature as man is only rivalled by the complexity of his environment.

Yet, astrologically speaking, we have dared to reduce him and his activities to a formula, something like this:

> What man does = planetary influence.
> How he does it = zodiacal sign influence.

No one (and especially no experienced astrologer) imagines that this formula sums up the totality that is man. For one thing, the whole is always greater than the sum of the parts. Nor do we imagine that one lifetime's study of astrology reveals all that is hidden in the words 'planetary influence' and 'zodiacal sign influence'. Nevertheless, we have been able to make a statement about man as a personality which we can grasp with our finite minds.

In the same way, the complexity of man's environment, while never fully understood, can be grasped by studying the various 'wheels within wheels', and if we limit our study again to describe our own position on the planet Earth in our own solar system, we can express it diagramatically and in terms of space and time measurements so that we can understand it.

For the sake of those who are reading this before setting up the birth chart, some of the information given in that chapter will be repeated here.

The star sphere which we can see appears to us as a great globe and we are looking at it from inside (rather like a goldfish in a goldfish bowl). To ourselves, we appear to be absolutely in the middle of it, because we can see distance equally in all directions. This is just a point of view, but it has been found convenient by

The Earth in the Celestial Sphere

astronomers to work with this concept of a celestial globe in order to be able to plot the positions of stars and planets as seen from Earth.

Now let us pretend that we can view this imaginary globe by looking down from above and outside it (a god's-eye view perhaps?). We can see the celestial globe itself as very like a large copy of the Earth, rotating between its own two pivots, a north and south pole (known as the north and south celestial poles) and we can imagine a girdle round it in the position midway between the two poles, which we call the *celestial equator*. From our position in outer space, the Earth is such a tiny speck that we begin to feel uncomfortable—so let us get back inside it.

From Earth's position inside the celestial sphere, it appears that the whole sphere rotates from east to west approximately every twenty-four hours, while we remain stationary, and this, of course, was what the ancient astronomers believed. We are now aware that it is the Earth which rotates from west to east in that time and gives us the illusion that the stars, the Sun and the Moon rise in the east and set in the west. The celestial north and south poles are the points where the earth's axis of rotation extended in both directions cuts the celestial globe, or, in other words, the line between the Earth's north and south poles, extended to the heavens (Figure 9).

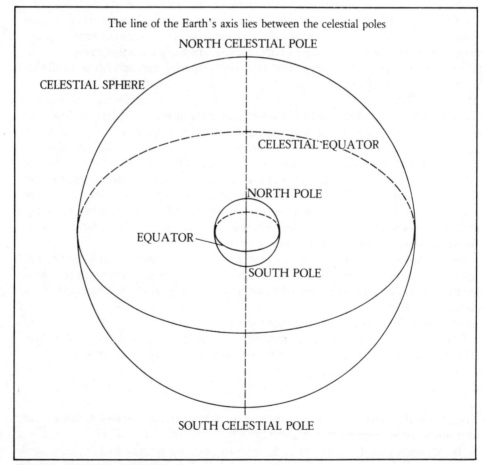

Figure 9. The Celestial Sphere.

Before we leave the concept of the Earth in the celestial globe, we must note that the time of twenty-four hours for the Earth's rotation is only approximate. In fact, it is almost four minutes short of that time, as can be checked by observing the night sky, when it will be found that a star observed in a certain precise position on one night will be in the same position about four minutes earlier the following night. This explains why some of the constellations which we can see in the autumn disappear completely in the spring—by that time, they are overhead during the daytime and so, invisible to us.

For astrologers, the important thing to realize is that we must make an adjustment for this four minutes per twenty-four hours, which equals ten seconds per hour. This is the adjustment which we made in the birth chart for each hour to or from Greenwich Mean Time and which is called *acceleration* or *the acceleration on the interval.*

We are referring here to the system containing the Sun, which is orbited by the Earth on which we live.

The Sun, is, in fact, a star and by no means a very large or significant one, when compared with other stars. Yet it dominates our system for three very good reasons. The first is that it is comparatively near to us (roughly 93 million miles away) while the nearest star, apart from our Sun, is more than 24 *million million* miles away. The second reason is that the Sun is huge in comparison to Earth (its diameter is about a hundred times greater). Thirdly, because it is a star, it gives light. The Earth and the other planets borrow their light from the Sun. So it is the focal point of our system, which consists of nine planets circling round it in regular elliptical orbits (the word 'regular' in this context means that the orbits are regular enough to be plotted for years ahead, with accuracy, and not that the orbits are perfect ellipses).

Nearest to the Sun are Mercury and Venus (in that order) then comes Earth, followed by Mars. In terms of the vast distances involved, these are all relatively close together and complete their orbits round the Sun comparatively quickly. Mercury takes a little less than three months, Venus about seven months, Earth takes one year and Mars nearly two years.

Then comes a great gap before we get to the outer planets. Jupiter and Saturn, which are next in order from the Sun, are the giants of our solar system in terms of size and they take approximately twelve and thirty years respectively to complete their orbits.

Astrologically, this means that Jupiter spends about one year in each zodiacal sign and Saturn will remain in each for about two and a half years.

The 'new' planets, Uranus, Neptune and Pluto, are out at still greater distances. Uranus takes about eighty-four years to complete its orbit, Neptune takes about 165 years and Pluto about 250 years. This explains why we say that these planets have an effect for a whole generation rather than a personal influence in many charts, since they stay in the same zodiacal sign for seven, fourteen and twenty-one years respectively (Figure 10).

The Moon is a satellite of the Earth, orbiting it in approximately $27\frac{1}{3}$ days, and because it continues to orbit the Earth while the Earth is orbiting the Sun it is obvious that it orbits the Sun as well.

The Earth in the Solar System

89

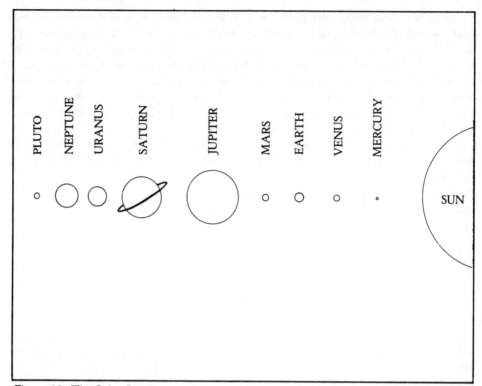

Figure 10. The Solar System.

Naturally, from the Earth we see all these movements against the background of the celestial globe and as if the Earth was at the centre of the whole picture, rather than the Sun.

So we see the Sun's apparent path through the heavens (known as the *ecliptic*) against the background of the *zodiac*. This is a band of about 16° (8° either side of the ecliptic) which we have divided into twelve 30° segments and to which we have given the names of the zodiacal signs. Because the planets and the moon are orbiting the Sun, they also follow the path of the Sun's ecliptic and appear to us against the background of the zodiac. All planets, except Pluto, are within the band of the zodiac, but Pluto can be as much as 17° away from ecliptic, though still following the same path.

The Obliquity of the Ecliptic   All this would be comparatively simple, but for the fact that the Earth's axis is not parallel with the plane of the ecliptic, but is inclined to it at an angle of 23½° (approximately). This angle is known as *the obliquity of the ecliptic.* This gives rise to some complication in finding the exact position of a planet. We were able by *reference to the celestial globe* to extend the axis between the Earth's north and south poles to get the celestial north and south poles, and to extend the Earth's equator to get the celestial equator. However, with *reference to the ecliptic,* since the Earth is not parallel with it, we cannot use the Earth's latitude and longitude positions produced to the heavens to give us a position along the ecliptic.

To be able to plot the position of a planet, astronomers need to have something corresponding to Earth's latitude and longitude, and as the Earth's measurements have a starting point of 0° longitude at Greenwich and 0° latitude at the Equator, so they needed a similar starting point for celestial latitude and longitude.

Plotting the Positions of the Planets

The ecliptic and the celestial equator intersect at two positions and the Sun crosses the points of intersection at the vernal (or spring) equinox and the autumnal equinox. These intersections are the *equinoctial points,* and 0° Aries (first point of Aries) is the point of reference which has been adopted by astronomers in order to plot the position of a planet, star or man-made satellite. This is the point where the Sun crosses the intersection at the vernal equinox (Figure 11).

From this point an astronomer can measure degrees, minutes and seconds along the *celestial equator,* in terms of *right ascension.* This corresponds to terrestrial longitude, but instead of measuring 180° East or West, as on Earth, right ascension measures eastwards along the celestial equator for 360°. It can also be measured in terms of hours (0 hours to 24 hours).

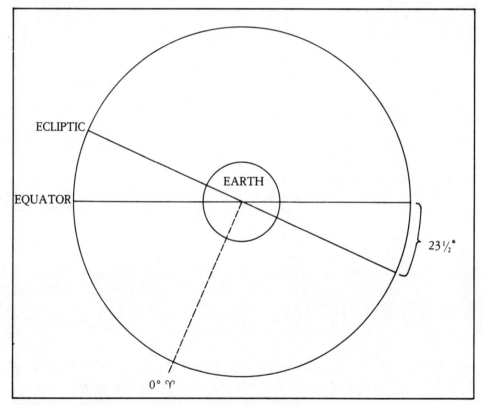

Figure 11. Obliquity of the Ecliptic and the Vernal Point.

The measurement north or south of the *celestial equator* is called *declination* (provision is made on printed birth chart forms to insert declinations. See final chapter).

Both of these measurements, of course, are by reference to the celestial globe and do not help us with regard to finding the position of a planet along the ecliptic.

So we need to measure along the *ecliptic* instead of the celestial equator. Again, the point of 0° Aries is a good starting point, and the measurement is made from there eastwards along the ecliptic and it is called *celestial longitude. Celestial latitude* is measured north of south of the *ecliptic.*

What is so puzzling to beginners is that the terms which one would expect to correspond to Earth's latitude and longitude, namely celestial latitude and celestial longitude, *do not* correspond, as they refer to measurements with reference to the *ecliptic* and not to the celestial globe. It is hoped that Figures 12 and 13 will make the situation clear.

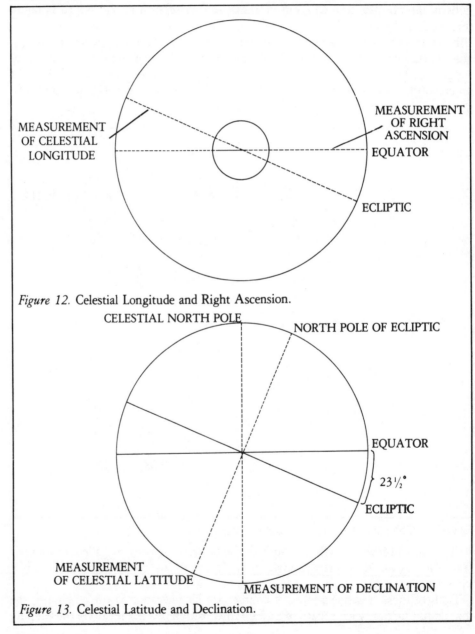

Figure 12. Celestial Longitude and Right Ascension.

Figure 13. Celestial Latitude and Declination.

Retrogradation

By observing the *superior planets* (i.e. the planets beyond the earth in distance from the Sun), it sometimes appears to us that they are moving backwards. We shall see the reason for this if we think of a large stadium with running tracks at great distances apart. It is obvious that the lap which the inside runner must complete in order to get back to his starting point is much shorter than that of the runners on the outer track. Now assuming that they all run at the same speed, the inside runner could look back at the others from time to time and see them at angles which suggested that they were moving backwards. Figure 14 should make this clear. Astrologically speaking, retrograde motion is always noted in the ephemerides by ℞ and when the planet again turns direct, 'D' will be noted by its position. The interpretation is doubtful and is discussed in the final chapter of this book. (The abbreviation Sta. is used to indicate when a planet is apparently stationary before turning from direct to retrograde or vice versa.)

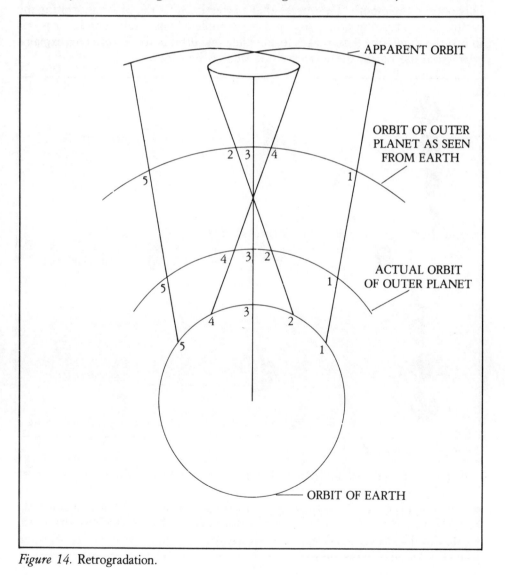

APPARENT ORBIT

ORBIT OF OUTER PLANET AS SEEN FROM EARTH

ACTUAL ORBIT OF OUTER PLANET

ORBIT OF EARTH

Figure 14. Retrogradation.

The Moon If you shine a torch in a dark room and the light happens to fall full on a round object, you will see half of it—the half that is facing you. All the planets and their moons are like that—completely in the dark except when illuminated by the Sun. Our own Moon is no exception, and for most of the month we can see some part of it, as it reflects the light of the Sun back to us. But sometimes in the month it is completely between the Earth and the Sun, and the Sun's light is then being reflected by the Moon back to the Sun, leaving the side of the Moon facing the Earth in complete darkness. A few nights after this, its position has altered slightly in the course of its monthly orbit of the Earth and we see a crescent of light—the 'new Moon' we say, though correctly this phrase applies to the dark of the Moon (Figure 15). The Moon's *lunation period* (i.e. from one new Moon to the next) is $29\frac{1}{2}$ days.

But, like the Earth, the Moon also rotates on its own axis from west to east but only once in the month. This means that all the time that the Moon is orbiting the earth it is also turning slowly so that it has completed one rotation on its own axis in just the same time that it takes to complete one orbit of the Earth. This explains why, from the Earth, we never see one side of the Moon.

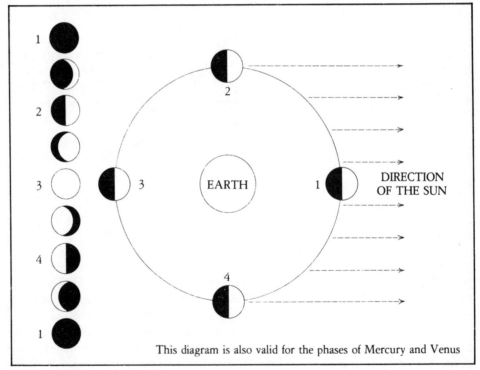

Figure 15. Phases of the Moon.

Eclipses can occur at full Moon (lunar eclipse) or a new Moon (solar eclipse), but neither of these occur every month or, indeed, in most months. A solar eclipse occurs when the new Moon is *exactly* lined up with the Sun, thus blocking the Sun's light to the Earth. Since the Moon's orbit is tilted with respect to that of the Earth, this does not occur often. You can see from Figure 15, that it can only occur when the Moon is in position 1.

In the *lunar eclipse,* the Earth's shadow falls on the Moon, and completely blocks off the sunlight from reaching the Moon (Figure 16).

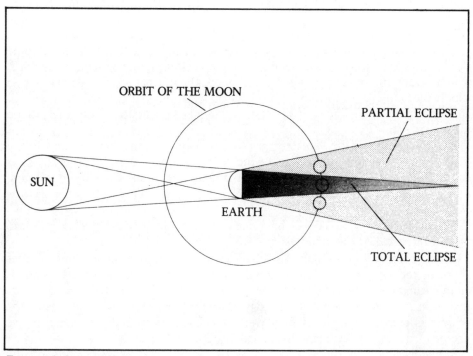

Figure 16. Lunar Eclipse.

The orbit of the Moon round the Earth is not circular and so the Moon is nearer to the Earth at some times than at others. At *apogee,* the most distant point of its orbit, it is about 27,000 miles further away from us than at *perigee,* the closest point of its orbit to the Earth.

Astrologically, the Moon appears to us against the background of the zodiac as though it completed the whole journey through the signs in a month, so that it is moving rapidly through them—far quicker than any of the planets. This means that we need to be most accurate with calculations involving the Moon.

The Moon's Nodes are the two points at which its orbit intersects the plane of the ecliptic as it moves from north to south or south to north latitude. The Latin names are *caput draconis* (the dragon's head—north node) and *cauda draconis* (the dragon's tail—south node). These are often abbreviated to *caput* and *cauda.*

The position of the north node is given in the ephemeris (see page 201, above the black line, column headed ☽'s node), and the south node will be at the opposite point. *Example:* 1 June 1949. North node 23° 25′ Aries. South node 23° 25′ Libra.

These are usually inserted in the chart in the appropriate positions, but it is not clear what the astrological interpretation should be. This question is discussed in the final chapter of this book.

The symbol for the north node (☊) is very like the symbol for Leo and you must be careful not to confuse the two. The south node is the same symbol reversed (☋).

Space and Time on Earth

So far, we have been considering the Earth as a whole in relation to the celestial globe and the solar system, but we know that we have to set up birth charts for the time and place of the nativity, so we will now look at the Earth itself, in relation to these two factors.

First of all, we must realize that there are different kinds of 'day' and of 'time'.

At any place on Earth, the *civil day* starts at midnight, local time, at which time the Sun transits the lower meridian of that place. (In fact, of course, it is the Earth which is moving, but it is convenient to adopt the normal form of description in which the Sun is said to move round the Earth from east to west, and we will continue to do this.) The *civil day* lasts for twenty-four hours. This is also called the *mean solar day*.

The time taken by the Sun to return to a given position as seen from Earth is a *solar day*. As it is, in fact, the Earth which is moving at a variable speed, the solar day is also variable in length. However, its average (or mean) is twenty-four hours, hence the adoption of twenty-four hours for the civil day. This is also referred to as *clock time*.

The addition or subtraction which needs to be made to convert solar time into mean time is called the *equation of time*.

The *sidereal day,* as we have already discovered, is approximately four minutes short of the civil day (or clock time). Sidereal time starts when 0° Aries is culminating (i.e. has reached its highest point) on the meridian of that place. From this, sidereal time at noon on any day thereafter will show what degree of the ecliptic is culminating (the Midheaven or MC position) and consequently the degree of the Ascendant can also be calculated.

Remembering that the Ascendant is the point of the ecliptic rising on the eastern horizon at the time and place of birth, you will realize that this will vary widely as to both time and place and can be, literally, any sign and degree of the zodiac. Moreover, although sidereal time is shown in the ephemeris as being roughly four minutes further advanced each day, a complete revolution of the Earth has already taken place and, therefore, every degree of the zodiac has passed the eastern horizon at some time during the day. The Earth has, in fact, completed one revolution and is four minutes into its next revolution in a twenty-four hour day.

Because it would be impractical to use local times so that each town (or even a smaller unit) had its own clock time which would differ by minutes from its nearest neighbours, most countries have adopted a *standard time* for use throughout the country, and, in the case of very large countries (America and Russia, for instance) they have divided the country into zones and adopted a *zone standard time*.

In Britain, *Greenwich Mean Time* has been adopted as the standard time for the whole country since 1880. This, of course, is the mean time at Greenwich. Because Greenwich is also the place of the Meridian line (0° longitude), most ephemerides relate their data to noon or midnight G.M.T.

Since most people will give their birth time in the standard time of their country (or zone), adjustments must be made to the time given to find its equivalent to Greenwich Time before the ephemeris can be used.

For instance, many European countries are one hour *fast* of Greenwich Time, so if the birth time was given as 1 p.m. German local time, we would subtract one hour to give noon G.M.T. Similarly, the eastern zone of the U.S.A. is five hours *slow* of G.M.T. If a birth time is given as 5 p.m. eastern standard time, we would *add* five hours to give a G.M.T. of 10 p.m.

Unfortunately, this is not the end of the time complications. In Britain, *Daylight Saving Time* was introduced in 1916. Clocks were put *forward* one hour in spring and put back again to G.M.T. in the autumn. (This was chiefly for agricultural purposes, so that work could be continued into the long summer evenings.) This came to be known as *British Summer Time* (B.S.T.). In 1941, during the last war, clocks were kept one hour fast all year round, and an extra hour fast in summer. This period was called *Double British Summer Time* (D.B.S.T.). It continued until 1945 and was reintroduced in 1947 for that one year only. Dates of both B.S.T. and D.B.S.T. are given in Appendix I (page 163).

Other countries also adopted the idea of daylight saving during the war, and the position is now so involved that complete books have been published to show the various times adopted in all parts of the world. (See booklists in Appendix IV, page 199.)

In practice, you should find that most of your clients will give their birth time in their own country's standard time (or zone time) and will also be able to tell you how it compares with G.M.T. by reference (if they do not already know it) to *Whitaker's Almanac* or similar reference books in their own country.

Figure 17 shows the twenty-four time zones of the world. The straight lines show hourly changes every 15° of longitude from Greenwich. This will give you an idea of the adjustment you will need to make for various parts of the world, but, because of zoning and daylight saving, you should regard it as nothing more than a rough guide.

I have just pointed out that the hour changes every 15° (since 24 × 15° = 360°, or a complete circle) and this means that every degree changes in four minutes or, to put it another way, four minutes equals one degree. This is the adjustment for longitude which we make in calculating the birth chart.

Before we leave the discussion on the various kinds of time, and for the sake of completeness, I should say a word about the terrestrial year. We think of a year as being 365 days, the approximate time that the Earth takes to complete its orbit round the Sun. This measurement is accurate enough for most purposes, but it needs adjusting (otherwise, over a long period of time, the seasons would gradually reverse) and so we have an extra day every fourth year. In fact, this adjustment over-compensates, as the Earth actually takes 365 days 6 hours and nearly 10 minutes to complete its orbit, and so, every century year there is no extra day unless the century is divisible by four, e.g. 1900 was not a leap year, but the year 2000 will be.

The Precession of the Equinoxes

Not so very long ago, a common criticism of astrology was that it had been proved wrong by the discovery of the precession of the equinoxes. The deluded critics based their statement on the fact that what is known as the first point of Aries, is, in fact, now in the *constellation* of Pisces; but, of course, modern astrologers are well aware that the twelve divisions of the zodiac each bearing the *name* of one of the star groups does not coincide with the constellation of the same name.

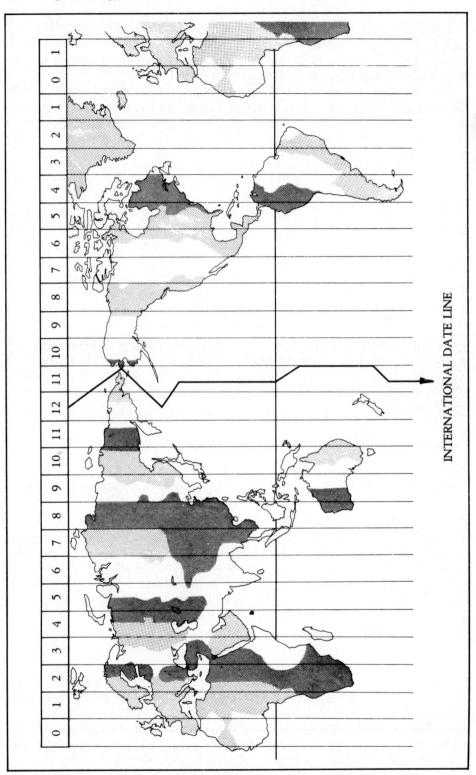

Figure 17. World Time Zones. Each line indicates one hour (= 15°).

The Sun crosses the equator at the vernal equinox about twenty minutes earlier each year and about half a minute further westwards along the ecliptic. This is known as the precession of the equinoxes and its rediscovery is reputed to have been made by Hipparchus, the Greek astronomer in 130 B.C.

The first point of Aries was in the constellation of Aries at the beginning of the Christian era. 2000 years before it was in Taurus. As you will realize, it is going *backwards* along the zodiac and is next due to go into Aquarius. Hence, this is 'the dawning of the Age of Aquarius'. The complete cycle of precession takes about 26,000 years.

The next chapter will deal with the question of house divisions, and is not entirely divorced from astronomy.

There follows a list of astronomical definitions, some of which are relevant to the next chapter, but are included here for convenience.

Although examiners will probably ask for definitions of astronomical terms, I would beg you *not* to learn them parrot fashion. Do try to understand the meaning of each. When you can do this, much that seems obscure will become clear to you.

ASTRONOMICAL TERMS

Aphelion. The point at which the orbit of a planet is furthest away from the Sun.

Apogee. The point at which the Moon's orbit is furthest from the Earth.

Aries, First Point of. The vernal equinox. The intersection of the celestial equator and the ecliptic.

Celestial equator. The projection of the Earth's equator on to the celestial sphere.

Celestial latitude. Latitude north or south of the ecliptic.

Celestial longitude. Measurement eastwards along the ecliptic from the vernal equinox (first point of Aries).

Celestial poles. Points on the celestial sphere in directions parallel to the Earth's axis.

Celestial sphere. An imaginary globe surrounding the earth, postulated for marking the positions of celestial objects. Also called star sphere or celestial globe.

Circumpolar. Describes the stars which appear, from the observer's position on earth, to be near the celestial poles, and which always remain above the horizon— i.e. they do not rise or set.

Constellation. A grouping of stars which appear to be together in the celestial sphere.

Declination. The measurement on the celestial sphere which corresponds to Earth's latitude. The declination of the celestial equator is 0° and of the celestial poles 90°.

Ecliptic. The apparent path of the Sun through the heavens as seen from Earth. (Actually, the line of intersection of the produced plane of the Earth's orbit with the star sphere.)

Equation of time. Difference between solar time and mean solar time.

Equinoctial points. The points at which the equator and ecliptic intersect. The Sun crosses them at the vernal and autumnal equinoxes.

Equinox. A point at which day and light are of equal length (at vernal and autumnal equinoxes—see above).

Geocentric. Pertaining to the centre of the Earth. An Earth-centred perspective. In astrology, the word is often used to describe aspects, which are angles made at the centre of the earth between lines produced from the two planets in aspect.

Great circle. Any circle, the plane of which passes through the centre of the Earth. Such a circle will have the same diameter as the Earth.

Greenwich Mean Time. Time system used in the British Isles in winter. The hour angle of the mean Sun at Greenwich plus twelve hours.

Greenwich sidereal time. The hour angle at Greenwich of the first point of Aries.

Hour angle. Angle at north or south celestial pole between the directions to a planet and the meridian of the observer. As this depends on the longitude of the observer it is called the local hour angle, Greenwich hour angle, etc.

Imum Coeli. Opposite point to Midheaven, often abbreviated to IC.

Inferior conjunction. Occurs when one of the inferior planets passes in orbit between the Earth and the Sun. At that stage it is at its nearest position to Earth.

Inferior planet. Mercury and Venus are so described as they lie between the Sun and the Earth.

Libra, First point of. The autumnal equinox.

Lunar eclipse. The Moon is eclipsed by the shadow of the Earth, which prevents the Sun's light from reaching it.

Lunes. The moon-shaped divisions between the house circles.

Meridian. Any great circle on the surface of the Earth, Sun, or any other planet, which passes through its poles. *The meridian* usually refers to the celestial sphere and hence, the circle passing through the celestial north pole and the celestial south pole. When referring to other objects it is usual to say 'The Sun's meridian', 'the Greenwich meridian', etc.

Meridian of longitude. This refers solely to terrestrial meridians and describes the great circle passing through the north and south poles of the Earth and the observer's zenith and nadir.

Midheaven (Medium Coeli or MC). The degree of celestial longitude culminating (i.e. at the highest point of any meridian of the birthplace for which the chart is erected.)

Moon's nodes. The two points at which the Moon's orbit cuts the plane of the ecliptic as it goes from north to south or south to north latitude. These are called the north node and the south node.

Nadir. The point on the star sphere which is vertically below the observer. The opposite point from the zenith.

Nonagesimal. The highest point of the ecliptic above the horizon, i.e. $90°$ from the Ascendant. (Note: only at the equator and at the equinox does the nonagesimal coincide with the MC.)

Obliquity of the ecliptic. The angle between the Earth's equatorial plane and the plane of its orbit round the Sun, i.e. the angle between the celestial equator and the ecliptic—about $23\frac{1}{2}°$.

Occultation. Passage of one celestial body behind a nearer one, as seen from Earth. In astrology, used of the Moon (chiefly) and the inferior planets.

Perigee. The point at which the Moon's orbit is nearest to the Earth.

Perihelion. The point on the orbit of any planet at which it is nearest to the Sun.

Plane of the ecliptic. The level of the great circle which the Sun *appears* to travel in orbit, produced to the celestial sphere.

Polar elevation. The height of the pole (north or south) above the horizon at any place on earth. The latitude of the place will equal the measurement, in degrees, of the polar elevation.

Prime vertical. The great circle which passes through the east point of the horizon, the zenith and the nadir.

Rational horizon. A great circle, parallel to the visible horizon produced to the celestial sphere.

Retrogradation. The apparent motion of a planet in a contrary direction to the general direction of the motion of planets in the solar system.

Right ascension. The measurement on the celestial sphere corresponding to terrestrial longitude.

Sidereal day. The true period of the rotation of the Earth, relative to the stars, taking 23 hours 56 minutes (approx.).

Solar Day. Time based on the hour angle of the Sun, and varying, but *mean* (average) *solar day* is twenty-four hours.

Solar eclipse. Phenomenon which occurs when the new moon lines up exactly with the Sun (see Figure 15 Phase 1).

Solstice. This takes place twice a year, when the Sun is at its greatest northerly declination (summer solstice, about 21 June) and its greatest southerly declination (winter solstice, about 21 December), i.e. furthest north or south of the celestial equator. (Astrologically, the time when the Sun enters Cancer and Capricorn.)

Superior conjunction. The inferior planets (Mercury and Venus) are in superior conjunction at their furthest orbit from the Earth. (See Figure 15, Phase 3).

Transit. The passage of one celestial body in front of a more distant one. The astrological meaning is slightly different, as we talk about planets in their present positions transiting natal planets.

Vertical circle. Any great circle which rises vertically from the horizon and passes through the zenith and nadir.

Visible horizon. The horizon which we see from our own position on Earth. The part-circle formed by the apparent meeting of Earth and sky.

Zenith. The point on the celestial sphere which is vertically above the observer on earth. The opposite point to the nadir.

Zodiac. The imaginary band stretching 8° each side of the ecliptic.

Zodiacal constellations. The star constellations near the plane of the ecliptic. Many of them have the same name as the zodiacal signs but *do not* coincide with them.

Zone time. Standard time adopted throughout a geographical zone.

EXERCISES

1. Explain in your own words:
   a) The celestial globe, celestial equator and celestial north pole.
   b) The solar system, listing the planets in order from the Sun.
   c) The ecliptic.
   d) The zodiac.
   e) The equinoctial points.
   f) Retrogradation.
   g) The phases of the Moon, together with solar and lunar eclipses.
2. Define the different types of time which may need to be taken into account in setting up a birth chart.
3. Why do we adjust for longitude at the rate of four minutes for each degree?
4. What is the ''acceleration on the interval''.
5. What is meant by the precession of the equinoxes?

CHAPTER 7

METHODS OF HOUSE DIVISION AND FURTHER COMPUTATIONS

Because astrology is a living and developing discipline there are certain areas where there is little or no agreement among astrologers. It would be completely wrong to think of astrology as something which had crystallized and that it was based on beliefs and techniques of the past. As we shall see, it is a source of inspiration to its practitioners today and many fertile minds are producing new ideas and better solutions to old problems.

In the final chapter of this book, I have discussed some of the areas where there is disagreement or where accepted beliefs of the past are now considered doubtful, but in this chapter I must deal with one of the most controversial subjects—the question of house division.

We are aware that the birth chart is a diagram of the planetary positions at the moment of a *beginning* (since it can refer equally well to the birth of a person, a business, a society, an animal, or a manufactured object) and that at this moment a certain degree of the ecliptic will be rising (on the Ascendant). Even a second or two later this pattern will have changed slightly, and in the course of the day, each degree of the ecliptic will have appeared on the eastern horizon of the observer in that position on Earth.

At the Earth's equator *and* at the time of the vernal or autumnal equinox (and only then), the divisions of the zodiac, represented by the zodiacal signs, will each take exactly the same time (two hours approximately) to pass the point of the Ascendant. In terms of house division, this means that at 6 a.m. 0° Aries may be on the Ascendant (and, therefore, forming the cusp of the first house) and at 8 a.m. 0° Taurus will be on the Ascendant, while 0° Aries will be forming the cusp of the twelfth house. As the signs continue to rise during the course of the day, 0° Aries will form the cusp of each house in turn, being on the cusp of the tenth house at noon (i.e. culminating), the seventh house at 6 p.m. and the fourth house at midnight, and similarly with all the other divisions of the zodiac.

But, because this is only true for the equator, and because of the obliquity of the ecliptic, some parts of the ecliptic rise over the horizon at a much quicker rate than others, depending on the latitude of the observer. In northern latitudes, the signs from Capricorn to Gemini are *signs of short ascension* and the signs from Cancer to Sagittarius are *signs of long ascension.* In southern latitudes the reverse is the case. In the polar regions, some signs do not rise at all.

In view of these difficulties, the question then arises as to how the houses should be charted, and various methods have had their supporters over the years.

The Equal House system, which we have used for Carol's chart, virtually ignores the latitude for which the chart is set up, and makes all the houses equal in length. Although it has no astronomical validity, it appears to work very well and has a large body of adherents. When we consider how much interpretative astrology is based on symbolism perhaps this is not surprising. It is one of the oldest systems known to us and can be used for any latitude. It has the advantage of being easy to learn and the major aspects can be seen at a glance by an experienced astrologer. In company with all the known systems, it starts with the Ascendant as the cusp of the first house, but then goes on to divide the ecliptic into twelve equal divisions.

The quadrant systems divide the birth chart into four quarters, by taking the Ascendant as the first house cusp and the Midheaven as the tenth house cusp. The Descendant and the IC are the opposite cusps (seventh house and fourth house respectively). The inventors of the various systems of division had their own methods of dividing the intermediate houses. As it is only at the equator and at the equinoxes that the MC is actually 90° away from the Ascendant, it follows that each quarter of the quadrant can be made up of different numbers of degrees. For instance, when signs of long ascension are rising, there might be 120° from the cusp of the tenth house to the cusp of the first house, and only 60° when signs of short ascension are rising. They can, in fact, be more or less than the degrees quoted—see Carol's chart, Figure 5 (page 66), where there are only 56° between Ascendant and MC.

Some of the astronomers and mathematicians chose one of the great circles to divide into twelve parts—these are known as the *space systems.*

Notable among these was a thirteenth-century mathematician, Johannes Campanus who divided the Prime Vertical by trigonometry. This system is still used, though not widely, being the most acceptable to the mathematically-minded. It consists of finding the position of the house cusps by working out where the ecliptic is cut by six circles of position passing through the Prime Vertical and the north and south points of the horizon. These give house cusps for first, second, third, tenth, eleventh and twelfth houses, the other houses being exactly opposite. *Example:* if the third house cusp was 18° Leo, the ninth house cusp would be 18° Aquarius.

In the fifteenth century, Johann Muller (who wrote under the name of Regiomontanus), an astronomer, divided the celestial equator in a similar manner (at the equator the two systems would be identical). His method is not widely used today, but the great William Lilly (seventeenth century—see Chapter 9) cast all his birth-charts by this system, which has survived on the continent of Europe.

In the sixteenth century, Jean Morin, another mathematician, used a similar system, and Morinus tables are still in use today. However, it was a contemporary of Morin, Placidus de Tito, who invented the system most widely used by modern astrologers. This was still based on the quadrant, but was a *time system*. It used the time taken for every degree of the ecliptic to rise from the lower meridian to the horizon and from the horizon to the upper meridian on its own parallel of declination. The arcs made by these movements were trisected to form the cusps of the houses. However, as some degrees of the ecliptic remain circumpolar for latitudes near the poles, and therefore never touch the horizon, it is obvious that this system simply does not work for births in the higher latitudes. These circumpolar degrees cannot form house cusps and this leads to great distortion in the size of the houses. For this reason, the method seems illogical, yet users of the Placidus houses are convinced that they are of great value.

The system was violently condemned at first, but the editor R. C. Smith, writing as Raphael, issued almanacs and ephemerides giving the Placidean tables of house division in the nineteenth century. These continue to be widely available and there is no doubt that they have been used by many astrologers simply because they are easily obtainable, and with no thought for the method used to obtain them.

As Derek and Julia Parker have pointed out in *The Compleat Astrologer,* whichever system is used, the conception of the 'houses' is man-made, whereas the ecliptic is not. It would appear to be at least as reasonable to divide the ecliptic equally (as in the equal house system) as to adopt a purely 'intellectual system that has evolved over the centuries as a result of the various findings of mathematicians' (Parkers) for an interpretative discipline which is largely based on symbolism.

It may be as well to make my own position clear at this stage, if only because you can then discount it, if you wish.

I believe that the practice of astrology is a very personal thing. After you have learned the 'basics' and have a little experience you will soon begin to get an urge to explore in your own direction—which may be in one particular branch of natal astrology, mundane astrology (connected with world affairs) or 'scientific' astrology (for want of a better name—dealing with, and perhaps computing, new methods and tables), or testing some of the old astrological beliefs to find out whether they are valid. In the same way, you will decide which methods to use— which 'work' for you. I believe that all methods have value in the hands of competent astrologers.

Of recent years, there has been some suggestion that the house meaning is strongest at the centre of the house, while tending to blend into the house before it, or the house following it, at the cusps, in the same way that a person born around the time when the Sun is on the cusp dividing two zodiacal signs may have some characteristics of both the signs involved. I am very strongly of the opinion that there is some such blending and that the traditional meanings of the houses should be regarded as a guide only, until such time as you have formed your own opinion. I may say that, when I have heard some quite acrimonious arguments on the relative merits of Equal House and Placidus, I have frequently felt 'a plague on both your houses', since I am sure that future astrologers will regard the matter as relatively unimportant.

I have used Equal House for teaching and for lecturing because of its clearness. I have usually set up charts for clients by Equal House and then checked to see whether any planets would be in a different house if I had used Placidus. If so, I have noted *both* significators and then decided which seemed to be most valid in considering the chart as a whole.

In order to give you the opportunity to judge for yourself, we will now set up Carol's chart according to Placidus, and I would suggest that you use both methods for each birth chart you set up until you have the experience to judge which you prefer.

Carol's Chart by Placidus

In Britain and America, it is usual to use a chart form on which the twelve houses have been given equal space, even though the houses themselves do not contain the same number of degrees. On the continent of Europe, the houses are drawn to the actual size. Both types are shown in Figures 18 and 19.

The ephemeris which we have been using gives the Placidean cusps.

If we turn to the Table of Houses for London (p. 204) and follow the line for the sidereal time of 15 hours 34 minutes 41 seconds, as we did before, we shall get the following information:

Tenth house, 26° Scorpio; eleventh house, 15° Sagittarius; twelfth house, 2° Capricorn; Ascendant, 21° 48' Capricorn; second house, 19° Pisces; third house, 0° Taurus.

The remaining six houses will have the same number of degrees on the cusp as the house opposite and, of course, the opposite sign of the zodiac.

When the house cusps are completed in this way, you will realize that there are four signs of the zodiac which do not appear on a cusp at all. These are Aquarius, which is all contained within the first house; Aries, which is all within the second house; Leo, which is all within the seventh house and Libra which is all within the eighth house. In fact, the first and seventh houses both contain 57° and the second and eighth houses both contain 41° of arc. The signs contained within the houses are called *intercepted signs*.

We can see by comparing Carol's Equal House chart (Figure 5) with the Placidus chart (Figure 18) that nearly all the planets have 'moved house', as follows:

	Equal House	*Placidus*
Mars	Fifth house	Third house
Sun	Fifth house	Fourth house
Mercury	Fifth house	Fourth house
Venus	Sixth house	Fifth house
Uranus	Sixth house	Fifth house
Moon	Eighth house	Seventh house
Saturn	Eighth house	Seventh house
Neptune	Ninth house	Eighth house

Only Jupiter in the first house and Pluto in the seventh remain in the same house by both systems.

It is unusual to have so many of the planets in different houses by the two systems. Of course, the houses tend to be more equal the nearer the latitude to 0° (i.e. the equator).

106

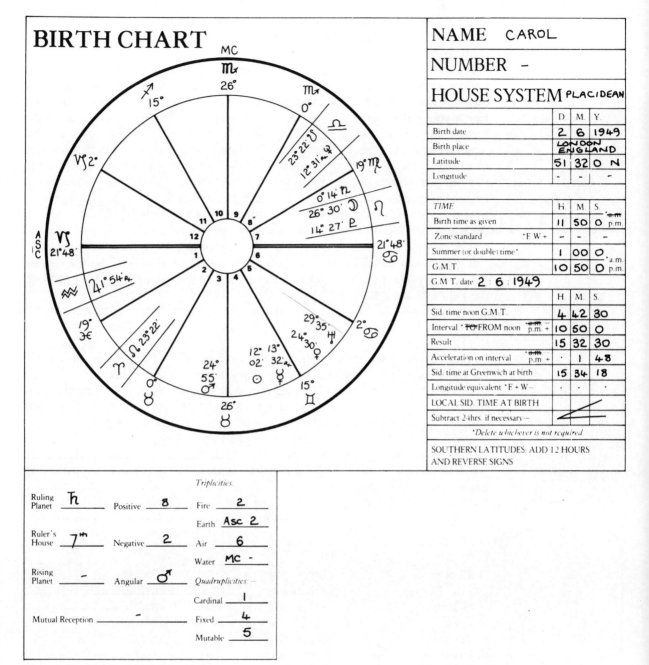

Figure 18. Carol's Chart (Placidus).

To complete Carol's chart, the Moon's nodes have been inserted. You will find the data on page 201 where the page for June 1949 has been reproduced. At the top of the page you will see the column headed ' ☽ Node', and you will see by the DM column that the position is given for alternate days. On 1 June, it is given as 23° ♈ 25′ and on 3 June it is 23° ♈ 19′. This is a difference of 6 minutes,

107

so for 2 June there would be a difference of 3 minutes, which gives 23° ♈ 22'. This position is the north node, which is inserted in the chart as shown. The south node is opposite it as 23° ♎ 22'.

Figure 19 is a Placidus chart for Leningrad (Latitude 59° 56' North) for a sidereal time of 15 hours 51 minutes. No attempt has been made to put in the places of planets, as they would be crowded together in the intercepted signs, but it illustrates clearly how much distortion occurs by the Placidus house system the further away from the equator. This proves conclusively, in my opinion, that while we need not reject Placidus as a *symbolic* system (like Equal House), it is ridiculous for its supporters to insist that it has a strong claim as a more accurate scientific method.

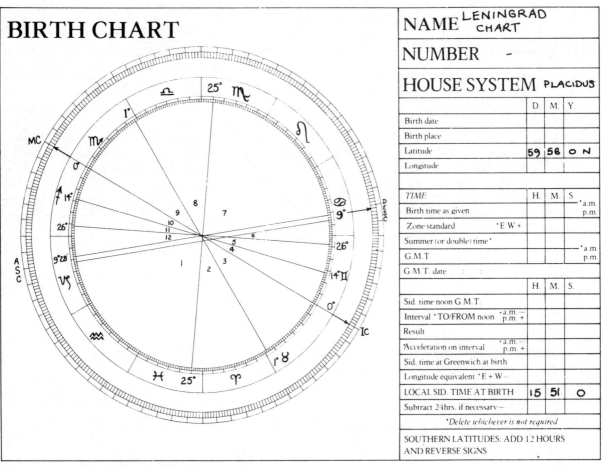

Figure 19. Leningrad Chart by Placidus.

Further Computations   In view of the 'houses' controversy and the fact that very few people can give their time of birth to the exact minute, you may very well feel that the nearest degree is quite accurate enough for the Ascendant and MC. However, you should know how to adjust for a sidereal time which is not given exactly in the tables of houses.

Turn to p. 204 where the tables of houses for London are reproduced. We will suppose that we wish to find the Ascendant and MC for a sidereal time of 14 hours 24 minutes 6 seconds. In order to do this, we work out the difference between the sidereal times given on each side of this time (i.e. 14 hours 22 minutes 31 seconds and 14 hours 26 minutes 25 seconds) and the difference between the Ascendants and MCs given for these times and then calculate the proportion of that difference which we need for the sidereal time we require. These are worked out by means of the log tables which we have already used.

Example: To find Ascendant and MC for S.T. 14 hours 24 minutes 6 seconds, using London table of houses and logs:

	Column 1 S.T.	Column 2 Asc.	Column 3 MC	Column 4 S.T.
Highest Required Lowest	14° 26′ 25″ — 14° 22′ 31″	3° 14′ — 2° 18′	9° — 8°	— 14° 24′ 6″ 14° 22′ 31″
Difference	3′ 54″	0° 56′	1° (60′)	1′ 35″

Note. When working with minutes and seconds, the top line headed 'Degrees or Hours' can be used for minutes and the column headed 'Min' can be used for seconds. If working with minutes only, the minute column should be used.

Column 4	1 min 35 secs		log 1.1806
Column 2	56 mins		+ log 1.4102
			Total 2.5908
Column 1	3 mins 54 secs		— log .7891
			Result 1.8017

log 1.8017 = anti-log 22′

Therefore, 22 minutes is the proportion which has to be added to the *lesser* Ascendant 2° 18′ + 22′ = 2° 40′ Capricorn.

To find the MC required:

Column 4	log (as before) 1.1806
Column 3	+ log of 60′ (1°) 1.3802
	Total 2.5608
Column 1	— log (as before) .7891
	1.7717

log of 1.7717 = anti-log 24′

Add 24′ to lower MC = MC 8° 24′ *Scorpio*

Adjustments for East and West Longitudes

So far, we have only found the sidereal times for a birth in London, which is on the Greenwich meridian (0° longitude), although you have already been told of the adjustment of 4 minutes for each degree of longitude.

Here are two examples to show exactly how this works in a calculation to find the local sidereal time.

Example 1. To find the local sidereal time for a birth at 7.30 a.m. G.M.T. on 1 December 1954 in Newark, Nottinghamshire (latitude 53° 6' N, longitude 0° 48' W).

The time has been given in G.M.T. and needs no adjustment for Summer Time, so we can take the sidereal time for noon at Greenwich as shown on page 202 where the ephemeris page for December 1954 has been reproduced.

	Hrs	Mins	Secs
Sidereal time (G.M.T. noon)	16	13	14
Interval from noon (*minus* for a.m.)	4	30	0
	11	43	14
Acceleration on interval (10 secs per hour, *minus* for a.m.)			45
Sidereal time, Greenwich, 7.30 a.m.	11	42	29
Longitude equivalent (4 minutes per degree, *minus* for West)		3	12
Local sidereal time at 7.30 a.m.	11	39	17

We should now proceed to set up the birth chart by going to the table of houses nearest in latitude to that of Newark. This would be the Liverpool table at latitude 53° 25' N (reproduced on p.205).

Example 2. To find the local sidereal time for a birth at 0.30 a.m. on 20 June 1949 in Norwich, Norfolk (latitude 52° 38' N, longitude 1° 17' E).

The first thing to notice in this example is that the time of 0.30 a.m. will almost certainly have been given in the local time prevailing in the United Kingdom at that time, which will be B.S.T., so that there will be a *change of birth date* when the conversion to G.M.T. is made, as follows:

	Hrs	Mins
Birth time as given	0	30
Less B.S.T.	1	00
G.M.T.	23	30

G.M.T. date = 19 June 1949.

From this point on we work on a birth date of 19 June 1949, as we are working with a G.M.T. ephemeris. The computation for local sidereal time is as follows (see page 201 for June 1949):

	Hrs	Mins	Secs
Sidereal time G.M.T. noon	5	49	31
Add interval from noon (new G.M.T. of 11.30 p.m.)	11	30	0
	17	19	31
Acceleration on interval (*add* for p.m.)		1	55
Sidereal time at *Greenwich* at 11.30 p.m.	17	21	26
Longitude equivalent (*add* for East)		5	8
Local sidereal time at 11.30 p.m.	17	26	34

Finding the Ascendant for any Latitude

When you have a book of tables of houses you will still find that not all latitudes are listed. In the case of Example 2, for the birth at Norwich (latitude 52° 38′ N), you would need to find the exact Ascendant and MC for a latitude between London (latitude 51° 32′ N) and Liverpool (latitude 53° 25′ N). Both of these tables are reproduced on pp. 204 and 205.

This is done in three stages.

(1) Find the *exact* Ascendant and MC for the local sidereal time, which we have just worked out as 17 hours 26 minutes and 34 seconds, *as if the latitude was for Liverpool* (we take this first because it is the higher of the two latitudes).

(2) Find the exact Ascendant and MC for the local sidereal time *as if the latitude was for London* (these two calculations are exactly as already explained).

(3) Adjust to interpolate the correct latitude between the two latitudes given.

Here are the calculations for Norwich (latitude 52° 38′ N) at local sidereal time 17 hours 26 minutes 34 seconds:

Step 1. Exact Ascendant and MC for S.T. 17 hours 26 minutes 34 seconds at latitude 53° 25′ N (Liverpool):

	Column 1 S.T.	Column 2 Asc.	Column 3 MC	Column 4 S.T.
Highest	17° 29′ 30″	10° 24′ Pisces	23° Sag	—
Required	—	—	—	17° 26′ 34″
Lowest	17° 25′ 09″	7° 46′ Pisces	22° Sag	17° 25′ 09″
Difference	4′ 21″	2° 38′	1°	1′ 25″

Logs for Ascendant

Column 4	1 min 25 secs	1.2289
Column 2	2° 38' (*add*)	.9597
		2.1886
Column 1	4 mins 21 secs (*subtract*)	.7417
		1.4469

Log 1.4469 = anti-log 52 mins
Add to lower Asc.
7° 46' Pisces + 52 mins = 8° 38' Pisces exact Ascendant

Logs for MC

Column 4	As above	1.2289
Column 3	1° (60 mins: *Add*)	1.3802
		2.6091
Column 1	As above (*subtract*)	0.7417
		1.8674

Log 1.8674 = anti-log 20 mins
Add to lower MC
22° Sagittarius + 20 mins = 22° 20' Sagittarius exact MC

Step 2. Exact Ascendant and MC for S.T. 17 hours 26 minutes 34 seconds at latitude 51° 32' N (London):

	Column 1 S.T.	Column 2 Asc.	Column 3 MC	Column 4 S.T.
Highest	17° 29' 30"	11° 54' Pisces	23° Sag	—
Required	—	—	—	17° 26' 34"
Lowest	17° 25' 09"	9° 26' Pisces	22° Sag	17° 25' 09"
Difference	4' 21"	2° 28'	1°	1' 25"

Logs for Ascendant

Column 4	1 min 25 secs (as Step 1)	1.2289
Column 2	2° 28' *(add)*	.9881
		2.2170
Column 1	*Subtract* 4 mins 21 secs (as Step 1)	.7417
		1.4753

Log 1.4753 = anti-log 48 mins
Add to lower Asc.
9° 26' Pisces + 48 mins = 10° 14' Pisces exact Ascendant

Note. Columns for MC remain exactly the same in both steps, so the exact MC is 22° 20' Sagittarius at this sidereal time for *all* northern latitudes.

Step 3. Interpolation between latitudes.

	Column 1 Lat.	Column 2 Exact Asc.	Column 3 Lat.
Highest latitude	53° 25'	8° 38' Pisces	—
Required latitude	—	—	52° 38'
Lowest latitude	51° 32'	10° 14' Pisces	51° 32'
Difference	1° 53'	1° 36'	1° 06'

Logs

Column 3	1° 6 mins	1.3388
Column 2	1° 35 mins *(add)*	1.1761
		2.5149
Column 1	1° 53 mins *(subtract)*	1.1053
		1.4096

Log 1.4096 = anti-log 56 mins
Subtract from Ascendant of *lower* latitude (because the difference between the latitudes is decreasing)
10° 14' Pisces less 56 mins = 9° 18' Pisces

Exact Ascendant for latitude 52° 38' N = *9° 18' Pisces*
Exact MC for latitude 52° 38' N (for sidereal time of 17 hours 26 minutes 34 seconds) = *22° 20' Sagittarius*

To Erect a Chart for a Southern Latitude

You now have the necessary information to enable you to set up a chart for anywhere in the northern hemisphere.

The adjustment for a chart in the southern hemisphere is extremely simple and can be summed up in one sentence:

Add twelve hours to the local sidereal time for the same latitude north and reverse the signs on the Ascendant and MC.

In practice you can either add or subtract twelve hours, whichever is more convenient. For instance, if you have a sidereal time of 23 hours and subtract 12, the result is 11 hours—exactly the same as if you had added 12 hours.

Example: Birth at Wellington, New Zealand (latitude 41° 17' S, longitude 174° 45' E) at 1 p.m. G.M.T. (i.e. local time already converted to G.M.T.) on 20 December 1954 (see December 1954—ephemeris in Appendix V).

	Hrs	Mins	Secs
Sidereal time, Greenwich, noon	17	54	9
Interval from noon (*add* for p.m.)	1	0	0
	18	54	9
Acceleration on interval (*add* for p.m.)			10
Sidereal time, Greenwich, 1 p.m.	18	54	19
Longitude equivalent, 174° 45' E (*add* for East)	11	39	0
Local sidereal time at birth for northern hemisphere	30	33	19
Subtract 12 hours	12	0	0
Local sidereal time for southern hemisphere	18	33	19

Alternatively, since local sidereal time for the northern hemisphere was over 24 hours, you can deduct 24 hours from it, leaving 6 hours 33 minutes 19 seconds and add the 12 hours for the southern hemisphere. The answer will be the same in either case.

To Find the Ascendant

Since the southern latitude is 41° 17' S, we can use the table of houses for New York (see p. 203), which is 40° 43' N. We will not make the exact adjustments as it is more important that you should grasp the principle at this stage.

The nearest sidereal time to 18 hours 33 minutes 19 seconds is 18 hours 34 minutes 51 seconds. The Ascendant is given as 15° 3' Aries and the MC is 8° Capricorn. Therefore, the Ascendant for the equivalent southern latitude is 15° 3' Libra and the MC is 8° Cancer.

Mental Computations

Once the computations in this chapter are thoroughly understood, together with the principles behind them, you will find that, in many cases, you can do interpolations mentally.

Absolutely accurate positions are only worth calculating where the birth time is known precisely, but it is necessary that you should understand how to do them. With the information you now have you should be able to set up a birth chart for anywhere in the world.

EXERCISES

1. Explain how the house cusps are formed.
2. What are signs of short and long ascension?
3. Write a short essay on the various methods of house division.
4. Transpose the New York chart to Placidus.
5. Write out the new interpretation for any planets which have changed house.
6. A client gives you a birth time of 1 a.m. 7 June 1945 in London, England. What adjustments are necessary before you can set up the chart using an ephemeris for noon G.M.T.?
7. Find the exact Ascendant and MC for a sidereal time of 13 hours 11 minutes 20 seconds using the Liverpool table of houses.
8. Find the exact Ascendant and MC for a birth at Waterford, Eire (latitude 52° 16′ N, longitude 7° 08′ W), at 7 a.m. G.M.T., 4 December 1954.
9. What is the Ascendant and Midheaven for a birth at Falkland Islands (S. America), latitude 51° 30′ S, 59° W? The birth time is given in G.M.T. as 11 p.m., 4 December 1954.

CHAPTER 8

ASSESSING FUTURE TRENDS

As the pattern of the planets at the time of birth enables us to interpret the psychology of the native, it seems logical that a study of their future positions may give us some clue as to how that future will affect him. This is the basis upon which astrologers assess future trends for their clients, and since the method used is to 'progress' the birth chart into the future, it is known as 'doing the progressions'.

First let us consider exactly what it is that we are doing. We are recognizing that, whatever the future holds, it will be related to the native's own psychology. For each of us, it is a very personal thing—not just *the* future, but *our* future. In attempting to interpret it, therefore, we need to relate the progressed positions of the planets to the natal positions. No two people, faced with the same situation, will react in exactly the same way. The progressions present us with a series of situations and the natal chart tells us how the native is likely to deal with them. It is possible to think of the major progressions as representing a lesson to be learned, and the part of the natal chart affected will give us some idea of the context of the lesson (i.e. home life, career, etc.).

If there are difficulties in the natal chart, a progressed planet coming exactly into aspect with the afflicted natal planet will spark off the same set of circumstances, time and again, throughout the life, so that the native is constantly being given the opportunity to deal with it. Sometimes it can be dealt with by 'breaking the pattern', that is, by refusing to react in the usual way, and thereby breaking a habit which, having once been broken, becomes increasingly easier to deal with. Some situations are not the result of the native's psychology and then they cause problems which cannot be overcome, but only outgrown. As time goes by, the native comes to terms with them, accepts them as part of his pattern and absorbs them so that they no longer have the power to disrupt his life.

Equally, progressions may also signify opportunities which, if taken, will open up new vistas and bring great good into the life. We are also presented with these situations many times in our lives, but sometimes they go unrecognized, or we feel fearful of taking a step in a new direction and so, for various reasons, good opportunities pass us by.

In dealing with clients' problems, all of these things can be explained and it should be emphasized that all progressions have something to teach and none should be regarded as disastrous. It is the very nature of the planets that the pattern is ever-changing and all situations, whether good or bad, pass in the fullness of time. Difficult aspects, when recognized, give us a chance to 'gird up our loins' for whatever comes and to get over the ground as lightly as possible— or, if there is no way to go but through, at least to 'go consenting', which can take the sting out of many of our difficult experiences.

Secondary Progressions

There are several methods of progressing a chart, and, as with the question of houses, the experienced astrologer often uses a combination of methods. The most common one is known as *secondary progressions.*

Of all the seemingly unreasonable assumptions on which the astrologer works, none seems to emanate from cloud cuckoo land more clearly than the one which is made in this connection. It is that one day in the life of the native represents one year in the future life of that person. As far as I am aware, there is no reason why this should work, but the plain fact is that it does—and in some cases (where the birth time is known precisely) with quite astounding accuracy.

The method is simple, requiring only two easy calculations, which I will explain by reference to the birth chart of Carol (born 2 June 1949).

Example: We are asked to assess the trends in Carol's life for the year 1977. This means from January to December 1977, so the first thing we need to do is to find out where to start. If a day is to represent a year, then it follows that half a day will represent half a year, and so on. In order to save laborious calculations for each year and to enable us to use an ephemeris giving the noon positions, we need to calculate first *which day in the year the noon position* represents. For instance, if Carol had been born at noon G.M.T. we could say that noon of the following day would represent an *exact* year in her life. The planets' positions at noon on that day would then represent the birth chart for 2 June 1950 (her first birthday). However, she was born at 10.50 p.m. G.M.T. and, therefore, by noon of the following day, she would be only 13 hours 10 minutes old—nothing like as much as the 24 hours which represents a complete year. So a calculation has to be made in order to find the noon date (i.e. the date to which the planets' positions at noon G.M.T. correspond). Because this remains valid for every year, once it has been calculated, it is known as the *perpetual noon date.* There are two methods of calculation, both of which I will explain.

Calculation to find Perpetual Noon Date: Method 1

This method involves the use of a table of reference, known as a noon date card, which is readily available (see stockists in Appendix IV). It contains two tables, one of which shows the day of the year at every date. For instance, 30 September is the 273rd day, while 31 December is, of course, the 365th day. In doing the calculations for noon date, it sometimes happens that a large number of days needs to be taken away from a smaller number, and it is then necessary to add a complete year, 365 days, to the smaller figure. For this reason, the table gives two figures for each date (e.g. 1 January is 1 and 366).

The other table gives the complete list of hours and minutes and the equivalent proportion of the year which they represent, for example,

12 hours	182.6 days (i.e. 6 months)
10 hours	152.2 days
50 minutes	12.7 days
1 minute	0.3 days.

As we saw with Carol, a birth which is *p.m.* means that a complete year is not represented by the following noon, as less than 24 hours has passed since the birth time until then, so we have to *subtract* the number of days represented by the time from noon to birth—in this case 10 hours 50 minutes, which, as shown by the part of the table given above, is:

10 hours	152.2 days
50 minutes	12.7 days
	165 days (to the nearest day)

From the noon date card, Carol's date of birth, 2 June equals 153 days, or 518 days (i.e. 153 + 365 days), and since we have to subtract 165 days, we must use the larger figure, thus:

2 June	518 days
10 hrs 50 mins (*Subtract* for p.m.)	165 days
	353 days

From the table, 353 days = 19 December.

So the *perpetual noon date* for Carol is 19 December, and because of the *p.m.* birth, the next day's noon G.M.T. (i.e. 3 June 1949) will represent 19 December *1949* (*not* 1950, because the proportion is far less than a year and December 1950 would be nearly a year and a half). The noon positions on 2 June 1949, the day of her birth, represented 19 December 1948, i.e. the December before she was born, and this would be correct because she was not, in fact, born by noon on that day.

If you turn to the ephemeris for June 1949 (page 201) you can now make a pencil note against *3 June* 'equals 19/12/49', and you will then realize that you need not do this calculation again for Carol's chart, since 4 June will represent 19 December 1950. 5 June equals 19 December 1951, and so on.

Since we are asked to do progressions for 1977, and the noon date of 19 December is very close to 1 January, we need only to look at 19 December 1976 to get a picture of the year ahead. In this case, it is easy to count down the page of the ephemeris and you will see that 30 June will equal 19 December 1976.

Sometimes this calculation can involve three months of the year, and rather than laboriously counting each line, you can use the noon date table. This is done, first of all, by finding the person's age for the year required. Carol was born in 1949, so in 1977 she will be 28. This is added to the days representing her date of birth:

2 June	153 days
Add age in 1977	28
	181 days

The noon date card will tell you that 181 days correspond to 30 June.

Before we go on to the second method (which does not require the noon date card) we will look at an example of an a.m. birth. Our subject was born at 7.30 a.m. G.M.T. on 1 December 1954 (ephemeris for December 1954 reproduced on p. 202).

As this is an *a.m.* birth, by noon on the following day, 2 December, the child was more than 24 hours old, so the *difference* from the time of birth *to noon* (i.e. 4 hours 30 minutes *not* 7 hours 30 minutes) has to be *added* to the date of birth. The noon date card shows that:

1 December	335 days
4 hrs 30 mins (*add* for a.m.)	69 days
	404 days

The equivalent date for 404 days is 8 February.

The *perpetual noon date* for this native is 8 February and the planet's positions at noon G.M.T. on 1 December 1954 corresponds to 8 February 1955.

It usually happens that a birth towards the end of the year which is *before noon* results in the noon date falling in the following year. The two examples given are the extremes and in many cases the noon date calculated will be in the same year as the birth day.

When the birth date is in a leap year the calculations may cross 29 February **Leap Year** which is not given in the tables. A correction is made to the day which is equivalent to the interval of time before or after noon, from which you *deduct 1 day*. Do this *before* you add it to (for an *a.m.* birth) or subtract it from (for a *p.m.* birth) the birth date.

Example: Birth date 2 March 1976 (Leap Year) at 3 p.m. G.M.T. Since a *p.m.* birth has to be *deducted,* the noon date will be *earlier* in the year than the birth date, so this one is certain to cross 29 February.

Interval from noon: 3 hrs	46 days
Deduct for Leap Year	1 day
	45 days

2 March	61 days
Interval from noon	45 days
(*subtract* for p.m.)	
	16 days

16 days = 16 January.

This is an example where the noon date falls in the same year as the birth date. 2 March 1976 equals noon date of 16 January 1976.

Note. *If an ephemeris based on Greenwich Mean Time is used it is essential that the birth date should be converted to Greenwich Mean Time and both Greenwich time and Greenwich date must be used.*

Method 2: Using the Sidereal Time

This method uses the adjustment of 4 minutes per day (or approximately 10 seconds per hour) by which sidereal time increases. The calculation is simple and can best be explained by examples. We shall use the same two examples as before.

Example 1: Birth at 2 June 1949 at 10.50 p.m. (i.e. Carol's birth date).

	Hrs	Mins	Secs
Interval to or from noon	10	50	0
Acceleration on interval (*add*)		1	48
Sidereal time interval	10	51	48
S.T. at noon G.M.T. on 2 June 1949	4	42	30
S.T. interval, as above			
(*subtract* for p.m.)	10	51	48
S.T. at noon G.M.T. (noon date)	17	50	42

The day in the year which has a sidereal time at noon nearest to 17 hours 50 minutes 42 seconds, will be the noon date. On 19 December 1949, the sidereal time was 17 hours 51 minutes 1 second, so the noon date is confirmed as 19 December.

Example 2: Birth on 1 December 1954 at 7.30 a.m. G.M.T.

	Hrs	Mins	Secs
Interval to or from noon	4	30	0
Acceleration on interval (*add*)			45
Sidereal time interval	4	30	45
S.T. at noon G.M.T. on 1 December 1954	16	39	14
S.T. interval, as above (*add* for a.m.)	4	30	45
S.T. at noon G.M.T. (noon date)	21	9	59

On 8 February 1955 the S.T. is 21 hours 11 minutes 17 seconds, which is the nearest date for the time, as calculated.

Once we have found the noon date, and the date which corresponds to the year for which we wish to 'do the progressions', we can read off the planets' places along the column for that date. These are referred to as the *progressed planets,* and it is usual to differentiate between them and the natal (or radical) planets, by the letters P and N or R. In order to avoid confusion with the retrograde sign, I shall use N for natal planets. We also need to calculate the *progressed Ascendant* and *MC.*

To do this, we take the new sidereal time (i.e. the one shown for the date which we are using for a particular year of progressions) and adjust it exactly as we did for the birth date.

Example: To illustrate this, we will continue to work with Carol's chart, and we will do the progressions for 1977. We have seen that 30 June 1949 equals 19 December 1976, and the planets' positions on 30 June 1949 will show us the likely trends in Carol's life for the year 19 December 1976 to 18 December 1977.

Progressed Asc. & MC

	Hrs	Mins	Secs
Sidereal time at 30 June 1949	6	32	53
Interval from noon (*add*) p.m.	10	50	
	17	22	53
Acceleration on interval (*add*) p.m.		1	48
Sidereal time at Greenwich	17	24	41

From the London table of houses (p. 204) we can see that the nearest sidereal time is 17 hours 25 minutes 9 seconds, which gives a progressed Ascendant of 9° 26′ ♓ and a progressed MC of 22° ♐

Most people find that it is a visual aid in interpreting the progressions to chart the progressed planets round the edges of the natal chart, as shown in Figure 20. It is possible to buy similar chart forms, which also come in a double sheet so that the aspects between natal and progressed planets can be tabulated. However, it is quite simple to tabulate your data on a blank sheet of paper and to put the progressed planets round the outside of the natal charts which you have drawn yourself. If you insert them in red you will not confuse them with natal planets.

If you follow the line for 30 June 1949 (page 201) you will be able to insert the progressed planets exactly as shown, beginning with the Sun at 8° 21′ ♋ (to the nearest minute), and so on. *The Moon's progressed position has been omitted for reasons which I will explain later.*

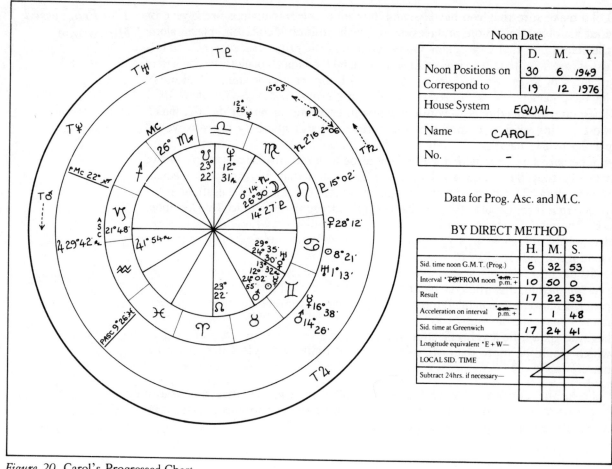

Figure 20. Carol's Progressed Chart.

Data for Prog. Asc. and M.C.

Noon Date

	D.	M.	Y.
Noon Positions on	30	6	1949
Correspond to	19	12	1976
House System	EQUAL		
Name	CAROL		
No.	–		

BY DIRECT METHOD

	H.	M.	S.
Sid. time noon G.M.T. (Prog.)	6	32	53
Interval *TO/FROM noon a.m. –/p.m. +*	10	50	0
Result	17	22	53
Acceleration on interval *a.m. –/p.m. +*	–	1	48
Sid. time at Greenwich	17	24	41
Longitude equivalent *E + W —*			
LOCAL SID. TIME			
Subtract 24hrs. if necessary —			

Tabulating the Aspects By far the easiest way to spot the aspects between natal and progressed planets (not forgetting the Ascendant and MC) is to list them in two columns in ascending order of the number of degrees (ignoring the zodiacal signs) which mark each planet's position. The two columns for Carol's chart would be listed like this:

Natal	*Progressed*
♄ 0.14 ♍	♅ 1.13 ♋
♃ 1.54 ♒	♄ 2.16 ♍
☉ 12.02 ♊	☉ 8.21 ♋
♆ 12.31 ♎	ASC. 9.26 ♓
☿ 13.32 ♊	♆ 12.25 ♎
♇ 14.27 ♌	♂ 14.26 ♊
ASC. 21.48 ♑	♇ 15.02 ♌
♀ 24.30 ♊	☿ 16.38 ♊
♂ 24.55 ♉	M.C. 22.00 ♐
M.C. 26.00 ♏	♀ 28.12 ♋
☽ 26.30 ♌	♃ 29.42 ♑
♅ 29.35 ♊	

To make sure that you have listed everything, check that there are twelve in your list of natal positions and eleven (i.e. twelve minus Moon) in the progressed planets.

There are several things to consider when interpreting progressions and one of these is the relative strengths of the various aspects made by the progressed planets to the natal ones. Only an orb of 1° is considered significant and the number of years over which this is operative will vary widely according to the speed of the planet concerned. In the case of a slow-moving planet which is retrograding at birth, the aspect may be in orb for the whole of the lifetime.

Strength of Progressed Aspects

Example: From the Pluto ephemeris (page 206) you will be able to see that someone who was born at noon G.M.T. on 11 January 1949 (and whose noon date would, therefore, be 11 January) would have Pluto retrograding in her natal chart at 15° 54′ ♌ . On 20 February, it is still within 1° orb of exactness and this is 40 days (i.e. 40 years) later. When interpreting the progressions for the early years of the life, this would be ignored as being merely a corroboration of the natal pattern. However, if natal Pluto was very active in the life and there had been many changes as a result, you would be able to tell your client that life would begin to get a little less hectic after the age of forty. (Pluto turns direct on 1 May, which would be more than 60 years later and unlikely to affect this particular native!)

Aspects made by the progressed Moon are also relatively unimportant since, because of the speed of the Moon's motion, they only affect a month or two in the year. There is one important exception to this. When the Moon is the Ascendant ruler or Sun ruler, the progressed aspects of the Moon will be of major importance. At this stage, we will calculate the progressed moon's position for Carol's birth chart.

Lunar Aspects

The mean motion of the Moon for the year is divided by twelve to get the position for each month. The day of the month when it is exact will be the day given by the progressed noon date. In Carol's chart this will be 19 December, 19 January, etc.

Calculating the Progressed Moon

The Moon's position on 30 June 1949 is 0° 55′ Virgo (nearest minute) and on 1 July 1949 it is 15° 3′ Virgo (seconds are ignored).

The Moon's motion is	15°	3′
Subtract	0°	55′
	14°	08′

Dividing by 12, we get 1° 10′ with 8 minutes over, so we will add an extra minute to the first 8 months. In practice, odd minutes can be added anywhere but they must not be overlooked or progressed positions will become increasingly inaccurate for later years.

We know that 30 June 1949 equals progressed noon date of 19 December 1976, so we have the following positions for 1977:

Progressed Moon

19 December 1976 — 0° 55′ ♍
19 January 1977 — 2° 06′ (adding 1° 11′)
19 February 1977 — 3° 17′
19 March 1977   — 4° 28′
19 April 1977   — 5° 39′
19 May 1977   — 6° 50′
19 June 1977   — 8° 01′
19 July 1977   — 9° 12′
19 August 1977   — 10° 23′
19 September 1977 — 11° 33′ (adding 1° 10′)
19 October 1977 — 12° 43′
19 November 1977 — 13° 53′
19 December 1977 — 15° 03′

In Carol's chart we have only had to work with one year to get the progressed positions for the whole of 1977, but if the progressed noon date had not fallen so conveniently near to 1 January it would be necessary to calculate into the next year to get the Moon's progressed positions for the months of January to December. In practice, clients often ask for a prediction for the next five years and it is comparatively rare to be working out progressions for one year only. We will discuss the easiest way to tabulate many years progressions later in this chapter.

Solar Aspects Aspects made by the progressed Sun are of major importance and will indicate years which affect the native *very personally*. The Sun moves about 1° in a year and the influence will be greatest in the year when the aspect comes to exactitude, but it will also affect the life for the year before and the year following, as the aspect will be within a 1° orb for all that time. As always, the aspect will work *according to the nature of the two planets involved*.

Example: Progressed Sun trining natal Jupiter would indicate an *expansion* or 'opening out' of the basic *personality*. It may exteriorize in various ways, which is why it is unwise to make precise predictions. For instance, one result of such an expansion might be that the native had sufficient confidence to launch out into a new career (this, of course, would be more likely if natal Jupiter and progressed Sun were in sixth and tenth houses). If Jupiter is involved there is almost always an opportunity available if the native wishes to take it. Progressed Sun making a favourable aspect to Saturn in the same houses—sixth and tenth—may indicate new *responsibilities* in the career, which would probably mean promotion, but in each case the *reason* would be that progressed Sun had affected the basic *personality* making the native *ready* for a new opportunity or increased responsibility. Such a change does not come about overnight and so one would expect to see it gradually taking place in the preceding year before its results are seen.

124

The aspects made by progressed Ascendant are similar in effect to the solar aspects and they are of equal importance *provided* the birth time is *accurate*. Unless this is so, they should be ignored, as a difference in *minutes* throws out progressions by *years*. The same caveat applies to the progressed MC, which, of course, affects the career and public standing of the native.

Progressed Ascendant and MC

Aspects between the other planets are called mutual aspects. Next in importance to the solar aspects are those made by the progressed ruler of the natal chart and then by the progressed Sun ruler. In Carol's chart this would be Saturn (ruler of Capricorn Ascendant) and Mercury (as she is a Sun Geminian).

Mutual Aspects

After these, take the planets in order from the Sun.

The fast-moving Mercury and Venus can be out of orb in just over a year. Mars, being slower will take about three years before its effects pass. Jupiter can take five to seven years to reach exactitude and then a similar time to separate from the aspect. You can see from Carol's chart that there is little difference between the natal positions and the progressed positions of the slower planets. For example, Saturn has moved only 2° 12′, Uranus 1° 38′, Neptune 6 minutes, and Pluto 35 minutes. (Neptune has, of course, moved more quickly than Pluto, but because it was retrograde and has now turned direct, it does not appear to have done so.)

Note that any planet which is retrograding, or about to retrograde, slows down considerably and will be in aspect much longer than the times given above. We can see by the June 1949 ephemeris that even Mercury, the fastest moving of the planets, takes eleven days (the equivalent of eleven years) to move from 9° 44′ to 9° 50′, being first retrograde and then moving direct in that time.

This means that we only need to consider the outer progressed planets when the aspects which they were making natally become exact. For instance, in Carol's natal chart Saturn is quincunx Jupiter within 1° 40′ and progressed Saturn closed this orb to exact in 1972 (i.e. on 26 June 1949 = 19 December 1972), when it was 1° 55′ ♍ on the noon date, Jupiter's natal position being 1° 54′ ♒ .

In the progressed chart, Saturn would be said to be *applying* to Jupiter and after it passes the exact aspect, it is said to be *separating* (i.e. the orb of the aspect is becoming greater and the planet will eventually become out of aspect).

Note. In a birth chart we would normally say 'Jupiter is applying to Saturn' because it is the faster planet that is moving into aspect with the slower one, but in the case of progressions, it is the progressed planet which is said to be applying to the natal one.

At the time when the aspect is exact, it becomes important even when a slow-moving planet is involved and we would expect it to manifest in the life of the native in an obvious way, but for the other years, when it remains within orb, it will only continue to reinforce the life pattern.

In all cases, a progressed aspect will have a much greater effect if there is a natal aspect between the two planets. *Natal aspects remain stronger than progressed aspects,* and a good progressed aspect to a difficult natal one may mitigate the difficulty for that time but will not reverse it.

Progressed planets in aspect to each other will only have a weak effect unless there is a natal aspect between them. You will not need to work these out, as the ephemeris lists them under the heading 'Mutual Aspects' in the last column at the top of the right-hand page. You will see that for 30 June (Carol's progressed date for 19 December 1976) the only aspect listed is P ♂ ⊡ P ♃ .

Progressions into New Zodiacal Signs

During a normal lifetime, the natal Sun will progress into the next sign of the zodiac two or three times. Again, the *basic* characteristics, as shown by the natal chart, do not disappear; instead, an extension of the personality seems to be added. In Carol's case, the Sun would have progressed from Gemini to Cancer when she was in her twentieth year. It is reasonable to suppose that she then became aware of the attractions of having her own home and someone to look after. The emotional and maternal side of her nature, which is almost absent in the natal chart, would have begun to blossom.

The progression of the Ascendant into a new sign has a similar effect, giving the native a fresh outlook on life and an interest in a new facet of life. By the time Carol was twenty-three, her progressed Ascendant was into Pisces, again adding the water element which was missing completely in the natal chart. For much of her young life it would have been passing through Aquarius, stressing her lively interest in unusual subjects and bringing a strong desire for freedom. Yet the basic Capricorn Ascendant practicality and sense of responsibility would remain, and will remain, an intrinsic part of her character.

The ruler of the chart and the Sun ruler should also show the effect of progression into a new sign, but these will be in accordance with the *nature* of the progressed planet.

For example, Carol's chart ruler is Saturn, which is in an early degree of Virgo and will remain in that sign all her life, but her Sun ruler, Mercury, moves into Cancer when she is thirty-eight years old, and we can expect that her *mental activities* will then be directed more to domestic affairs. This is the time at which she might be expected to retire from business life and settle down at home full-time. Note that Mercury does not normally take so long to change signs. Fifteen years later it has progressed into Leo, but it is retrograde in the natal chart and so has slowed up considerably in her earlier years.

Carol's Progressions

A full list of these are given on the progressions sheet (Figure 21), but at this stage of your training you should concentrate on major aspects only—the conjunction, opposition, square and trine. If you look back to p. 122, where we listed the natal and progressed positions in ascending order of degrees, you will be able to see these very quickly. Remember the order of importance.

1. *The Sun.* The progressed Sun is at 8° 21′ Cancer. None of the natal planets are within 1° orb of this, so there are no solar aspects.
2. *Ascendant.* The progressed Ascendant is at 9° 26′ Pisces and, again, there are no natal planets within 1° orb of this.
3. *Chart ruler.* Progressed Saturn is at 2° 16′ Virgo. This is within 1° orb of

natal Jupiter. This is a quincunx aspect, confirming the natal quincunx, but Saturn is a slow-moving planet and it has already passed the exact aspect and is separating, so we would not consider it, even if it were one of the major aspects.

4. *Sun ruler.* Progressed Mercury is at 16° 38′ Gemini, and there is no natal planet within 1° orb.

5. *Other planets in order from the Sun:*

   a) *Venus.* Progressed Venus is at 28° 12′ Cancer, and there is no natal planet within orb.

   b) *Mars.* Progressed Mars is at 14° 26′ Gemini. Natal Mercury is at 13° 32′ Gemini, so we have P ♂ conjunct ☿ N.

   Note that this conjunction would have been exact in 1975/6 and is now separating, so the effect is passing. Progressed Mars is also sextile to natal Pluto and it is almost exact in December 1976 and *applying* (i.e. closing to exactness).

   c) *Jupiter.* Progressed Jupiter at 29° 42′ Capricorn is quincunx natal Uranus in December 1976. Do not be misled into thinking that Jupiter is separating, as it is *retrograde* and is therefore applying to Uranus. In fact, it is exact on 1 July 1949, noon, which is December 1977. (You should not be concerned with this aspect in considering only the major ones.)

   d) *Uranus.* (Saturn was considered earlier, being the chart ruler.) With progressed Uranus, we are now concerned with the very slow-moving planets. This is not making an *exact* aspect and can be ignored. The same applies to progressed *Neptune* and *Pluto.*

6. *Progressed planets in aspect.* You will see from the list of progressed aspects that progressed Mars is sextile progressed Pluto. (This reinforces the P ♂ ✶ ♇ N.) This becomes exact in 1977/8, because Pluto is the slower planet and Mars is gaining on it. In the same way, Progressed Venus is not yet within 1° orb of progressed Jupiter, but this opposition aspect also becomes exact during 1977/8.

7. *Change of Sign.* To see if any planets have progressed into another sign it is only necessary to glance along the line of the ephemeris for 30 June 1949. In this case, there have been no changes.

8. *Lunar Aspects.* We have each month's position for the progressed Moon listed on page 124. These are compared with the natal positions in exactly the same way, and you should get the results shown on the progressions sheet (Figure 21).

Transits

The final step in judging progressions is to look at the current ephemeris (in Carol's case the ephemeris for 1977) and to see whether the planet's *present* positions make any aspects with those on the natal chart. Why this should affect the native is another astrological mystery, since the present planet (said to be 'transiting' the natal one, because the aspect is transitory) is making an aspect to a position where a planet was many years before, i.e. at the birth of the native. In practice, however, there is no doubt that a transit very often 'touches off' a natal

NATAL PLANETS NUMERICAL ORDER	PROGRESSED PLANETS AT 19th DEC 1976	ASPECTS TO NATAL PLANETS	ASPECTS TO PROGRESSED PLANETS	O.D'S FOR YEAR 1977
♄ 0°14' ♏	♅ 1° 13' ♋			
♃ 1°54' ♒	♄ 2° 16' ♏		♀ ☍ ♃ 1977/8	☽ □ ♀
☉ 12°02' ♊	☉ 8° 21' ♋			☽ △ ♂
♆ 12° 31' R ♎	ASC 9° 26' ♓			
☿ 13° 32' R ♊	♆ 12° 25' ♎	p ♂ ✱ ♇	♂ ✱ ♇ EXACT 1977/8	♃ △ ♅
♇ 14° 27' ♌	♂ 14° 26' ♊			
ASC 21° 48' ♑	♇ 15° 02' ♌			♇ □ ☉
♀ 24° 30' ♊	☿ 16° 38' ♊			
♂ 24° 55' ♉	MC 22° 00' ♐			
MC 26° 00' ♏	♀ 28° 12' ♋			
☽ 26° 30' ♌	♃ 29° 42' ♑			
♅ 29° 35' ♊				

LUNAR ASPECTS — TRANSITS — NOTES

Date 19th Month 1977	Moon's Long. ♍	To Natal	To Prog.	♂	♃	♄	♅	♆	♇
JAN	2° 06'	⚻ ♃	☌ ♄	29. ☌ ASC		20. ☌ ♇			
FEB	3° 17'			12. ☌ ♃	3. △ Asc	1. ✱ ☿ 15. ✱ ♆ 20. ✱ ☉			
MAR	4° 28'				5. ☌ ♂ 12. ☍ MC 15. □ ☽				7. △ ☿
APL	5° 39'				4. □ ♄ 13. △ ♃				17. ☌ ♆
MAY	6° 50'				28. ☌ ☉ 30. △ ♆	30. ✱ ☉			2. △ ☉
JUNE	8° 01'		✱ ☉		3. ☌ ☿ 7. ✱ ♇	6 ✱ ♆ 16 ✱ ☿		17. △ ♇	
JULY	9° 12'		☍ ASC	10. ☌ ♂	22. ☌ ♀			30. ☍ ☿	
AUG	10° 23'			4. ☌ ☉ 6. ☌ ☿ 23. ☌ ♂ 31. ☌ ♅	1. ✱ ☽ 18. ☌ ♅ 22. ✱ ♄				9. △ ☉ 29. ☌ ♆
SEP	11° 33.					15. ✱ ♀ 18. □ ♂ 28. □ MC		19. ☍ ☿	24. △ ☿
OCT	12° 43.					3. ☌ ☽			15. ✱ ♇
NOV	13° 53'	□ ☿				8. ✱ ♅ 23. ☌ ♄			
DEC	15° 03'		□ ♂		29. ✱ ♄		14. □ ♇		

NOTES

NO TRANSITS LESS THAN SEXTILE

MARS: CONJUNCTIONS ONLY.

NEW MOONS

JAN 19th: ☌ ♃
FEB 18th: △ ♅ ☍ ♄
MAR 19th: □ ♅ ✱ ♃
APL 18th: (ECLIPSE) △ ☽ ✱ ♅
MAY 18th: □ ☽ ☍ MC
JUNE 16th: ☌ ♀ ✱ ☽
JULY 16th: ☍ ASC △ MC ✱ ♂
AUG 14th: ☌ ☽ W
SEPT 13th: △ Asc
OCT 12th (ECLIPSE) NO ASPECTS
NOV 11th: NO ASPECTS
DEC 10th: NO ASPECTS

Figure 21. Tabulation of Carol's Progressions.

aspect in much the same way that a match activates a firework. The natal aspect is always there—always part of the native's make up—but not, necessarily, manifesting all the time.

In judging aspects made by transits, the slow-moving planets are the most important, since they stay in aspect for weeks. The same is only true of the fast-moving planets if they are retrograding, otherwise we can disregard Mercury and Venus transits altogether. Transits of Mars are only considered where the aspect is a conjunction, unless Mars is 'strong' in the natal chart. If there are solar or lunar aspects to Mars in that year, transiting Mars will become more important and will probably indicate the time when these aspects will 'activate'.

In the case of the other transiting planets, only major aspects are considered— conjunction, opposition, trine, sextile and square. With the slower ones, you can see from the ephemeris how many degrees they move in the whole year and then compare them with the natal planets in those degrees.

Example: On 1 January 1977, Pluto is at 14° 7′ Libra. It turns retrograde on 18 January at 14° 11′ Libra and retrogrades to 11° 24′ Libra before turning direct on 24 June and finishes the year at 16° 35′ Libra. For transits of Pluto, therefore, we need only consider the natal planets at 11° 24′ to 16° 35′. We can see from our list of natal planets that transiting Pluto will trine the natal Sun at 12° 2′ Gemini and the 1977 ephemeris will show us that this will happen twice during the year—once on 2 May 1977 when Pluto is retrograding and again on 9 August 1977 when it is moving direct. Similarly, the transiting planet trines natal Mercury twice, and conjuncts natal Neptune twice. The ephemeris will tell you when these aspects are exact but you must not forget that they will be within 1° orb for weeks at a time. Like the progressions, the transits will be more effective if there is a natal aspect between the planets involved. Transits made to progressed aspects may scarcely be noticeable. The letter T is used to denote a transiting planet, e.g. T ♂ △ ☉ N.

Lunations of the Moon

When noting the transits (i.e. in the current year's ephemeris—1977 in Carol's case) it is usual to note the new Moons. These do not require any calculation as the date and time of them is printed in the ephemeris. (See June 1949 where the new Moon is shown at the very top of the left-hand page—New Moon. 26 June at 10 hours 1 minute 52 seconds a.m.) If the new Moon aspects a natal planet it will continue to do so each month for some months. See the tabulation sheet (Figure 21), where the new Moon's have been listed. The new Moon in January 1977 conjuncts natal Jupiter; in February it has not been noted because the aspect is slightly wide of a semi-sextile, but in March it is sextile to natal Jupiter. If there had been a natal aspect between Moon and Jupiter, the transiting new Moon might be expected to activate this. Similarly, there are aspects to Uranus in February, March and April. In general, new Moons are considered extremely significant by some astrologers, especially in a year when there is much activity by progressions.

Eclipses Eclipses of the Sun and Moon are noted in the ephemeris under the heading 'Lunar Aspects' in the last column on the right-hand side under the black line (the mutual aspects are shown above it). The eclipse of the Sun is shown by a blocked-out conjunction ☌ and the eclipse of the Moon by a blocked out opposition ☍ . You can see the solar eclipse marked in 25 December 1954 (page 202). These are also listed under 'Phenomena', which occupies a full page towards the back of each year's ephemeris in *Raphael's Astronomical Ephemeris*.

The effect of a solar eclipse strengthens the activity likely to be engendered by the new Moon. It is doubtful whether lunar eclipses are of great significance, but this is something to decide for yourself when you have the experience to do so.

For a full explanation of lunations and eclipses see the chapter on Astronomy (page 94).

Influence of Progressed Planets Remember that in all things, the planets will 'work' according to their own nature, so that Mars, for instance, whether by progression or transit, will always 'get a move on', while Saturn will tend to delay and frustrate plans while his influence is in orb (though it is noticeable with the 'great teacher' how often one lives to be thankful that plans *were* frustrated or delayed).

While you are still at the elementary stage of learning, it will be quite sufficient to concentrate on the progressions and ignore transits altogether. Later you can begin using the major ones and, as your experience increases, you will be able to decide for yourself how much work and time you wish to put into 'doing the progressions'.

Working for Several Years If you are likely to have clients who come back to you year after year for guidance as to the future trends, it will save you time to look at five or ten years' progressions at once, and list the aspects so formed under the appropriate year. For instance, from the June 1949 ephemeris, we can read off the progressed planets' positions from Carol's first year to her twenty-eighth year (remembering of course that the noon date represented is 19 December).

Unless you have an ephemeris which gives information for some years ahead, you will not be able to list the transits, but the progressions are far more important and will indicate the life-trends.

When the birth time is accurate, the progressed Ascendant and MC can also be obtained for some years ahead, simply by adding the difference between the progressed date sidereal time and the birth date sidereal time to the local sidereal time at birth, and looking up the progressed local sidereal time in the table of houses.

Example (using Carol's data).

Progressed date 30 June 1949 S.T.	6°	32′	53″
Birth date 2 June 1949 S.T.	4°	42′	30″
Difference	1°	50′	23″
Add local S.T. on 2 June	15°	34′	18″
Local S.T. on 30 June	17°	24′	41″

From table of houses for London (nearest S.T. 17° 25′ 9″):
P. Asc. = 9° 26′ ♓ P.MC = 22° ♐ (corresponds to 19 December 1976).
   This is a shorter method of working out the P.Asc. and P.MC than that shown on page 121 and you will see that the result is the same. Working out future years can now be done mentally. On 1 July 1949 the sidereal time is 6° 36′ 50″ and you will realize that this is 3° 57′ more than the previous day. You need only add this to the local S.T. for 30 June and your new local S.T. for the progressed date is 17° 28′ 38″.
   Looking this up in the London table of houses we can see that Carol's progressed Ascendant for 19 December 1977 is 11° 54′ ♓ and her progressed MC is 23° ♐ for the nearest S.T. of 17° 29′ 30″. By using the interpolation method shown on page 111 the P.Asc. and P.MC for the exact sidereal time can be found.

OTHER METHODS OF PROGRESSING THE BIRTH CHART

It is not suggested that the beginner should be concerned with the following methods, but they are mentioned here for the sake of completeness. There is no harm in 'looking at the O.Ds' (see below), which are simple to do and which I have sometimes found very significant; but, as in so many areas of astrology, experienced practitioners eventually find the methods which 'work' for them. This is a matter of, firstly, experiment over a considerable period, and then of familiarity with the preferred technique.

The 'One-Degree' Method

This is often abbreviated to O.D. It consists of adding to the natal planets the number of degrees equivalent to the age of the native in the year under consideration. For example, in 1977, Carol is 28. Adding this figure to her natal planets we get:

$$♄ 0° 14′ + 28 = 28° 14′ \text{ Virgo}$$
$$♃ 1° 54′ + 28 = 29° 54′ \text{ Aquarius, and so on.}$$

   Comparing these with the natal planets (listed in numerical order) we can see at a glance that O.D. Saturn will not make an aspect in 1977, but will square Uranus in 1978 (P ♄ □ ♅ N 1978), and that O.D. Jupiter will trine Uranus in 1977 and be in opposition to Saturn in 1978. Care must be taken when the addition of a number of degrees means a change of zodiacal sign, e.g. Carol's natal sun is at 12° Gemini and the addition of 28° will give progressed position of 10° Cancer. A full list of O.Ds for Carol is given in the tabulation sheet.   131

The Radix Method   This is similar to the O.D. method, but 52 seconds less than 1° is added for each year. It is possible to get tables to work this out.

The Primary System   This is based on the rotation of the earth, and 1° of Right Ascension is taken as being equal to 1 year of life. It is little used as it raises all the difficulties of the various house systems and depends on the absolute accuracy of the birth time.

Converse Aspects (or Directions)   Instead of progressing the planets' positions forward from the time of birth, the positions are regressed to the years before birth, the first year before birth being equivalent to the first year of life, and so on. The aspects formed by the regressed planets to the natal ones have been found significant and are used by many astrologers.

A BRIEF INTERPRETATION OF CAROL'S PROGRESSIONS

Before interpreting progressions we should know something of the events in the life of the native, as we can expect that the natal aspects activated by the same planet will have similar effects all through the life. In particular, we should keep in mind that a 'difficult' natal aspect will not turn into an easy one just because a progressed planet is making a good aspect to it. It may bring some relief in the area where the difficult natal aspect operates, and it may well indicate that an attempt to deal with the difficulty in a new way or in a *new frame of mind* may have a good chance of being successful.

Here is Carol's biography of herself.

I come from an upper middle-class background. My mother was a strong, dominant woman and my father was a rather weak character with whom I had very little contact. My brother is two and a half years younger than me and we are very close [typical Gemini]. We sided with each other against our parents and saw things from the same point of view. From an early age, I deceived and lied to my mother in order to avoid arguments with this dominant woman whose values were so different from mine.

My parents were money- and position-oriented. We had maids and I went to a private girls' school in a hired Rolls Royce. I hated this and would make the chauffeur put me down away from the school so that I could walk in like a 'normal' girl.

In my eleventh year my formal education ceased. I went into hospital for operations on my legs and this was a turning point in my life and a maturing experience. [Jupiter, the planet of maturity, was conjunct the progressed Ascendant by O.D. during the period she was in hospital.] I knew that I would be out of hospital in six months, but most of the people there were grown-ups who knew they would not recover. It made me think a lot about death and the reason why I was in the world. I read lots of books on alternative medicine and on the arts, especially music, which was a love of my life.

After my legs came out of plaster, I had to learn to walk again. I had always been interested in movement and someone suggested a dancing school to strengthen my legs. I went to ballet school and eventually became a full-time dance student.

When I was seventeen my brother nearly died of some brain trouble. I was very distressed and spent hours practising at the piano for comfort. I got so good at this that someone suggested I should apply for entrance to a music school. I did it for a joke and got a scholarship. So at the age of eighteen I was studying music and was in my second year of ballet. Although I passed all my piano exams up to Diploma, I actually got a diploma for guitar playing.

I got married at twenty, at a difficult time in my life. An impressario wanted to send me to Paris for further training and to go on the stage, but my parents wouldn't hear of it and, once again, I felt my life was completely dominated by them. The man I married was in a similar position and we saw marriage as a way of each getting away from parents. We didn't love each other, but I wanted the baby I was expecting very much—I would have liked to have the baby without marriage, but with my social background that was impossible. We married in January 1971 and my baby was born in the August. *On the day I married I felt that I was myself for the first time.* In the five years we were together I really did do the things I wanted to do. My second baby was born in March 1974. We broke up soon after. We had always gone our own way, and it was quite an amicable divorce.

In September 1974 my ex-husband went to India and before he went he introduced me to the man I fell in love with and with whom I am still living. He is a teacher of karate and yoga and with my dancing we have a lot in common. During my marriage, I had learned to be a psychotherapist and I became a vegetarian. I learned to meditate and I became a Buddhist. The man I am with is all of these things and he is my teacher as well as my lover.

I see our future as continuing together. It is a good relationship which becomes stronger all the time. It is important to us both that we should be ourselves. I want to have his children but I feel my own children must be stable in our relationship before the time will be right for this.

1977 is obviously not a year of major change in Carol's life. There are no solar progressions, and no exact aspects involving the Ascendant and MC by secondary progressions.

There is only one mutual aspect: Progressed Mars sextile natal Pluto (P ♂ ⚹ ♇ N). This has no natal aspect, i.e. Mars and Pluto are not in aspect on the natal chart. The effect is general and not likely to be very strongly marked, but 1977 will tend to be a year of changes (Pluto), some of which may come quickly or more quickly than planned. There is a general feeling of 'getting on with things' this year.

It is by no means uncommon to find many years in the life when nothing much seems to be happening. This does not mean that much progress may not be made, even in a quiet way. However, one of the great difficulties of doing progressions is that it is quite common to do them for five years and find nothing of great significance. We should not be surprised at this as our own experience tells us that many years are *not* outstanding in our lives, but it does make it difficult to know what to say to a client!

It is at this stage that we turn to the transits and give a month-by-month indication of the *trends* and the *possible dates* of events. It should always be stressed that they are only approximate as it is common to find that a transit of Mars tends to show *before* it becomes exact and a transit of Saturn is often *later*.

Let us consider what shows up in Carol's transits for the month of January.

1. The progressed Moon (not strictly a transit, but treated as such because its effects only last for the month) is conjunct progressed Saturn. Since there is also a natal conjunction between these planets, it is likely to be significant and to colour the whole month. The new moon on the 19th conjuncts Jupiter (no natal aspect).

2. Transiting Mars is conjunct the Ascendant about 29 January (this is a natal opposition).

3. Transiting Saturn conjuncts natal Pluto about 20 January and is in orb from 7 January to the end of the month (no natal aspect).

The only other aspects are those to progressed planets, which are not very significant. If you wish to consider them, they are treated in the same way as the natal planets, i.e. an orb of 1° is allowed and the slower ones will remain within orb for long periods. The interpretation is the same except that the effects will be weaker.

Interpretation Our interpretation to Carol might begin something like this (the signifactors are inserted here, but would not appear on her copy):

P ♂ ✳ ♇N This is not an outstanding year in your life, but the major trend is for
5th-7th quite a lot of beneficial changes, which seem likely to affect your
houses children and your partner.

January:
P ☽ ♂ P♄ You start the year with some feelings of frustration, perhaps because
of increased responsibilities, and there may well be some annoying
T♄ ♂ ♇N delays which prevent you from making changes just now.
New ☽   There should be a pleasant day about 19 January, when you feel
♂ ♃ N generally more optimistic and relaxed and this should set the tone for
T♂ ♂ Asc. the next month. By 29 January (probably a little before), things get
moving in a way which brings you a lot of personal satisfaction.

The report would then be continued through each month of the year and end with a forecast of the trends for future years. You will see that there are quite a few aspects by O.D. and these, too, can be interpreted if you wish. They will obviously be stronger where they are borne out by secondary progressions.

Before leaving Carol's progressions, let us glance quickly at 1971 (24 June equals 19 December 1970). This was the year in which she married. We have already mentioned that progressed Sun had moved into Cancer, so that she would have been thinking of her own home and family. In that year, progressed Venus was in opposition to the natal Ascendant, which means, of course, that it was just going into the seventh house—the house of partnerships. Progressed Moon was conjunct the natal Sun and natal Mercury during that year. Finally, progressed Neptune turned direct and, of course, was still in trine to natal Sun, as it had been at the day of her birth.

Note that, although her marriage ended in divorce, she herself recognised it as being the means of enabling her to become truly herself (P ☽ ☌ ☉ N) for the first time. However, it is not surprising that Neptune comes into the picture, as there must have been confusion and 'nebulous' feelings both in connection with the baby, which she wanted desperately (Sun in fifth house), but would have preferred to have without the husband, and in her feeling that this was the only way to get away from her dominating mother.

If you like to do the progressions in full for 1971 you will probably find the main trends borne out by transits, progressed Moon, etc. As with the natal chart, something which is strong in the life pattern tends to be 'backed up' by the lesser significators.

Clients with Problems

It is usually easier to deal with the progressions for clients who have problems. These are likely to 'show up' in the present progressed birth chart and you will be in no doubt as to what the 'significators' are likely to be. If the problem is of a Venusian nature, the transits of Venus (even though they may only be in orb for a day or two) may indicate very clearly when the next significant event will take place. Similarly with Mercury. If it is likely to be a significator, then the transits need to be considered. Otherwise their effect is, indeed, transitory and is hardly worth reporting.

I feel very strongly that it is dangerous to let clients get obsessional about their progressions and transits and I do not encourage the ones who ring up to ask 'Is it a good day to go to the hairdresser?' (Yes, that is an actual example!) Nevertheless, it is a fact that daily trends may show up very clearly in your own life. I have often found that a day when I particularly wanted to do some writing was bedevilled by telephone calls, which broke my concentration, only to find that Mercury was 'touching off' a sensitive point on my own birth chart and I would have been far better employed doing gardening.

If you are dealing with a client's problem you need to know as much about it as possible. It may affect more than one area of life and you will need to look at changes of house position by progressed planets.

Example: A client comes to you because she feels that her marriage is breaking up. The complicating factors are that both husband and wife want the children, the wife wants to keep on the family home, and there are certain to be financial and legal difficulties. This is likely, at the very least, to involve fourth house (the home), fifth house (the children), seventh house (the partnership), eighth house (litigation), together with the planets ruling these. You would need to come to a clear understanding with your client as to how much work you are expected to do and the approximate fee for this. Obviously, it would be very time-consuming. Of course you are not going to be handling client's problems until you are well qualified to do so, but it is information that you need to have when that time comes.

135

A full interpretation of a birth chart and progressions will be found in Appendix II

EXERCISES

1. Using the sidereal time method, work out the perpetual noon date for Philip (born in New York at 10 a.m. E.S.T. on 4 December 1954).
2. You are asked to work out the progressions from Philip's sixteenth birthday for five years. Work through each stage according to the chapter you have just read (omit transits).
3. Summarize your findings as if you were writing to the parents on the question of further education and career prospects.
4. Work out Carol's progressions for 1974 and say which aspects by progression might indicate:
   a) The birth of her second child.
   b) The ending of her marriage.
   c) The meeting with her present partner.
   If you have a 1974 ephemeris, see if the transits are significant for any of the above happenings.

CHAPTER 9

THE HISTORY OF ASTROLOGY

The Background

No one who has experienced a total solar eclipse in broad daylight is ever likely to forget it. The sudden hush as the birds fall silent, the temperature drops abruptly and an eerie twilight falls as the dark Moon begins to take a melon-shaped wedge out of the Sun is enough to send a *frisson* down the spine of the most sophisticated. We are, after all, not far removed from our ancestors, who cried out in fear as the dread fell upon them that something evil was eating up their God, and that they would never see the light again.

When we realize that they were nomadic peoples, whose very existence was governed by the seasons, and who lived night and day under the open sky, it is not difficult to appreciate how familiar they would have been with all the planetary and lunar motions.

In the novel *Far from the Madding Crowd,* Thomas Hardy tells how the shepherd becomes alert to the storm which is brewing by observing the movements of a toad, a slug and two spiders. In the same way, ancient man would have picked up such slight clues from the heavens and learned to interpret them in terms of the fertility of the soil, seed time and harvest, seasonal changes of weather and so on.

It was, of course, a naked-eye observation only, and so the movements of the Moon were more obvious than those of the Sun, which was too bright to be studied. The appearance and disappearance of the constellations of stars, according to the time of year, was also familiar to them. So we can assume that they began to connect the seasons of their year with the entry of the new Moon into the various constellations. (The new Moon in their interpretation meant the crescent Moon. The astronomical New Moon—the dark of the Moon—was regarded by them as an evil omen).

The Naming of the Constellations

Thus it seems likely that the zodiacal constellations got their names according to the position of the Moon rather than the position of the Sun. The Egyptians are credited with having named them according to the events which were taking place at the time, so that the *constellation* of Libra (the scales) would appear in the evening sky when the Sun was in Aries (February/March). This was the time when the harvest was weighed (balance) and sold. Similarly the stars of Capricorn rose after sunset (about 1000 B.C.) during June/July (Sun in Cancer), when the sun of midsummer was at maximum elevation at midday. This they symbolized as 'The Goat on the Mountain' and because it was at the time when water began to increase in the Nile, the goat became a goat-fish or sea goat.

The constellation of Aries, rose in September (Sun in Libra), when the Nile was likely to be in flood. The ewes were separated from the rams at that time. The stars of Cancer rose in December (Sun in Capricorn), the turning point of the year when the Sun's light began to increase. This was regarded as the rebirth of the Sun, represented by the sacred scarab beetle, the symbol of Kheper, the god of rebirth. Rameses II (c. 1300 B.C.) is credited with the establishment of the four cardinal signs.

Astrology in Various Civilizations

How it was first realized that the movements of the solar system affected events and people, as well as seasons and crops, we shall never know. The story of astrology goes back to at least 3000 B.C. and appears to have developed at about the same time in both the Middle East and the Far East.

Astronomy and astrology were the inseparable twins for so long that any history of one would be unthinkable without the history of the other. Thus we know that from the reign of Sargon of Agade (c. 2870 B.C.) predictions were made from the positions of the lights and the known planets, but star charts from Egypt have been dated much earlier (around 4200 B.C.). Monuments, also, tell of astronomical observations from early times—from the ziggurats at Babylon and Ur (dated around 2000 B.C.) to Stonehenge in England (possibly built about 2500 B.C.), which was almost certainly used to predict eclipses, and the pyramids of Egypt which were oriented to the (then) north pole of the heavens and were certainly used for observation purposes, as well as for tombs of kings.

It is very difficult to find any consensus of opinion as to the probable dates of the astrological 'firsts'. For instance, one source says that the **Babylonians** invented the zodiac 'probably not earlier than 500 B.C.'. Another source puts it at least 300 years earlier, and yet a third says 'in the early Greek period'. According to the same source, the early Greeks learned their astrology from the Babylonian Berosus (c. 250 B.C.), but another writer says that it was probably Cleostratus of Tenedos who introduced the Babylonian Zodiac into Greece in c. 600 B.C.

Traces of the early astrological beliefs have been found in most parts of the known world. In old Mexico, the Mayan civilization built the Caracol monument which was used for astronomical observation, and both the Mayans and their successors, the **Aztecs,** are said to have used astrology to decree the future profession of each new baby boy so that he could be given the appropriate training.

The Chaldeans produced the first written ephemerides in the reign of the Assyrian King Assurbanipal (668-626 B.C.). They were the 'priests of Nabu (Nebo)', whose temple at Kalakh housed the libraries of Assurbanipal, Sargon II, and Sennacherib. These libraries were later removed to Nineveh.

The Chaldeans are credited with teaching the Egyptians astrology, but at least one source makes a good case for the reverse. It became quite common to refer to any astrologer as a 'Chaldean'. Juvenal, for instance, referred to the astrologers of Tiberius as 'his herd of Chaldeans'. (Most of the Roman Emperors encouraged astrology. It is well known that Augustus had his Moon sign, Capricorn, on his coinage.)

Indian astrology flourished (and continues to flourish) along with that of the rest of the world. It is interesting to note that the traditional horoscopes for the Hindu heroes always showed the planets in their signs of exaltation (or dignity). Their astrology is still bound up with their religious beliefs and they have never adopted the tropical zodiac, but continue to use the sidereal zodiac which places the planets in the *constellations* of the fixed stars. Although some western astrologers use the sidereal zodiac, it is comparatively rare now, but originally all civilizations used it.

Chinese astrology is in a decline (or at least, has gone underground) in the communist republic of China. It was blessed by Confucius, and developed in a very original way, and appears to owe very little to other astrological traditions. The number five plays a great part, there being five elements (air has been discarded and wood and metal substituted), five planets only, plus the Sun and Moon, and the universe is divided into five 'palaces'. Their zodiac divides the equator, not the ecliptic, and each sign of the zodiac is an animal—so we get the year of the horse, the year of the tiger, etc. The Japanese zodiac is similar.

Arabic astrology seems to have started later than in other parts of the Middle East, but once they had grasped its import the Arabians' flair for precision and numerology contributed largely to our knowledge. They improved many astronomical devices, notably the brass astrolabes which were used for finding the altitudes of stars. They bequeathed to us names such as 'nadir' and 'zenith', as well as many of the names of the fixed stars. They were skilled in medicine and astronomy especially, so that medical astrology continued to flourish in their culture at a time when it was beginning to decline in Europe.

How the Philosophers Explained the Universe

As long ago as c. 3000 B.C. the Sumerian civilization pictured the earth as being surrounded by water, with a dome above it in which the heavenly bodies were to be found. They believed that the gods ruled man through these heavenly bodies. By the sixth century B.C., the Greek philosopher **Thales** (624-546 B.C.), who was considered one of the seven wise men of Ancient Greece, expressed the belief that water was the primary substance of the universe. He also made several astronomical discoveries and predicted eclipses.

Anaximander, a pupil of Thales, disagreed with his tutor in believing that the cosmos was fire, surrounded by mist with solid, cold matter in the centre. He was a practical scientist, who is credited with inventing the sundial and preparing the first map of the universe.

Pythagoras, who was working from 540 to 510 B.C., was a philosopher and mathematician. He saw the universe as 'energy descending into matter'. For him the planets were 'living intelligences'. He is best known for his theories of the transmigration of souls and of 'heavenly harmony'—or 'the music of the spheres'. His contemporaries apparently stood in some awe of him for his reported powers of divination and other supernatural practices. He is credited with being the originator of the idea that the earth, moon and planets revolved round the sun.

Heraclitus, yet another Greek philosopher, believed that fire was the prime substance of the universe and that the sun was the source of life. He was a pupil of **Aristotle,** who published books on the heavens and on meteorology and who is believed to be the first teacher to insist on correct scientific procedure. Aristotle (384-322 B.C.) believed that the fixed Earth was the centre of the universe.

ASTRONOMERS AND ASTROLOGERS

First Century B.C. to A.D. 500

At the beginning of this period (first century B.C. to A.D. 500) Greek astronomy was flourishing. As always at such times, there were major disagreements between the practitioners. Although the Julian calendar had been introduced in c. 22 B.C., most astronomers continued to use the Egyptian one into the third century.

But the main bone of contention was the precise degree of the vernal equinoctial point. The sidereal zodiac was, of course, still in use, and the Egyptian astronomers had always used certain fixed stars as markers, notably Spica in Virgo. Presumably, they knew of precession from their own observations. If so, whether from reluctance to impart all their knowledge to another civilization or by an inadvertent omission, they had certainly not passed on this information to the Greeks.

Hipparchus (190-120 B.C.), in comparing the distance of the autumnal point from Spica with that recorded 150 years previously, is credited with having discovered the precession of the equinoxes ('rediscovered' would seem to be the more appropriate term. How many other astronomical and astrological facts may have been lost in antiquity?) However, this did not settle the question immediately. His findings were rejected by his contemporaries and for two or three centuries astrologers were still using 8° or 10° Aries as the equinoctial point.

Hipparchus was a fine observational astronomer. He is credited with discovering a new star and with measuring the obliquity of the ecliptic.

Ptolemy (Claudius Ptolemaeus, c. A.D. 120-180), an Alexandrian astronomer/astrologer, conceived the idea of the universe which was accepted for well over 1200 years. This was that the earth was the fixed centre of a perfect sphere. Around it were layers of water, air and fire, then the sphere of the Moon, the sphere of the Sun and, in ever increasing circles, the spheres of the five known planets in their correct order. Then came the sphere of the fixed stars and finally the sphere of the Prime Mover which enclosed the total universe.

Beyond the universe was the home of the gods. This theory was described in his book *Almagest.* He is also credited with having written the *Tetrabiblos,* though recent scholarship suggests that it may have been a collection of early astrological writings from Egypt, Babylon and Greece. It was certainly the first astrological textbook of note.

He gave some fascinating explanations of the exaltations, as follows:

The Sun is exalted in Aries because the length of days and the heat began to increase in that sign (which was true then because the spring equinox was at the beginning of the *constellation* of Aries, not, as now, in Pisces).

Saturn, being cold and of the opposite nature to the sun, is exalted in the opposite sign, Libra.

The Moon is exalted in Taurus because it was the next sign to that of the Sun's exaltation, Aries.

Jupiter, which produced the north winds, is exalted in the most northern constellation, Cancer.

Mars, because of its heat, is exalted in the most southern constellation, Capricorn.

Venus, because of its moist nature, is exalted in Pisces—representing the moisture of spring.

Mercury, because of its dryness, is exalted in the dry autumnal sign of Virgo.

By the time of Ptolemy, the exaltations were, of course, already ancient, and it is not known whether he had any previous source for his statements.

He is said to have catalogued over a thousand stars, many for the first time.

The Siderealists claim that it was with Ptolemy's writings that the great 'blunder' of the tropical zodiac was made. They say that, at that time, the vernal equinoctial point was within 1° of the beginning of the *constellation* of Aries, so that the sidereal and tropical zodiacs were virtually the same, and that the *Tetrabiblos* is the sole authority for the moving zodiac, which was not Ptolemy's intention. One wonders why this is no longer a 'live' issue in the west today.

Manilius (Marcus or Gaius) was a Roman poet of the first century A.D. He wrote a learned astrological poem, *Astronomica,* in five books.

Porphyry (Porphyrios, c. A.D. 233-301) a Greek Neoplatonist, wrote a life of Pythagoras among other books and also a commentary on the *Tetrabiblos.* He is known in astrological circles for a quadrant system of house division.

Firmicus (Julius Firmicus Maternus, c. A.D. 300). The author of eight books on astrology, he was also the person responsible for the publication of Manilius' *Astronomica.*

Shortly after this, and chiefly as a result of religious intolerance, interest in astrology began to decline in Europe. It was then that the Arabians were developing their interest in the subject and we have to thank them for keeping it alive and, eventually, for reintroducing it to Europe. From this period, the name of **Albumasur** (eighth century) is well known for his *Introductorium in Astronomiam.* It was the translation of this which appeared in Europe during the Middle Ages and greatly helped the revival of interest in astrology and astronomy. During this time, Baghdad was the seat of such learning, having a magnificent observatory and library.

The Middle Ages

This era began with the conflict between the church and the practice of astrology. (When astrology does not cause controversy, it will be dead, indeed!) Albertus Magnus and, a little later, St Thomas Aquinas (c. 1230-80) both realized that astrology had a religious value as long as it could be divorced from pagan beliefs and fortune-telling, and it was their view which eventually prevailed. Astrology then found a place in the universities, became respectable and endowed its practitioners with esteem. Dante and Chaucer both showed great knowledge of it in their writings and it found favour with several Popes. Of course, natal astrology was still limited to the rich and famous, but horary and mundane astrology were widely used (see Chapter 10).

Campanus (Johannes—late thirteenth century), a mathematician and physician to Pope Urban IV, is chiefly remembered as the inventor of one of the quadrant systems.

Regiomontanus (Johann Muller, 1436-1476), who was a German astronomer, also invented a quadrant system of house division. He equipped the first European observatory and made the instruments for it. He also printed (on his own printing press) tables of ephemerides and a translation of the Almagest. He was helping in the reformation of the calendar for Pope Sixtus IV in Rome when he died of the plague. His early death has undoubtedly deprived the world of much valuable knowledge.

Copernicus (Nicolaus, 1473-1543) was the Polish astronomer who wrote *De Revolutionibus Orbinum Coelestium* ('On the Revolution of the Heavenly Bodies') in 1530, although it was not published until 1543, when he was dying. This postulated the theory that the Sun was the centre of the solar system and that the Earth revolved round it. The opposition to his theory came from both scientific and theological circles, for he had displaced man from the centre of the universe and was also accused of 'ignoring the ancient wisdom'. It seems likely that the publication was deliberately delayed because he realized that it was likely to cause such a storm of protest. The book includes an introduction by his pupil *Rhaeticus,* in favour of astrology. It has been said that Copernicus was anti-astrology, but this hardly seems likely in the circumstances. Like most astronomers of his time, he was also a fine mathematician and physician.

Paracelsus (Theophrastus Bombast von Hohenheim, 1490-1541) was a Swiss physician who also studied alchemy, minerology and astrology. He held that the 'influence' of the planets was strong but not all-powerful—'the stars incline, but do not compel'. He was, of course, interested in medical astrology and, in particular, linked the lack of blood with a deficiency of iron, the metal of Mars. Robert Browning wrote a poem, called *Paracelsus* of which he is the subject. His interest in alchemy caused him to be credited with keeping a small devil prisoner in the pommel of his sword!

Jerome Cardan (Girolama Cardano, 1501-1576) was an Italian philosopher, who was also skilled in mathematics and medicine. His *Ars Magna* (1545) was an important mathematical work. He is reputed to have learned astrology from his father. He wrote a book on the work of Ptolemy and Regiomontanus.

Nostradamus (Michel de Nostre-Dame, 1503-1566), a French astrologer and physician, published a book of prophecies in 1555, called *Centuries* which is currently enjoying a revival. Although the prophecies were couched in obscure terms, it is possible to read into them a true forecast of many world events. It is certain that Nostradamus predicted the death (and the manner of it) of Henri II and that he was then regarded as a sorcerer. Catherine de Medici however, who had hired him to cast the horoscopes of the royal children, continued her patronage. His book of prophecies continued to cause controversy and it was condemned by a papal court in 1781.

During most of the Middle Ages, and certainly in this period, knowledge of astrology was widespread among the ordinary people. One has only to read almost any of Shakespeare's plays to find numerous allusions to it—some in the form of jokes, which most people find obscure today, but which Shakespeare obviously expected his audience to appreciate. I am indebted to Derek Parker for drawing my attention to the passage in *All's Well That Ends Well* where Helena suggests that Parolles must have been born under Mars 'retrograde'—because 'you go so much backwards when you fight'. Of course, the belief in astrology was still widely held by the aristocracy: Queen Elizabeth consulted Dr John Dee, the court consulted Simon Forman. Sir Walter Raleigh wrote of the influence of 'the beautiful stars'. In some universities, students were not allowed to take a medical degree without a knowledge of astrology. It is hardly surprising that this period produced some of our ablest astronomers and astrologers.

Renaissance to the Eighteenth Century

Tycho Brahe (1546-1601) was both. A Danish court astrologer, he is reported to have been a most accurate observer of the planetary motions. He corrected the tables made by Copernicus and designed more accurate instruments for observation purposes, but was unable to accept the Copernican theory that the Earth moved round the Sun, saying that 'the heavy and sluggish Earth is not fitted to move'. He is believed to have predicted the birth and conquests of Gustavus Adolphus of Sweden.

After the death of his patron, King Frederick of Denmark, he moved to Prague, where he was joined by Kepler (see below).

During this time, **John Napier**, Earl of Merchiston, a Scottish mathematician (1550-1617), published his work *Mirifici Logarithmorum Canonis Descriptio* (1614), in which he explained his new invention, logarithms.

Francis Bacon (1561-1626), who became Lord Chancellor of England in 1618, with the title of Lord Verulam (and later, Viscount St Albans), was a philosopher and essayist. He was very much against the method of reasoning by citing the ancient authorities and appealed for a much more scientific approach, by observation and testing of theories by experiment—a modern approach to science, in fact.

He applied this to astrology also, believing that much of the current astrology was nothing but superstition. In his book *Astrologia Sana* he wrote that it should be tested by scientific research and, if found to be correct, should be accepted. He believed that the celestial bodies had an influence and that it was possible to predict from them. In his essay *On Prophecies* he refers to Nostrodamus predicting the death of Henri II as having been related to him, in detail, when he was in France himself.

John Dee (1527-1608), an English mathematician and astrologer, was the son of a courtier of Henry VIII. He was a Fellow of Trinity College, Cambridge. He was also interested in magic and alchemy and had the reputation of being a sorcerer from the early age of twenty.

He seems to have enjoyed the confidence of all the progeny of Henry VIII, being first employed by Edward VI, then Mary and Elizabeth. His discussion of Mary's horoscope with Elizabeth landed him in prison on a charge of practising sorcery on Queen Mary's life. He was released in 1555 and began a long association with Elizabeth. He chose the date for her coronation and continued to advise her for many years.

He travelled extensively in Europe and it is believed that he was often an agent for the Queen.

He is believed to have predicted the invention of the telescope.

Simon Forman (1560-1620). What John Dee was to royalty, Forman appears to have been to the nobility. He learned his astrology in Holland and on his return he soon had a distinguished clientele in London. A colourful character, he is the subject of a biography by Dr A. L. Rowse. His predictions include some real 'bloomers' (to which William Lilly was happy to draw attention), including one in which his predictions of a knighthood for himself eventuated as a spell in Newgate gaol.

Kepler (Johannes, 1571-1630), a German astronomer, is one of the giants in the story of astronomy. He became assistant to Tycho Brahe in Prague, about 1600. He worked on the precise data which Brahe had left and discovered that the planets moved in elliptical orbits, and, as Copernicus had said, with the Sun as their centre. He was something of a mathematical genius. He formulated the three great laws of planetary motion (see Figure 22), anticipating Newton's discovery of the laws of gravitation, though not specifically stating them.

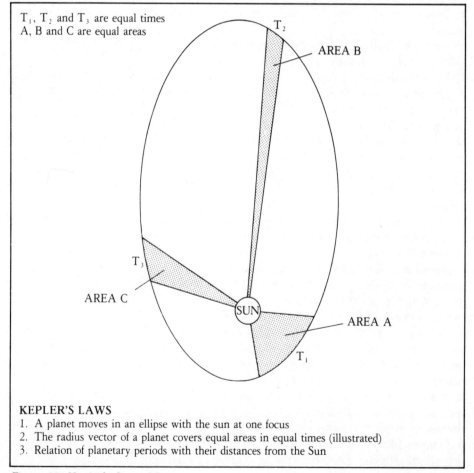

T_1, T_2 and T_3 are equal times
A, B and C are equal areas

KEPLER'S LAWS
1. A planet moves in an ellipse with the sun at one focus
2. The radius vector of a planet covers equal areas in equal times (illustrated)
3. Relation of planetary periods with their distances from the Sun

Figure 22. Kepler's Second Law.

Although he later became the court astronomer, he was, for some years, forced to earn a living by astrology. No doubt he regarded this as the necessary evil which enabled him to devote his spare time to his real interests (astronomy and mathematics). Kepler is credited with calling astrology 'the foolish daughter' of the wise mother, astronomy—'without which the wise mother would starve'. However, he left plenty of evidence that he had proved astrology valid and, indeed, went so far as to say that the evidence for it was so convincing that it could only be denied by those who had not studied it. Like Paracelsus, he believed that the planets might influence men but could not dominate a man's own will to rise above his circumstances.

His proof of the movement of the planets round the Sun was an earth-shaking event. Ever since Ptolemy constructed his theory of the universe it had been accepted as gospel. The church continued to oppose the correct assumptions made by Copernicus and proved by Kepler, and Copernicus *Revolution of Heavenly Bodies* was supressed by the Vatican until the nineteenth century.

Galileo (Galileo Gallilei, 1564-1642) was to strike the final death blow to the old Earth-centred universe. This Italian astronomer, physicist and philosopher had the enquiring and persistent type of mind which could not fail to yield results. In 1583 he discovered the isochronism of the pendulum and in 1586, hydrostatic balance. In 1610, he discovered some of Jupiter's satellites and the Sun spots, following his construction of one of the first telescopes to be made.

From his own observations he was satisfied that Copernicus was correct, and in 1632 he published his *Dialogue on Great World Systems.* This brought him into direct conflict with the church and he was tried before the Inquisition in 1633 for heresy. He recanted, but, according to legend, he muttered 'but it still moves' (meaning, the Earth). Despite his recantation he spent the remainder of his life under virtual house arrest. He was also a practising astrologer.

Morin (Jean Baptiste, 1583-1656). This French physician and mathematician was a prolific author on the subject of astrology. His *Astrologica Gallica* was suppressed by the church, despite the patronage of Pope Urban VIII. He was the personal astrologer of Cardinal Richelieu and had much success in accurately predicting the deaths of several contemporary well-known figures.

He invented one of the house systems which is still in use. It is said that his contemporaries regarded him as the best astrologer of the time.

Placidus (Placidus de Tito, 1603-1668) was an Italian professor of mathematics who invented the house system which is most widely used today, despite the fact that it was rejected by his contemporaries.

Lilly (William, 1602-1681). This son of the soil (his father was a farmer) is one of the first non-scientific and, relatively speaking, uneducated of the great astrologers. He achieved enough money to study astrology by marrying a wealthy widow. His predictions were too good for his own comfort and in 1666 he was required to convince Parliament that he had not started the Great Fire of London in order to make his prediction of it (fifteen years earlier) come true. He issued a series of predictive almanacs between 1644 and 1680 and published *Christian Astrology* in 1647. He is satirized by Samuel Butler in *Hudibras* under the name of Sidrophel.

Gadbury (John, 1627-1692) was a pupil of Lilly. He published *Genethliacal Astrology* and *The Doctrine of Nativities* (1658).

145

Culpeper (Nicholas, 1616-1654) was a physician and herbalist. Like Hippocrates, he taught that astrology and medicine were interdependent. He set up birth charts for the first onset of illness and prescribed accordingly. He classified each herb according to its ruling planet and gathered it at a time when it would be most efficacious according to the position of that planet. His book *The Complete Herbal* is still in demand today.

Flamsteed (Rev. John, 1646-1719) was the first Astronomer Royal. He set up an electional birth chart for the opening of the Greenwich observatory in 1675. This observatory contains the meridian line (0°) from which all degrees of longitude are reckoned.

Newton (Sir Isaac, 1642-1727), the great English mathematician, who discovered the law of gravity, is proclaimed throughout the world as a genius. His other discoveries, the method of fluxions, which has helped to modernize calculus, and the law of the composition of light, were explained in his best known book *Principia.* He also published books on optics and on the *Chronology of Ancient Kingdoms.*

You will find much written about him in many scientific books, but you are unlikely to read that he was also an astrologer. Whether or not he really made the famous remark attributed to him 'Sir, I have studied it, you have not', when challenged by Halley on his belief in it, there is no doubt that he understood and accepted it as valid.

The Fall and Rise of Astrology

When Flamsteed drew up his electional chart for the Greenwich observatory, he wrote 'Friend, are you laughing' below it. A sign of the times, indeed, for the ideas of astrology which had been accepted and revered for thousands of years were now beginning to be held up to ridicule. The new scientists took themselves very seriously—they had better instruments, better instruction and scientific rules of conduct. If something could not be proved by scientific methods, it did not exist for them. Their rationalist views were accepted by the majority and astrology suffered a decline which was to last almost two hundred years.

This time it was Britain which kept it alive and eventually gave it back to the western world. On the Continent it either died out completely or survived only in superstition.

What kept it alive in Britain was the publication by the Stationers' Company of a series of annual almanacs. These had been compiled from the time of William Lilly by well-known astrologers, including Lilly and his contemporaries John Gadbury, William Salmon, William Andrews, and John Partridge. As they died, the almanacs continued unchanged, i.e. still under their names (much as 'Raphael's' ephemeris does today).

The *Astrologer's Magazine,* appearing for the first time in 1793, referred to the 'revival of astrology', but apparently the revival was slow, as the magazine only survived for seven issues. Another one *The Urania* appeared only once, in June 1814. In the same year, the *London Correspondent,* containing astronomical and astrological articles, survived for eight monthly issues.

One almanac, however, achieved a stunning success—for no apparent reason, and certainly not for the fulfilment of its predictions! This was *Vox Stellarum* by

Francis Moore (c. 1657-1715), which survived until 1896 more than 170 years after his death. In 1768, it sold in excess of a hundred thousand copies. The copyright was sold in the early years of this century and Moore probably gave his name to the 'Old Moore's Almanac' which still survives.

Several astrologers of dubious integrity and talents were practising at this time —many combined it with magic, the making of talismans and alchemy.

One who appears to be worthy of note was **John Worsdale** (1766-1826), who was particularly interested in medical astrology, and who regarded his discipline as a science worthy of the most exact mathematical calculations. He published *Napoleon Bonaparte's Nativity* in 1814, having 'rectified' the birth time (like several other people, none of whom agreed with any of the others). In 1820, he published *Astronomy and Elementary Philosophy* and, posthumously in 1828, *Celestial Philosophy or Genethliacal Astronomy*. He seems to have taken great pleasure from predicting deaths both for clients and for anyone who offended him, he had no qualms in telling the victims themselves, which must have been shattering for them as he was invariably correct!

Robert Cross Smith ('Raphael') and **Richard James Morrison** ('Zadkiel') were both born in 1795. Both became well known as the publishers of various journals which contained predictions and astrological articles of a greater interest to the general public than had appeared in former journals. In addition, 'Raphael' ensured his survival (to the present day) by publishing the Placidean tables of house division.

This period produced the man who really got serious astrology on the move again.

Alan Leo (William Frederick Allan, 1860-1917) founded a group that lectured widely in England. He edited *Modern Astrology* a periodical previously known as *The Astrologer's Magazine*. Through his friendship with Walter Old ('Sepharial') he was introduced to the Theosophists, and in 1915 he founded the Astrological Lodge of the Theosophical Society in London, which still flourishes. He was a prolific writer, publishing over thirty books. His genius was directed towards the psychology of the native as shown by the birth chart and his ethical standards raised the whole status of astrology.

Evangeline Adams (Mrs G. E. Jordan, 1865-1932) is worth a mention as the successful American astrologer who was prosecuted for fortune-telling in 1914 (as was Alan Leo, in the same year). In *The Compleat Astrologer* Julia and Derek Parker relate how she was given a horoscope to interpret during her trial. The horoscope was that of the judge's son, and the judge announced that it was interpreted so accurately that, in his opinion, Miss Adams had 'raised astrology to the dignity of an exact science'. The case was, of course, dismissed (as was Leo's).

Charles Carter (1887-1968) virtually carried on the work of Alan Leo. He became President of the Astrological Lodge in 1922 and was the first Principal of the Faculty of Astrological Studies, which was sponsored by the Astrological Lodge in 1948.

Like Leo, he was an outstanding writer, interpreting the old astrological teachings in the light of his own observations. Many of his books appear in the 'Suggested Reading' of the teaching bodies (see booklist).

Nineteenth Century to Present Day

147

In 1954 he retired as Principal of the Faculty and was made Principal Emeritus. He forecast his own death in 1968 (one of a number of well-known astrologers who have done this).

Margaret Hone (1892-1969) succeeded Charles Carter as Principal of the Faculty of Astrological Studies, writing two textbooks for them *The Modern Textbook of Astrology* and *Applied Astrology*. Her high standards of teaching and the standard which she set for the award of the Diploma of the Faculty of Astrological Studies has made the diploma a recognized and worthwhile qualification throughout the world.

Brigadier Roy C. Firebrace (1889-1974) was a co-founder of the Astrological Association and its first President. He was also a Vice-President of the Faculty and the Astrological Lodge. After a distinguished military career he was able to devote his energies to astrology and he published the magazine *Spica*, which was devoted to sidereal astrology, on which subject he frequently lectured. He deserves our respect for being content to be 'a voice crying in the wilderness' and it is to be hoped that active interest in the sidereal zodiac will survive him.

The Situation Today

Once again, astrology is flourishing all over the western world. In Germany the team of **Rheinhold Ebertin**, his wife and his son, Dr Baldur Ebertin, has produced advanced astrological textbooks. Helped by a team of neurologists, chemists and physicists, they also continue to explore the field of medical astrology and cosmobiology.

Holland and France also have active astrological societies.

America has a number of flourishing associations and several distinguished exponents.

I have hesitated before including any living astrologer among the 'potted biographies'. Where so many are working hard to raise the standard, comparisons are invidious, but one name cannot be omitted.

John Addey (born 1920) was a member of the Astrological Lodge, where he became known to Charles Carter. From 1951 to 1958 he was Vice-President of that body. In 1958 he founded the Astrological Association with Brigadier Firebrace and Joan Rodgers. He was its Secretary until 1961 and then its President (combining this role with that of Editor of its journal—*The Astrological Journal*) for much of that time.

His interest in astrology has been philosophical and scientific. A writer of stimulating and witty articles for the *Journal*, he has published *Astrology Reborn*, a collection of his articles, and, recently, his great work on *Harmonics in Astrology*, setting out his thesis that astrology is based on the harmonies of cosmic periods.

The Future

Never has the outlook been brighter for astrology. As we go into the Age of Aquarius, serious interest is being shown on all sides. Scientists are no longer content to sweep aside those things which cannot be explained in terms of their present knowledge and there is more willingness to investigate.

The growth of reputable teaching bodies has resulted in a new breed of well-trained astrologers, from all walks of life, and thriving astrological societies, conferences and well-produced journals all speak of the vitality of our discipline.

The next great step must be a step back—back to the universities where it rightly belongs.

EXERCISES

1. Write a short history of astrology, introducing the figures who seem particularly significant to you.
2. Who explained the exaltations of the planets and what explanations did he give?
3. Who were the outstanding astrologers of the Middle Ages?
4. Why did the Church accept astrology and then reject it?
5. Write (after further research) a life of one of the outstanding astrologers of the sixteenth to eighteenth centuries.
6. Which country was responsible for the survival of astrology after its fall from recognition in the eighteenth century? Why was this? Who were the chief people who ensured its survival?

CHAPTER 10

A MISCELLANY OF FURTHER INFORMATION

The best training for an astrologer, congruent with formal teaching and lots of practice, is wide reading and attendance at lectures.

It is hoped that you will join one or more of the astrological societies, attend their lectures, whenever possible, and read their journals. Your initial reaction to both is likely to be that they are way above your head. Don't worry! We have all felt the same and you will find no shortage of people who will be willing to share their knowledge with you.

The reason for your bewilderment will be two-fold. The first is that astrology is such a huge subject that you must choose your special fields and be content to have only a basic knowledge of the others. The second reason is that astrology is 'alive and well' all over the world and so there are new ideas and new techniques coming along all the time. You are likely to hear lectures or read articles which are as new to experienced astrologers as they are to you.

This chapter is an attempt to give you at least a nodding aquaintance with some of the more common things which you may hear discussed.

TYPES OF ASTROLOGY

In this book we have concentrated on natal astrology. This remains the most popular—understandably so, since 'the proper study of mankind is Man'. But many astrologers are interested in other ways of using their discipline, and a description of some of these follows.

Mundane Astrology   As its name implies, this relates to happenings in the world. Each country has its relevant birth chart—in the case of 'old' countries, there are many such charts, while the newer ones would have only the chart for their 'Independence Day'. For a country like Britain, the charts commonly used are those for the coronation of

William the Conqueror, the unification of Great Britain and Nothern Ireland, the coronation of the reigning monarch, and so on.

All of these can be 'progressed' and the transits noted. Astrologers who are particularly concerned with economics would also study the charts of the leading economists—and of course, the Prime Minister and Chancellor of the Exchequer. These would then be compared with the major charts of the country (see Synastry). This is a specialized subject in that those practising it need to have a wide knowledge of world affairs, and a specialized knowledge of their particular interests in them. Mundane astrology also covers the physical geography of the world, including such things as earthquakes, weather generally and so on. The actual conditions prevailing at the times of the *Ingresses* (the four times when the Sun enters the cardinal signs each year) are compared with the main charts of the country to give some idea of the conditions likely to prevail for the next few months. The Spring Ingress, when the Sun enters Aries, is regarded as the most important. This, of course, is exactly the same as 'doing the transits' for a natal map. For a monthly assessment, the astrologer would look at the *lunation* charts, that is the 'birth chart' of each new Moon.

If there has been any outstanding event, or series of events (such as a series of air disasters), you may often hear a lecture about this, explaining the conditions prevailing at the time and their relationship to a country's 'birth chart'.

One of the difficulties which arises from using the charts of political figures in this way is that of deciding what is personal and what is likely to affect the whole country. The progressed chart of the President of the United States, for instance, might show a strain which materialized as a family bereavement and did not affect the country. If, however, the Independence Day chart of the United States was subjected to stresses at the same time most astrologers would conclude that the two were related.

If you find that it appeals to you, you can study mundane astrology by reading some of the books suggested in the booklist (Appendix IV).

Synastry has been defined as 'the coincidence of stellar influences' and in order to find coincidence one *compares* two or more things. In the practice of synastry, birth charts are compared to each other to find whether there is interaction between them.   ***Synastry***

We had a very small example of this in the questions at the end of Chapter 2 (page 50) when you were asked to say what Sun and Moon signs would be suitable for two people in (a) a marriage partnership and (b) a business partnership.

Synastry is used widely in both natal and mundane astrology and for a wide variety of reasons. It can be used, for instance, to see what influence a new partner is likely to have in a business firm. Does his chart indicate that he would get on well with the other partners? Are his skills likely to fill a need in the firm or are they merely a duplication of skills already here? If so, is the duplication likely to be a good thing? Perhaps the progressions will indicate the loss of a partner shortly and the 'back up' of the new partner may be needed.

Similarly, on the appointment of a new economics adviser, it may be that his own birth chart compares well with the birth chart of his country and also the

151

birth chart of the time when he was appointed. Such a result would, indeed, suggest that the 'moment had produced the man'.

The most frequent use of synastry techniques is in the choice of marriage partner. In the eastern world it is still usual for the birth charts of the boy and girl to be consulted before the wedding is arranged—and of course, the birth chart of the wedding day also has to be suitable.

Since you will almost certainly become involved in 'doing synastry' in some form or other, you should keep the following precepts in mind.

1. *Never make a comparison of two charts without first studying each of the charts in detail.* It is fatally simple to set up charts for an engaged couple, list their natal planets in order of orb and work out that (for instance) his Mars and her Venus are in good aspect (suggesting mutual attraction and a lively love life), and that his Sun is trine her Ascendant (indicating a lasting partnership) and conclude that they are going to make out very well together.

A *full* examination of both charts might reveal some deeply-felt psychological wounds as a result of an unfortunate childhood in one case, while the other chart indicated the type of person who completely lacked the imagination and understanding to deal with such a situation.

The practice of synastry is comparatively simple, but it must be done in detail. If you are not prepared to take the time, it is better not to undertake such work.

2. *Before commencing, decide which questions you want to answer.* This depends, entirely, on the reason for which the comparison is required. Two people who are thinking of forming a business partnership may not be very interested in how they would get on together. One may be buying stock for the other to sell. They may not come into a great deal of contact during the day, but they will want to know whether each is likely to be good at his own part of the job and whether their business ethics are reliable and their aims compatible. These are very different questions from those you would ask for a couple who were thinking of marriage, and different again for friends who wanted to share a house together, but each lead their own lives.

There is always the necessity to study the charts in detail, but you will appreciate that the comparison between charts for different reasons will give rise to different questions with emphasis on different planets, signs and houses.

As always, the planets work in accordance with their own principles. The Ascendant, Sun and Moon represent the sum total of the person; Mercury, the mentality; Venus, the attitude to relationships, and so on.

3. *Take into account the progressions and the transits.* It is common experience in the practice of astrology for the consultant to be asked to compare the charts of two people who intend to start a project together (whether it be marriage, business or an expedition) and to find that, although the comparison of the two charts is satisfactory (or inconclusive), a look at the transits indicates that their interest in the projects is 'transitory' and will not last beyond the duration of the transit. Similarly, progressions may indicate some deep water ahead, and while this would not necessarily indicate that a marriage should not take place, it may well be that a proposed business partnership would be best forgotten about, or at least, postponed.

4. *State the facts; do not give advice.* One has to learn very early in practising astrology how to avoid being put into the position of 'playing God'. The super-

stitious may credit you with all sorts of powers (I have even been asked to remove a curse!), and even the less credulous tend to want you to tell them what to do once they accept that you know your job. It is an insidious form of flattery, but one that must be resisted at all costs.

Firstly, you take autonomy away from a person when you tell them what to do. Secondly, if the advice is taken and does not turn out well, you will get the blame!

Put the facts honestly, but tactfully. A couple who believe themselves to be deeply in love are not going to take kindly to being told that this is a passing infatuation, but a suggestion that next spring (i.e. when the transit has passed) would be a more beneficial time for a wedding than the coming autumn may get you a hearing. Similarly with the couple who seem made for each other but who are likely to encounter one particular difficulty—tell them honestly what it is. They will probably recognize the possibility and decide what they are going to do about it before it arises. One young woman who was very 'home' oriented, on being told that her fiancé was likely to have a spectacular career, which might take him abroad for long periods at a time, wisely decided that he meant more to her than home and that she would accompany him whenever possible. They were very well suited and she was glad to have the opportunity to face up to this problem before it arose.

In practising synastry, the orb of the aspects should be limited to 3°. Do not forget that the outer planets will be close to a conjunction between the charts of people who are about the same age. These only indicate a 'generation influence' unless the planet is the Sun ruler or Ascendant ruler of the chart. Only major aspects are considered important, but triplicity links should also be considered.

This is an example of a married couple whose chart links are strong. They have been married over thirty years.

The 'good' significators:

a) Both are primarily negative/earth/water.

b) Both have Moon in Taurus, so their responses will be similar, and both have much interest in Taurean hobbies—gardening, music, etc.

c) His Venus is in *exact* trine to her Venus (4° Virgo to 4° Taurus)—indicates harmony in relationships.

d) His Moon is conjunct her Venus (within 2° orb).

e) His MC is in *exact* sextile to her Venus (she has sympathy with his career objectives).

f) His Sun in twelfth house is in *exact* sextile to her Pluto (in her eighth house). They have shared a common interest in 'matters of life and death' and of unusual and 'hidden' matters. It may be assumed that they have had a refining influence on each other. Their marriage has been subject to many changes of home over a wide area of the United Kingdom, and of occupations. These changes have been willingly accepted and have made their lives varied and interesting.

g) His Jupiter is in *exact* trine to her Moon and *exact* sextile to her Jupiter. (Both have enlarged the horizons of the other and each has been concerned to make life happy for the other. Both have encouraged the other to expand their own personality.)

153

The 'difficult' significators:

There is only one within orb: His Mars is square her Ascendant (within 1°). As might be expected of Mars, this works out in quick, sharp arguments which provoke her to retaliate (her Ascendant is in Scorpio) and both can be 'cutting' at such times.

The marriage, of course, is quite secure enough to withstand the occasional argument.

Such close aspects often show also in the charts of parents and children, and it is quite common to find the same zodiacal signs emphasized in the charts of a whole family.

There are now several good books on the subject of synastry (see booklist).

Electional and Inceptional Astrology

Now that more people have some knowledge of astrology, it is quite common for an astrologer to be asked to choose a favourable time for the beginning of a new project. This is known as *electional astrology,* since we are free to elect when this should be. The subjects for electional astrology range from wedding days (a very popular one) to the date of a business concern going public (i.e. becoming a quoted company on the Stock Exchange).

Similar questions apply when making an electional chart as applied to synastry. You need to determine what questions must be asked and which planets must be favourable. For instance, if the time required was that for the floating of a new oil rig, you would want a favourable Neptune (since this planet rules both oil and the sea). There is always a certain risk, and even danger, at such times and so you would want a favourable Mars also. In such a project, a planet like Venus would be comparatively unimportant, in contrast to an electional map for a wedding, where it would be a dominant consideration.

Since the election is made for the exact moment of beginning, it is usually possible to find an Ascendant which is helpful and, by choosing the exact degree, it is often possible to arrange that the important planets are in appropriate houses.

Where the election chart is for the beginning of something which is very personal to the native, synastry techniques must be used to make sure that the proposed electional chart compares well with the native's chart. In the case of the wedding day, you would, of course, consider the charts of both partners.

Inceptional charts are birth charts which are for things rather than for people. That is, they are for the moment of a beginning where no election has been possible, either because the 'birth time' has already passed before the astrologer is consulted or because circumstances have already dictated the time at which the project should commence.

Horary Astrology

This form of astrology, in which a question is posed and a birth chart is set up for the exact time at which the question is asked, was very popular in the golden days of astrology. The 'birth chart' of the question time is interpreted to provide the answer to the question. In England, William Lilly was one of its great exponents. It is still practised today, though one hears very little about it.

It is an esoteric type of astrology, since the questioner has to be 'in tune with the time' so that the question is asked at the *right* time, i.e. the time for which the answer can be deduced.

In the practice of horary astrology, the consultant normally takes the time at which the question is put to him by the client. If it is put in a letter, the client should state the time when the question formed in his mind. Where this is not known, the time when the letter reaches the astrologer can be taken.

The interpretation is not difficult, provided the question is stated precisely. A question like 'Will I move house?' is not the same as 'If I put my house on the market, will it sell within the next two months?' Possibly, they may amount to the same thing, but in one case the querent is primarily concerned with the *move* and in the other case with the *sale.*

The Ascendant ruler is taken to represent the querent and the ruler of the sign on the cusp of the house which is chiefly connected with the matter is taken as the significator. So the first thing to decide is which house is the significator. This is not always easy. In a business matter, the tenth house (worldly position) and the second house (financial gain) might appear to be equally important, hence the significance of obtaining an exact question.

Having established the two planets representing the querent and the question, the aspect between them is judged to give the answer to the question, i.e. an 'easy' aspect indicating a favourable answer. The snag in this traditional form of judging horaries is that there may be no aspect.

Because of the houses controversy and because of the difficulty in deciding which are the significators, I prefer to judge the chart as a whole—giving due weight, of course, to the planets which are likely to be the most significant. I also like to compare the birth chart of the querent.

As so often happens, experienced astrologers usually have their own methods which, they find, work for them.

Here is an example of an horary chart.

I began this part of the book on 3 July 1977. I had just written the heading 'Horary Astrology' when the question occured to me 'Will this book be published and be a success?' The time was then 10.20 a.m. B.S.T. (London).

I knew that I was hoping for success in terms of recognition (tenth house) as a competent astrologer and writer and also for financial success (second house) by teaching (Mercury/Gemini/third house).

On setting up the chart, I found 9° 33′ Virgo rising (teaching, writing and Mercury ruler). The MC was 3° Gemini in ninth house (further education). In tenth house, also in Gemini, was Jupiter (the fortunate planet and the significator of publishing). Mercury and Sun were in eleventh house (groups of people—also natural house of Aquarius, the astrologer's 'ruler') in Cancer—the ruler of Cancer, the Moon, was in Aquarius in the sixth house (work and service). Pluto in Libra in the second was in exact trine to the Moon, and also in second house was Uranus (the astrologer's planet) in Scorpio (my own Ascending sign). Although Pluto was also in exact square to the Sun, I really felt that I had got a resounding 'yes' from my horary chart, but was I 'in tune with the time?'—time alone will tell.

Medical Astrology

To people who are medically trained, the birth chart is an asset to indicate the physiological make-up of the native. Hippocrates, the Father of Medicine, did not think a doctor was properly qualified unless he understood astrology. Herbalists also use it, not only to decide which herbs will be beneficial to their patients, but also to judge the best time to sow and gather herbs.

This is just another fascinating area of astrology (there are so many), but it is best left to the experts.

RECENT DEVELOPMENTS IN ASTROLOGY

The advent of the computer has made it a comparatively quick and simple matter to test new theories for validity. We now have valuable statistics to support our theses, and among the new ideas which have gained recognition in recent years are the following.

Midpoints

This theory states that midpoints between any two planets, the Lights, Ascendant or Midheaven, are highly significant, being the point at which their influences intermingle. The midpoint, as its name implies, is the degree of the ecliptic exactly half way between the two. In Figure 4 the Moon is 2° Taurus and the Sun 7° Virgo. The number of degrees between them is 125° (4 complete signs plus 7°-2°). Therefore, the midpoint between them will be half of 125° or $62\frac{1}{2}$° on from 2° Taurus. This falls at $4\frac{1}{2}$° Cancer, at which point is the MC. Most midpoints will not be marked by another planet or significant point, as in this case. The interpretation of midpoints requires some skill in working with progressions and transits and should not be undertaken by a learner.

Unaspected Planets

A planet which makes no aspects to any other planet in a birth chart indicates an area in the life of the native which is not integrated with the rest of the personality. Sometimes there are two or more groups of planets in a chart which are in aspect to each other in the same group but which are not connected to the other groups. At the time of writing, some very interesting work is being done on the likely results of this.

Harmonics

The work of John Addey M.A. in harmonics has been the major new contribution to astrological thought. Since the 1950s he has been engaged in statistical experiments from which has arisen his thesis that the universe vibrates to different waveforms, much as a violin string vibrates to different chords. The implications of his work for all astrologers is not yet fully understood, although it is already clear that astrology will never be the same again. The subject is certainly not one for a 'trainee' astrologer to study, but you are bound to hear or read references to it.

SOME DOUBTS AND DIFFICULTIES

Apart from the obvious areas of disagreement, such as the houses question, there are several other things about which the interpretation is doubtful. Perhaps the most troublesome of these (certainly to the beginner) is the precise role of the *Sun* and the *Ascendant* in the natal chart. It is usual to find the Sun interpreted as the 'basic self', while the Ascendant is the persona, or the face we show to the world. This would seem to indicate that everyone puts on an actor's mask, and I would prefer to interpret it as the personality we portray—not a false image, but a very real part of ourselves. I have heard astrologers say 'The Ascendant is *now,* the MC is the *becoming*', and 'The Sun is the continuing soul, the Ascendant is for *this* lifetime.' (This presupposes that *all* astrologers believe in reincarnation. Such a belief is, indeed, widespread, but to get *all* astrologers to agree on anything would be unlikely, since we are all 'Urania's children'!) For what it is worth, my own opinion is that the Ascendant indicates our lesson for this lifetime.

While you are learning, it is wise to regard the Ascendant and the Sun as similar in meaning and of equal importance. Later, in the light of experience, you will form your own theory.

The Nodes of the Moon

It is usual to insert these into a birth chart, but there has been no research to date (1977) to decide on how they should be interpreted. The north node (the one shown in the ephemeris) is felt to be the one by which the native gains, and the house tenanted by it will indicate the area of life in which the native may be fortunate. The south node is said to have the opposite effect. For example, the north node falling in tenth house would indicate gains from wordly status and the south node would then fall in fourth house, indicating losses in home life. Indian astrologers believe the reverse, i.e. that the south node is the fortunate one, while some Tibetan astrologers regard both nodes as aggressive. Lately, there has been a suggestion that the gains and losses should be interpreted on a much more spiritual level and this may well prove to be the case.

Parallels of Declination

If you turn to the June 1949 ephemeris you will find the declinations of the Sun and Moon in the columns headed ☉ Dec. and ☽ Dec. under the black line, and you will find the declinations of the planets above the line. Those for Carol's chart are as shown in Figure 8. When two planets are at the same declination (only 1° orb allowed) they are said to be *in parallel* and the interpretation is that this is similar to a conjunction between them. It seems doubtful if many astrologers now accept this, since very few of them seem to use it. Nor does there seem any good reason for assuming this to be true. As shown on Carol's chart, there are three planets within orb of a parallel, Venus, Uranus and Pluto. As Pluto is in Leo, while Venus and Uranus are in Gemini, the fact that all of them are equidistant from the celestial equator seems to be irrelevant, since they can be many degrees distant on the ecliptic. In the case of Uranus and Venus, which are already conjunct on the ecliptic, it is likely that the parallel strengthens the conjunction. If

157

the conjunction and declination were exact, they would, of course, be in occult-ation. They are indicated on the grid by P or ‖ .

Rectification The problem of the unknown birth time is always with us. Many people have no idea of their time of birth while others know it only within a few hours. Even among those who give a precise time, the number which are exactly on the half or quarter hour is highly suspicious.

In the case of the person who can only give a birth date and has no one who can help with an approximate time, the astrologer should inform such a client that the birth chart can only be general and will apply to anyone born on that day in the same area. A chart can then be erected for noon on that day. If the Moon was in the same sign all day, the zodiacal signs of all the planets and Lights will be known and aspects (except those of the Moon) can be calculated, but there will be no Ascendant, no MC and no house positions. Such a chart should be marked 'Speculative'.

Where the time is known to within an hour or two, the Ascendant could be in two, or at most, three, possible signs. A little discussion on the nature of each will often result in the client deciding which one sounds relevant and this will give a starting point for the process of rectification.

As its name implies, this is an attempt to rectify the chart and it is done by reference to the major events in the native's life. The simple way to do it is to use the One Degree method.

Example: Ann married at the age of twenty-two. On her natal chart, Venus is at 4° Taurus. Adding one degree for each year of her age, progressed Venus would be at 26° Taurus when she married. Her Ascendant is believed to be in the later degrees of Scorpio. If it were taken as 26° Scorpio, progressed Venus would have come into opposition with the Ascendant (and, therefore be entering the seventh house of partnerships) at the time of marriage. This gives a possible degree for the Ascendant, which can then be tested (in the same way) by reference to other important events in the life.

There are other methods of rectification, some of which are quite complicated. None have a blameless record.

Charts for well-known people have been 'rectified' and later the exact birth time has become known. In such cases, the rectified Ascendant has often been wildly wrong, especially in cases where the birth time was not known at all. It is important to remember that a speculative chart remains just that—speculative.

Another clue to the Ascendant is found in how the progressions actually work out. If you are working with the same client for some years, you may get a comment such as 'some of the events you predict for me, seem to work out later than you forecast.' You should always ask your client to keep a note of the exact dates of any major events through the year, not only to enable you to rectify the chart but also to see how the various progressed aspects work out for him.

Because retrogradation is only an optical illusion, in effect, there seems no reason *Retrogradation*
why it should be considered detrimental in a birth chart. However, astrology is a
science of symbolism and it would be a bold astrologer who was prepared to say
that it had no significance. There are, certainly, some who believe that it inhibits
the full expression of the principle of the planet which is retrograding. If this is so,
it seems reasonable to expect that the difference would be marked when the planet
turned direct, by progression. This may well prove to be the case, but sufficient
evidence is lacking at present.

Modern astrology has a long inheritance from the past and from a wide variety of *The Arabian*
cultures. Many of the ancient techniques and beliefs have been discarded, but one *Parts*
which is still used today is the technique of finding sensitive points on the chart
known as the *parts,* and in particular, the *Part of Fortune,* (Latin—*Pars Fortuna,*
often abbreviated to *Fortuna* and even to *Pars*). To find these parts, the longitude
of the planet, is added to the longitude of the Ascendant and from the result is
subtracted the longitude of the Sun. (*Example:* the planet Venus is used to find the
Part of Marriage.) It is usual to find the Part of Fortune entered on the birth chart,
the glyph being ⊕ . To find this, the longitude of the Moon is used instead of one
of the planets.

    Example: On Carol's chart the Part of Fortune is calculated as follows:

Moon	26° 30′ Leo	= 146° 30′ (i.e. 4 whole signs from
	Add	0° Aries, plus 26° 30′)
Ascendant	21° 48′ Capricorn	= 291° 48′
	Minus	438.18
Sun	12° 02′ Gemini	= 72° 02′
		366° 16′

As this is more than the whole circle deduct 360°

Result: 6° 16′ Aries

    The Part of Fortune would fall in Carol's third house and the interpretation is
that her aim in life is in the matters connected with this house. Since it is the
natural house of Gemini and she is a Sun Geminian this may well be true, but
there is little agreement among astrologers as to whether Fortuna is of value.

    If you use it, a quick check that your computation is correct can be made by
observing the relative positions of the Sun and Moon. The Ascendant and
Fortuna should be in the same relationship. In the example, the Moon is two
houses further along the ecliptic than the Sun plus 14° 28′. Fortuna is two houses
away from the Ascendant plus 14° 28′ (in the same relationship, although it has
started another cycle along the ecliptic).

The Asteroids Most people know that the asteroids lie between the orbits of Mars and Jupiter. They are probably the fragments of an old planet. They vary greatly in size and it seems likely that the largest ones may have an astrological significance. It is now possible to get ephemerides for Pallas and Ceres but much more research needs to be done before we can come to any conclusions.

Vulcan and Lilith *Vulcan* is the name given to the, as yet, undiscovered planet, which is believed to be inside the orbit of Mercury. Until the astronomers can identify it and let us have ephemerides for its movements there seems little point in speculating about it. However, some astrologers have suggested that it would, if it exists, be a likely ruler for Virgo.

Lilith is the name given to a dark moon which is said to be a satellite of Earth. It was given much more credence in the eighteenth and nineteenth centuries than it is today and its interpretation was usually that of beckoning the native to his own doom! It is said to have been discovered about 1720 by its shadow cast on the face of the Sun. Although most astrologers are sceptical about it, one still hears the occasional lecture or reads an article on the subject—it would appear that the fatal fascination which is Lilith's trade mark is exercised on some astrologers who do not quite believe in it but cannot leave it alone. Perhaps we shall hear more of this dark lady.

SOME FURTHER DEFINITIONS

Decans By dividing each sign into three parts of ten degrees each, we get the first, second and third decans or decanates. The first decanate is reckoned to be the most potent part of the sign, partaking fully of the nature of, and ruled by its natural ruler.

The second decanate is ruled by the planet which rules the next sign in the same triplicity and the third decanate is ruled by the ruler of the final sign in the same triplicity.

Example (Figure 4):
The first decanate of Gemini—ruled Mercury (natural ruler—Air).
The second decanate of Gemini—ruled Venus (Libra—Air).
The third decanate of Gemini—ruled Uranus (Aquarius—Air).

Dispositors When a planet is in a sign which it does not rule, it is said to be disposited by the natural ruler. Thus, Venus in Aries—dispositor Mars.

It is possible to find a whole series of dispositors in a birth chart where no planet is in its own sign.

Example (see Figure 4):
Mercury in Libra —dispositor *Venus*
Venus in Virgo —dispositor *Mercury*
Mars in Leo —dispositor *Sun*
Sun in Virgo —dispositor *Mercury*

Jupiter in Scorpio —dispositor Pluto
Pluto in Cancer —dispositor Moon
Moon in Taurus —dispositor *Venus*
Saturn in Libra —dispositor *Venus*
Uranus in Pisces —dispositor Neptune
Neptune in Leo —dispositor *Sun*

In this chart Sun and Mercury are dispositors twice and Venus is dispositor three times. Venus is, therefore, the dispositor of the whole chart and due weight should be given to this planet when judging the chart as a whole. However, I am of the opinion that it is nothing like as strong as a planet in its own sign.

Genethliacal Astrology

This is an old name for natal astrology, which is still used occasionally.

The Great Year

The time which is taken by the Earth to pass through each of the Ages (e.g. the Age of Aquarius) in all the twelve signs of the zodiac. This takes more than 25,000 years, each Age lasting about 2000 years (see Precession of the Equinoxes, page 97).

Lunar Returns

The Moon returns at some point each month to the *exact* position which it occupies on any natal chart. The ephemeris will show when this happens and the positions of other planets at the same time can be compared with the natal chart and interpreted in the same way as transits. From the work of Dr Jonas in Czechoslovakia, it seems likely that this is the time of maximum fertility in the month for women.

Solar Returns

The time in the year when the Sun reaches the exact position which it occupies on the natal chart. A chart for the time of a solar return can be judged by itself, but will have greater impact if it also makes aspects to the natal chart.

Orrery

An orrery is a working model of our solar system. They can be found in science museums, and are well worth studying.

SOME FINAL DOs AND DON'Ts

Like all respected professions, astrology has a strict code of ethics. This is especially important when you are dealing with members of the general public, who are likely to confide in you.

161

You should respect all such confidences. Your own reputation will suffer if you do not; and so will the reputations of other astrologers.

You should not publish or lecture on any chart without the permission of the native. I always ask for permission at the time when I first analyze the chart, otherwise I may have lost touch with the client when I wish to use it.

Many clients will ask you to forecast deaths—either of themselves or of a relative. This is both difficult and dangerous. Difficult because it is impossible to say whether an accident or illness will be fatal or just severe, and because the significators of death can be anything from Jupiter (a happy release) to Uranus (a sudden upheaval) or Pluto (a welcoming of one door closing and another opening). It is also dangerous because, if your forecast is incorrect you may be blamed and if not, you lay yourself open to a charge of fortune-telling, thus debasing the true nature of astrology, so you should always refuse to do it.

Do not be drawn into doing work for a client who will tell you nothing and just wishes you to 'prove' astrology. Astrology does not need proving, any more than medicine or any other science. It is much more dignified (and will do astrology no harm) to explain that it is not a 'guessing game' but a valid method of helping people to understand themselves better, and to realize their own potentialities.

If you become too busy to do work for a client within a month of accepting it, do let him know how much delay there will be.

In dealings with your own colleagues, do share your own discoveries and theories, so that the body of astrological knowledge may grow. Similarly, if you are using someone else's ideas, do acknowledge the source of your quotations from them.

While you are learning, do not be afraid to ask for help. Astrologers are all rugged individualists but they are always willing to help others (like true children of Aquarius). When you have more experience, you, too, will find great pleasure in helping the beginners.

Never lose an opportunity to hear a lecture by someone who really knows his subject. Extend your range of knowledge by attending conferences whenever possible.

Finally, for yourself—be careful not to become obsessed with the planetary movements in your own chart. It is fascinating to watch them and see how they work out, but you are here to stand on your own feet and not to offer your planetary afflictions as excuses. As Shakespeare said, 'The fault, dear Brutus, is not in our stars, but in ourselves, that we are underlings.'

Above all, keep your sense of humour. Astrology is absorbing, a never-ending study, but above all—a source of great enjoyment. Enjoy it.

APPENDIX I

BRITISH SUMMER TIME TABLE AND WORLD TIME CHART

During the periods listed below the clocks were put forward by *one hour*, except for **1941-45** and **1947** (marked with an asterisk) when they were put forward for a total of *two hours* (Double Summer Time). All changes were at 2 a.m. G.M.T.

1916 21 May to 1 October	*1941 1 January to 31 December**
1917 8 April to 17 September	*1942 1 January to 31 December**
1918 24 March to 30 September	*1943 1 January to 31 December**
1919 30 March to 29 September	*1944 1 January to 31 December**
1920 28 March to 25 October	*1945 1 January to 7 October**
1921 3 April to 3 October	1946 14 April to 6 October
1922 26 March to 8 October	*1947 16 March to 2 November**
1923 22 April to 16 September	1948 14 March to 31 October
1924 13 April to 21 September	1949 3 April to 30 October
1925 19 April to 4 October	1950 16 April to 22 October
1926 18 April to 3 October	1951 15 April to 21 October
1927 10 April to 2 October	1952 20 April to 26 October
1928 22 April to 7 October	1953 19 April to 4 October
1929 21 April to 6 October	1954 11 April to 3 October
1930 13 April to 5 October	1955 17 April to 2 October
1931 19 April to 4 October	1956 22 April to 7 October
1932 17 April to 2 October	1957 14 April to 6 October
1933 9 April to 8 October	1958 20 April to 5 October
1934 22 April to 7 October	1959 19 April to 4 October
1935 14 April to 6 October	1960 10 April to 2 October
1936 19 April to 4 October	1961 26 March to 29 October
1937 18 April to 3 October	1962 25 March to 28 October
1938 10 April to 2 October	1963 31 March to 27 October
1939 16 April to 19 November	1964 22 March to 25 October
1940 25 February to 31 December	1965 21 March to 24 October

163

1966 20 March to 23 October	1973 18 March to 28 October
1967 19 March to 29 October	1974 17 March to 27 October
1968 18 February to 31 October	
to 1971 (inclusive)	
1972 19 March to 29 October	

From 1974, B.S.T. was from 2 a.m. G.M.T. on the *third Sunday in March* until 2 a.m. G.M.T. on the *fourth Sunday in October.*

Double British Summer Time (see above*)

1941	4 May to 10 August	1944	2 April to 17 September
1942	5 April to 9 August	1945	2 April to 15 July
1943	4 April to 15 August	1947	13 April to 10 August

World Time Chart

The countries listed overleaf are *east of Greenwich* and therefore the time given in hours and minutes should be *added* to G.M.T. to give local time or *subtracted* from local time to give G.M.T. Further information may be found in the *Nautical Almanac.* (S) indicates that Summer Time may be kept.

EAST OF GREENWICH

Albania (S)	01 00	Lebanon	02 00
Algeria	01 00	Luxembourg	01 00
Angola	01 00	Malagassy Republic	03 00
Australia		Malaya	07 30
Capital Territory	10 00	Malta (S)	01 00
New South Wales	10 00	Mozambique	02 00
Northern Territory	09 30	Netherlands	01 00
Queensland	10 00	New Zealand	12 00
South Australia	09 30	Nigeria	01 00
Victoria	10 00	Norway (S)	01 00
Western Australia	08 00	Oman	04 00
Austria	01 00	Pakistan	05 00
Bahrain	04 00	Poland (S)	01 00
Belgium	01 00	Rhodesia	02 00
Botswana	02 00	Rumania	02 00
Bulgaria	02 00	Singapore	07 30
Burma	06 30	South Africa	02 00
China	08 00	Sri Lanka	05 30
Congo Republic		Sudan, Republic of,	02 00
West	01 00	Sweden	01 00
East	02 00	Switzerland	01 00
Crete	02 00	Syria (S)	02 00
Cyprus	02 00	Tanzania	03 00
Denmark	01 00	Tunisia	01 00
Egypt (S)	02 00	Turkey	02 00
Finland	02 00	Uganda	03 00
France (S)	01 00	USSR	
German Federal Republic	01 00	W of 40°E	02 00
Gibraltar	01 00	40°E to 52°E	03 00
Greece	02 00	52°E to 67½°E	04 00
Hong Kong (S)	08 00	67½°E to 82½°E	05 00
Hungary	01 00	82½°E to 97½°E	06 00
India	05 30	97½°E to 112½°E	07 00
Iran	03 30	112½°E to 127½°E	08 00
Iraq	03 00	127½°E to 142½°E	09 00
Israel	02 00	142½°E to 157½°E	10 00
Italy (S)	01 00	157½°E to 172½°E	11 00
Japan	09 00	E of 172½°E	12 00
Jordan	02 00	Yugoslavia	01 00
Kenya	03 00		

Countries Normally Keeping G.M.T.

Eire	Portugal (S)
Gambia	Sierra Leone
Ghana	UK

Note: For countries west of Greenwich, the time given should be *subtracted* from G.M.T. to give local time or *added* to local time to give G.M.T.

WEST OF GREENWICH			
Bahamas	05 00	Indiana	05 06
Brazil		Iowa	06 00
East	03 00	Kansas	06 00
Central	04 00	Kentucky	06 00
West	05 00	Louisiana	06 00
Canada		Maine	05 00
Alberta (S)	07 00	Maryland	05 00
British Columbia (S)	08 00	Massachusetts	05 00
Manitoba (S)	06 00	Michigan	05 00
Northwest Territories (S)	04 08	Minnesota	06 00
Ontario (S)		Mississippi	06 00
E of 90°W	05 00	Missouri	06 00
W of 90°W	06 00	Montana	07 00
Quebec (S)		Nebraska	
E of 60°W	04 00	East	06 00
W of 60°W	05 00	West	07 00
Saskatchewan (S)	-	Nevada	08 00
SE	06 00	New Hampshire	05 00
Remainder	07 00	New Jersey	05 00
Yukon	09 00	New Mexico	07 00
Chile	04 00	New York	05 00
Equador	05 00	North Carolina	05 00
Haiti	05 00	North Dakota	06 00
Madeira (S)	01 00	Ohio	05 00
Mexico (some variations)	06 00	Oklahoma	06 00
Panama	05 00	Pennsylvania	05 00
Paraguay	04 00	Rhode Island	05 00
Peru	05 00	South Carolina	05 00
Uruguay (S)	03 00	South Dakota	
USA		East	06 00
Alabama	06 00	West	07 00
Alaska	08 11	Tennessee	06 00
Arizona	07 00	Texas	06 00
Arkansas	06 00	Utah	07 00
California	08 00	Vermont	05 00
Connecticut	05 00	Virginia	05 00
Delaware	05 00	Washington	08 00
Florida	05 06	Washington D.C.	05 00
Georgia	05 00	West Virginia	05 00
Hawaii	10 00	Wisconsin	06 00
Idaho	07 00	Wyoming	07 00
Illinois	06 00		

Notes

Summer Time is used in many parts of the USA. During the Second World War, *from 2 February 1942 to 30 September 1945,* all time zones in the USA advanced one hour.

The above listings are by no means exhaustive. To list all possible time variations would be a lengthy task. They do, however, indicate the considerable changes which may be encountered.

These lists relate to *time zones*. Actual calculation of precise time differences from G.M.T. should be made on the basis of every 15° east or west of Greenwich equalling one hour in advance or behind respectively. Thus, *every degree will make a difference of four minutes.*

APPENDIX II

EXAMPLE OF A COMPLETE ANALYSIS

The following is an analysis which was done for a client who was widowed in 1972. Since that time she had had two disappointing friendships with men, which had the effect of making her doubtful of ever having a successful relationship with a man again. She asked whether there was a possibility of remarriage in the future. Her chart is shown in Figure 23 and her progressions in Figure 24.

☉ ♌   I expect that you have often wondered whether your Sun was in Cancer or in Leo, as you will have found that, in newspaper and magazine astrology, your date of birth is sometimes included in one and sometimes in the other. In your case, this must have been very confusing as your Sun is actually in the sign of Leo, but you have four other Planets in Cancer, and therefore your character will certainly be a mixture of both. In addition, you have the Ascendant in Virgo and the Moon in Capricorn.

☽ ♑ ☍ ☿ ♋   I was interested that in your letter you used the phrase 'I shall just have to try and muddle through as I have been doing.' The reason why this particularly interested me was that your chart shows that you have a very strong intuition which is usually to be trusted.
☽ △ ♆   However, I think that your feelings and emotions colour this too
☿ ✶ ♆   much and you do not trust your own intuition and, consequently, get
Water   into a state of 'muddle'.
Asc. ☌ ♆

Water   Although you have a good brain, I am sure that you would always say 'I feel' rather than 'I think'. (This is not a criticism, as I am

168

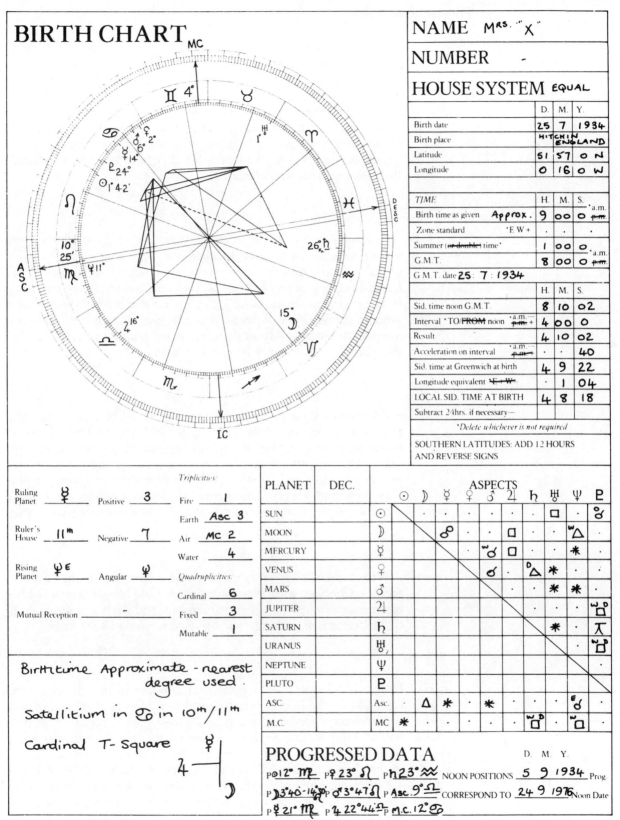

Figure 23. Mrs X's Chart.

☿ ♋   rather like this myself.) All it means is that you do have the intuition to know what to do if you could only quieten your emotions and nervous reactions and listen to what your own intuition tells you. I would have liked the chance of meeting you because when one is doing a birth chart, one has to keep in mind that this is exactly what it is; that is, the chart as at the time of birth and, of course, people modify this psychological background as they grow up. Usually, I can tell easily by talking to people whether they have learnt how to handle their own psychological 'mixture'.

Ψ in 1
in ♍

☉ ☿ ♇ in 11   It is not possible for me to answer the question as to whether you will marry again or not, but I realize from your chart that you ought to have (and probably do have) a very active social life. Your friendships may be much above average and they tend to be enduring. In addition, you should belong to societies and clubs and have some office in connection with them. If you do not, you are inhibiting your life pattern considerably as there are many pointers towards the fact that this should certainly be part of your life.

♀ ♋ in 10

☉ in ♌

♄ in ♒ in 6

♀ ✶ ♅

♀ △ ♄ (D)   As regards the closer relationships, it would be true to say that there are certain difficulties. There is no doubt that you would be very lonely without a partner of any kind and also that you are strongly sexed. On the other hand, you have a great feeling for your own personal freedom and I think that, if you do not marry again, you may very well find a very satisfactory life for yourself in your social activities, with your friends and, possibly, in a business partnership.

♃ in ♎

♀ ♂ ♂

♄ ♒

☉ ♌ in 11

♀ ✶ ♅

♃ in ♎

♀ △ ♄

What I would like you to do is to take a look at your life as it is at present. Consider what is the worst that could happen if you did not make another close personal relationship, and what you could do in that case towards making your life as you would like it to be.

Ψ ♂ Asc.

☿ ♂ ✶ Ψ

MC ♊

☽ ♑ in 5

Sat. in ♋

Asc. ♍

Ψ in 1

(benasp)

I say this because I see a great deal of potential in your chart and especially in the field of intuitive and artistic work. I think that you would make a good teacher, as you have a great capacity for dealing with children and, in general, for looking after people. I wonder if you have ever thought of writing for children? There are various factors in the chart which make me feel that you would be able to do this. I see that your sense of rhythm is very well developed and it occurs to me that you could also find outlets in poetry, music, dancing and drama.

I expect that some of your own self-expression has been limited by the fact that you have had children to bring up and, judging by their present ages, I should think it would now be a very good time for you to look at what you would really like to do with the rest of your life. At your age, many things are open to you.

☽ ♑ ☍ ☿

♀ ☿ ♇ ♂ ♋

☉ □ ♅

☿ ♂ ♂

I can see that one of your great difficulties is that your emotional level is high and that you find it difficult to release your nervous tensions. I think that you feel very deeply and are easily hurt (and possibly rather resentful) but you tend to keep your emotions 'bottled up' and this has a bad effect on your nerves. It is also possible for you to work to the state of nervous exhaustion and you should be aware of this.

☉ ♌

♂ ♋

☽ ♑ ☍ ☿

As regards your health generally, I would expect this to be good, but I see that your energy fluctuates quite a bit. This is likely to be caused by sluggish circulation which could, when you are older, lead to things like rheumatism and colds. The best way of combating this is to practise deep breathing. If you do not know how to do this properly get someone to show you.

Asc. ♍

♄ in 6

I expect that, with your Virgo Ascendant, you are interested in health matters generally. You would very much benefit from a diet of natural foods and you may like to find out more about this.

☿ in 11

Asc. ♍

MC ♊

♅ in 8

☉ ♌ in 11

☽ ♑ △ ♆

☽ □ ♃

♃ ♎ in 2

You have a powerful mind which is very original and there is a possibility of you making money in unusual ways. I would expect that, before you had a family, you were quite an ambitious person, and I hope that you will still feel that there is a great deal that you can do. I do not know if there is something which you particularly want to do, but, if so, you should be aware that you have both the organizing ability and the capacity to deal with details to make it a success. One thing, however, which is rather weak is your ability to deal with your own money, and if you are thinking in terms of investments (or even the best way of planning your financial affairs) it would be as well to get expert advice. I expect you can be extravagant at times and that you very much enjoy the little luxuries of life. Your chart suggests that you could certainly be financially successful.

Sat. in ♋   One of the things which appears constantly in your chart tells me
that you are a great worrier—even to the point of worrying if there is
Asc. ♍   nothing to worry about. You have plenty of self-control in other
ways, and you should bring your practicality to bear upon the subject
of worrying. As one who comes from a long line of worriers, I am able
☽ ☍ ☿   to tell you that you can train yourself not to worry about things that
you cannot do anything about. I have done this and I know that it is
☽ in ♑   not easy, but every time that you do this it makes it easier for the next
time. When such a situation occurs, and there is nothing which can
be done, turn your mind resolutely from it and find something else to
♄ in 6   occupy your thoughts.

☿ ♋   You have a very good memory and you find anything to do with the
past attractive. You would make quite a good historian or an antique
collector, etc. However, there is also a tendency to live in the past,
and I would like you to turn your attention to the future and make up
your mind where you want to go. I believe that you can go anywhere
♀ ☌ ♋   that you wish and I hope that this report may encourage you to do so.

Asc. ♍   I see that you are a hard worker (although you much enjoy being
♄ in 6   lazy when you are relaxing), but you should not be in a dull or boring
♃ in ♎   job. Your mind is too lively to accept confining conditions.
MC ♊

Present Position   You are now moving into a positive phase of your life and I hope that
and Future   this report will encourage you to take every advantage of it.
Trends

From the information which you have given me, your birth time
seems to be pretty accurate. I think that there is a possibility that it is,
in fact, about five minutes out, but, from the point of view of what I
am about to tell you, this will not make any practical difficulties.

I was able to pinpoint the date of marriage, the births of your
children and your husband's death from the information that you
gave me, and it all seems to correspond very well with this time.

172

NATAL PLANETS NUMERICAL ORDER	PROGRESSED PLANETS AT 24ᵗʰ SEPT 1976	ASPECTS TO NATAL PLANETS	ASPECTS TO PROGRESSED PLANETS	O.D's FOR YEAR 1976/7
♅ 1° ♉	♅ 1° 07' ℞ ♉		☉ ♂ ♆	☉ ✱ ☿
☉ 1°42 ♌	♂ 3° 47' ♌		☉ ✱ MC	
♀ 2° ♋	Asc 9° ♎	p ♂ ✱ MC		☿ ♂ ♄
MC 4° ♊	MC 12° ♋			
♂ 6° ♋	♆ 12° 08' ♏		♀ ✱ ♃	♇ ✱ ♂
Asc 10°25' ♍	☉ 12° 13' ♍		♀ ♂ ♄	
♀ 11° ♍	☿ 21° 27' ♍	p ☉ ✱ ☿ 1978/9		MC □ ♃
☿ 14° ♋	♃ 22° 44' ♎			
☽ 15° ♑	♀ 23° 03' ♌	p MC ♂ ☿ 1978/9	♀ ✱ MC	
♃ 16° ♎	♄ 23° 30' ℞ ♒			
♇ 24° ♋	♇ 25° 26' ♋			
♄ 26° ℞ ♒				

LUNAR ASPECTS				TRANSITS						NOTES
Date 24 Month 1976	Moon's Long. ♌	To Natal	To Prog.	♂	♃	♄	♅	♆	♇	NO TRANSITS LESS THAN SEXTILE MARS: CONJUNCTIONS ONLY
SEP	3°40'		♂ ♂					□ ♆		
OCT	4°40'	✱ MC			✱ ♃	△ ♂				
NOV	5°39'				□ ♄ ✱ ♃					NEW MOONS Sept 23rd
DEC	6°38'			1-4 ✱ ♇	✱ ♃	✱ Asc	□ ☿			□ ♀♏ ✱ ☉♏
1977 JAN	7°37'		20. ♂ ☽	26- ✱ ♇		✱ ♆	□ ☿			
FEB	8°36'					✱ ♆ ✱ ♃	□ ☿			Oct 23rd (ECLIPSE) ♂ ♅ △ ♀ □ ☉
MAR	9°35'	✱ Asc	15- ♂ ♄	12- □ ♄		✱ ♆ ✱ ♃				
APL	10°34'			12.✱ ☉ 23 ♂ MC	14. ✱ Asc	✱ ♃				Nov 21st No ASPECTS
MAY	11°33'			21 □ Asc 23 □ ♀						
JUNE	12°32'		7. ♂ ♅	16 △ ♃						Dec 21st △ ♅ ♏
JULY	13°31'		23. ♂ MC	30. △ ♄						
AUG	14°30'			26- ✱ ♅						

Figure 24. Tabulation of Mrs X's Progressions.

This may make some slight difference to the actual dates which I am going to give you and I would be grateful if you would make a note and see how they work out. You may find that they are one month or just a few days behind the dates actually given. I do not think that they will be ahead.

I do not believe that astrology is a sharp enough tool with which to make accurate forecasts and say that something *will* happen on such-and-such a date. For one thing, there are many different ways in which the planets can work out.

P ♀ ♂ P ♄   I can tell you, however, that the situation which has been, I might say, 'dogging your footsteps' just before the death of your husband and right up to now, is moving away and I think that you have every

P ♀ ✳ P ♃   reason to expect a brighter future.

First of all, I am giving you the main trends for the whole year from September 1976 to September 1977. These are the important things. The things which follow and which only last for a short period are transitory and, although they may seem important at the time, will not necessarily affect your whole life.

P ♂ ✳ MC   However, the trends for the whole year are very strong and very clear. There is absolutely no doubt at all that if you decided to launch out on a different career this year you could make a great success. I do not know whether your mind has been turning to this at all, but I see that your whole personality could benefit from your career prospects and that there is an energizing force which will make it almost certain that there will be a great advance in this area. It may mean that you

P ☉ ✳ P MC   will continue to do the same job but will have some promotion or added responsibility which will make it more interesting for you. It seems to affect your whole status (or standing in the world) and may not necessarily mean an actual job but a boost to your social standing as against your private life. I see you being very busy in this area for the next year. [This lady opened her own catering business with a

Sat. in ♋   male partner during the year in question.]

P ☉ ☌ P Ψ

P Ψ P MC

P ☽ ✶ MC

From early October and for the year onwards, your intuition seems to tie in very well with your basic personality and I think you may at that time be able to get things a lot more clear in your own mind as to what you really want out of the rest of your life. In other words, you could be making long-term plans which are very satisfying and it could be that the energy and vitality brought to the social life or career could very well tie in with this.

P ₊ ☍ P ♄

As regards the area of personal relationships, it appears, as I have already told you in a letter, that the frustrations and delays concerned with this will continue until about mid-1977. This situation will then begin to change. I do not say that it will change rapidly from that time, but the difficulty which has been impeding this area of your life is certainly moving away and will not return during your lifetime. [As at July 1977, the business partnership appeared to be developing into something closer.]

P ☉ ✶ ☿

P MC ☌ ☿

In two years from now (that is to say, September 1978 to September 1979), you will have an extremely good year both personally and again in the public sector of your life. These both seem to be affected very much by your mentality and by your nervous system, both of which are strengthened by this.

May I suggest that, if you make another relationship which looks as though it may be permanent, you should let an astrologer compare your birth chart with the chart of your partner to see whether it is the case that this could be a permanent relationship and also, if you decide that it is to be so, to let you know of the likelihood of the areas of difficulty and the areas where you would be of great help to each other.

I am now coming to the 'day-to-day' forecast and, as I have already said, this may be delayed for some days, depending on the accuracy of the birth time that you gave me. These I have done just to the end of December 1976. I am willing to do further forecasts for you, if you find that these are helpful.

T ♆ □ ♆ N

Usually, your intuition is extremely good but I would like you not to trust it for the month of September and up to 16 October. It appears that you may be subject to deception (and this can include self-deception) about this time. If there is any chance of you having to sign any contracts or anything of that type, please do get legal advice. It would also be as well if you were not to take people at their face value or to make any snap judgements of anyone that you should meet around that time.

T ♅ △ ♂ N
(Natal ⚹)
☽ ☌ P ♂
☽ ⚹ MC
New ☽ ⚹ ☉ △ ♅
T ♅ ⚹ Asc

You should find the period from 24 September to 22 October a very exciting and unexpected time. There seems to be a lot of energy or life put into unexpected happenings which will be of a pleasant nature. If there are changes about then, they should work out very well in the future. This is one of the few dates which might be earlier than I have said. This is due to the presence of the planet Mars, which often speeds things up! There is a smaller aspect (i.e. unexpected but pleasurable happenings) from 12 December and into the New Year.

T ♄ ⚹ ♃ N
T ♃ □ ♄ N

From 28 October, all through November and to 28 December, there is gain to you from taking extra responsibilities. This looks like a time when you will have some hard work to do but which you will find pleasurable as well as financially rewarding. There may be a short period during this time (12 to 18 November) when you will not find the hard work so pleasurable and this could be because you are really overdoing it. If possible, try to slow down for that short time.

T ♃ ⚹ ♇ N

Towards the end of the year (27 November to 4 December) there is a suggestion that you may find one door closing and another opening. This will work out very well. I hope that you will welcome these changes and go along with them, as they are certainly for your own good. You should find an expansion of your personality, and indeed of your life, by making the changes as they come along.

The client confirmed the analysis as being largely correct—in particular with reference to worrying, need for secure relationships, but also regarding the need for personal freedom, lack of trust in her own intuition and the 'bottling up' of emotion with resultant tension. She also has a good memory and a love of antiques. She does not recognize her own potential, but admits that her partner says the analysis is also correct about this.

APPENDIX III

A SHORT INTERPRETATION OF THE ASPECTS

1. It must be clearly understood that the aspects, like all other significators in a birth chart, should be interpreted according to the indications in the chart *as a whole*. One would not expect an 'easy' aspect in the chart of a top athlete, for instance, to work in the same way as it would in the chart of a lethargic work-shy individual. In the latter case, the aspect would be merely a reinforcement of a situation which was already undesirable and in no way could it be described as a 'good' aspect for that person. *Notes*

2. 'Difficult' aspects are often the spurs which drive us on, in much the same way that a critical parent may encourage a child to develop an 'I'll show him' attitude and so increase the child's determination to succeed. While the easy aspects will be pleasant to live with, the difficult ones may bring the rewards.

3. An aspect between two planets is a link between the principles which they represent. *Both* principles will combine, whether easily or with difficulty, and the aspect will be modified by the aspects made to it by other planets. *Example:* A Sun-Uranus conjunction, indicating powerful use of originality and inventive traits, may be inhibited by a difficult aspect from Saturn, which will impose limitation. The chart, *as a whole,* will give a good indication as to whether the native will let this crush his natural aptitude or whether he will accept it as a challenge and submit willingly to the discipline.

4. As with the planets, so with the aspects. Some may be 'strong' in comparison with others for any of the following reasons:

   1. The Sun is one of the planets involved.
   2. The ruling planet is involved.
   3. One planet, or both, is 'strong' in its own sign.

5. Dissassociated aspects are considerably weaker than the normal aspects. In some cases, they seem to have the opposite effect. For instance, a trine which is dissassociated usually means that five signs separate the two planets in aspect,

177

therefore they do not have a triplicity in common (or even a quadruplicity). Such a trine may tend to be a 'difficult' aspect. However, a square which spreads into four signs means that the two planets are in the same triplicity and it is difficult to avoid the conclusion that they will have a lot in common and this may prove to be an 'easy' rather than a 'difficult' aspect.

ASPECTS TO THE SUN

The Moon Lack of an aspect between the Sun and Moon indicates a dichotomy in the personality which may be difficult to live with. The native sometimes experiences a feeling of watching himself acting a part. Even though there may be no aspect 'in orb' this situation will be mitigated if the Lights are in 'compatible' signs.

The Conjunction. While the basic personality and the instincts are very similar, so that the subject is free from conflicts of the personality, there is a tendency to imbalance in that the sign containing both the Lights is heavily 'weighted' in comparison with others. The likelihood that Mercury (and possibly Venus) will be in the same sign, may indicate a limited personality with very little adaptability. Much depends on the sign and house tenanted.

The Opposition. There is often considerable mental ability with this aspect, but the feelings will be at variance with the personality. The houses and signs tenanted will give an indication of where these difficulties are likely to occur.

Easy aspects. The native will be psychologically integrated, and, consequently, will be contented and peaceful. If the Moon sign shows intuitive qualities these will be brought into the outer life and used positively.

Difficult aspects. There may be personality difficulties, and these often originate in childhood, as a result of conflicts between the parents and the child. The native is often extremely self-willed and restlessness is common.

Mercury The only possible aspect to the Sun is the conjunction, as Mercury is never further away from it than 28°.

The conjunction. Has a weakening effect on the critical faculties. It will be appreciated that, as often happens, Mercury in the same sign as the Sun indicates that the mentality and personality are alike. Where, in addition, the two are within 5° of each other, the mind cannot get away from the influence of the personality, so that judgement tends to be biased—everything is coloured by how it effects the native.

Venus This planet is always within 48° of the Sun and the only strong aspect will be the conjunction.

The conjunction brings Venusian charm to all aspects of the native's personality, together with warmth of manner and friendliness. There is a great interest in all Venusian pursuits.

The semi-sextile is similar, but weaker.

The semi-square, though considered a 'weak' aspect, indicates difficulties in partnerships (particularly the marriage partnership). In all other matters it is similar to the conjunction. In women's charts it seems to indicate rather excitable and unstable people with exaggerated emotions.

The Sun and Mars are both powerful; both much connected with energy and   ***Mars***
health. They are traditionally linked by the exaltation of the Sun in Aries.

The conjunction makes for a powerful and vital personality. The zodiacal sign
(and the rest of the chart) will indicate whether this can be handled well. It is
excellent for hard, physical work, but even this can be carried to extremes. Sometimes the excess energy shown by this aspect can be too much for the native to
cope with.

The opposition. Like all oppositions, this can indicate excellent balance (in this
case, in the expenditure of energy) if it is handled well. Otherwise, it should be
interpreted as for 'difficult' aspects.

Easy aspects. These indicate a vital and energetic personality. The health is
usually good and the native enjoys being active.

Difficult aspects. Arguments and quarrels may be frequent. Restlessness and a
tendency to overwork are present. There is often enjoyment of potentially
dangerous situations.

The conjunction. The great benefic in conjunction with the Sun certainly bestows   ***Jupiter***
its blessings. The native should be optimistic, relaxed, tolerant and generous.

The opposition. The nature of these two planets tends to make the opposition
similar to the conjunction. There may however, be restlessness or, in contrast, an
easy-going attitude to life which is carried to excess.

Easy aspects. Contentment and a relaxed attitude often combine with an
expansive mind to portray the typical philosopher—a very Jupiterian personality.

Difficult aspects. As with the opposition, restlessness is common with these
aspects. The native should leave his financial affairs to the experts. He can be
wildly extravagant. There is a tendency to over-expand in all areas of life.

The conjunction. The Sun will 'spark off' the Saturn ambition and the native may   ***Saturn***
achieve a powerful worldly position, but not without the dedication and serious-
ness of purpose which leaves little time for the lighter side of life.

The opposition is similar to the conjunction, and may, in fact, work out more
easily, the native achieving a 'balance' between the energizing, life-giving Sun
characteristics and the responsible determined attitude indicated by Saturn. People
with this aspect often find their enjoyment in activities which seem like work to
other people!

Easy aspects. Since the characteristics of the Sun and Saturn are not in
harmony, even the easy aspects will only help the native by the exercise of
responsibility and hard work. He will be well-organized and health will usually be
good. These contacts give durability in all aspects of life and the native often lives
to a ripe old age.

Difficult aspects. The Saturnian keyword of 'limitation' exactly expresses the
likely result of these aspects. Results of hard work may be limited by
circumstances beyond the control of the native. There is often a responsibility
forced on him (possibly for someone else—see houses involved). Health may lack
vitality and the native may suffer from feelings of inferiority.

Uranus *The conjunction.* The originality and inventiveness of Uranus is given a powerful thrust by the conjunction with the Sun. The urge for freedom contributes wilfulness and a need for independence is very marked. This often makes the native a difficult person to live with.

The opposition. The effect is similar to that of the conjunction. The signs tenanted will indicate whether balance can be achieved. In 'strong' signs the self-will fights the basic personality and can result in the native losing what he most desires—either through nervous or mental strain or because he 'throws a spanner in the works' himself.

Easy aspects. A very strong combination which will accentuate originality. The native may excel in unusual ways and is capable of leadership. These aspects sometimes indicate a man who is ahead of his time.

Difficult aspects. Similar to the worst effects of the opposition. A strongly revolutionary tendency may cause much trouble, especially if nervous tensions are allowed to build up and become explosive.

Neptune Remember that these aspects are very slow-moving and tend to have a 'generation' influence, unless Neptune is strong in the birth chart.

The conjunction. There should be an easy expression of creative talent, especially in the inspirational field. The native may be mediumistic. Creative gifts will 'materialize' into the writing of fiction or poetry, etc., if the conjunction occurs in one of the practical (Earth) signs, or if Saturn is helpful.

The opposition. The tendency to live in a dream world may be very strong and confusion is common, especially in dealings with others.

Easy aspects. As for the conjunction, but inspirational gifts will remain nebulous unless there is strength by sign or from other planets in aspect.

Difficult aspects. These can indicate a highly emotional person, too easily ruled by the feelings. Deception and self-deception may be present. This will be mitigated if there are good aspects from Mercury to Neptune.

Pluto As with Neptune, the 'generation influence' needs to be considered.

The conjunction. Either the Scorpion or the Eagle can be expressed and the rest of the birth chart will show which this is likely to be. Intensity of feeling is bound to be present and requires a legitimate outlet. Pluto has been in Leo in recent years and this exaggerates the effect of Sun/Pluto contacts. In this sign there is a danger that the native will seek to dominate others.

The opposition. Dramatic changes are likely to occur at intervals during the native's life. When the opposition is activated by progressions, the native may change his mode of life completely.

Easy aspects. These should help, psychologically, by enabling the native to 'exteriorize' the areas of conflict in his own personality and discard those which are unhelpful.

Difficult aspects. Intensity manifests as tension and can undermine self-confidence and damage health unless the tensions can be released.

The conjunction. As with the Moon/Sun conjunction, this aspect indicates a very **The Ascendant**
integrated personality. However, the sign which both occupy will be heavily-
weighted as against the rest of the chart and may result in a lack of adaptability.
The Sun will be strengthened if in the first house and all the characteristics of the
sign tenanted will be much emphasized. The native will be very self-oriented. This
tendency will be mitigated if the Sun is in the twelfth house, where a need for
privacy is shown. The native may then be very self-contained and tend to be a
loner.

The opposition. This is almost always a good aspect and indicates a well-
balanced personality, particularly if the Sun is in the seventh house, where it will
emphasize good and enduring relationships. In the sixth house, the native will be
much concerned with matters of work and health.

Easy aspects emphasize the well-integrated personality which should give
freedom from mental conflicts.

Difficult aspects. The native finds difficulty in reconciling two sides of the
personality, with consequent strain. The house in which the Sun falls will show
the area of life where this is most likely to be felt.

The conjunction. The worldly standing, either in terms of a career or of a social **Midheaven**
position, will be the chief concern of the native. There is a great need to be
recognized as 'someone'. If other aspects are helpful, the occupation will be a
source of enjoyment.

The opposition. The native may be completely uninterested in his worldly
position and be perfectly happy in home surroundings. However, he may merely
have feelings of inferiority with regard to his own capabilities. The signs tenanted
will show which is most likely, together with planets near the MC.

Easy aspects. Work will be enjoyable, but not over-emphasized. The native will
take a sensible attitude towards the attainment of his objectives and not set his
sights impossibly high. Ambitions will be attainable.

Difficult aspects. As with the opposition, feelings of inferiority are common—
often because the native is a perfectionist in matters to do with the career.

ASPECTS TO THE MOON

The conjunction. This is a happy combination of the mentality with the intuition. **Mercury**
The native should be both intelligent and imaginative. The memory is usually
good.

The opposition. May be quite similar to the conjunction in mentality, but there
may be fluctuation in the nervous energy. This will be noticeable if Cancer, Virgo
or Capricorn are tenanted.

Easy aspects. As for the conjunction, with plenty of nervous energy and a
practical mind.

Difficult aspects. Intelligence may be misdirected and become over-concerned
with the affairs of others. The ebb and flow of the Moon characteristics is very
noticeable and the subject changes his mind often. Not good for the nervous
system, unless strengthened by the other aspects.

181

Venus   *The conjunction.* The two compatible planets emphasize all the good Venusian traits—excellent for friendship and all the artistic pursuits. Emotionally relaxed.

The opposition. Unless badly aspected by other planets this favours development of artistic pursuits where imagination is also required (artistic designing, for instance).

Easy aspects. As for the conjunction. The marriage partnership will be stable and the home life pleasant.

Difficult aspects. Home life lacks harmony and there is difficulty in expressing the emotions. Each planet seems to inhibit the normal function of the other.

Mars   *The conjunction.* This enlivens the emotions and often over-activates responses. The Martian tendency to rush into things needs control. Health, and especially nerves, are strengthened by this aspect. If the conjunction receives strong difficult aspects, there may be too much propensity to risk-taking. Plenty of will power.

The opposition. The energy fluctuates, especially if Mars is not in a strong sign. Worrying and emotionalism may drain the vitality.

Easy aspects. Excellent for health. The Martian characteristics will predominate. The native will be a good judge of other people. Very self-oriented and guileless.

Difficult aspects. As with the opposition, energy is drained by the strength of the emotions. There may be frequent quarrels and lack of self-control.

Jupiter   *The conjunction.* Optimistic and relaxed. Generous but can be pompous. The intuition works well with the Jupiterian expansiveness to give a flair for handling large projects.

The opposition. Health will certainly suffer if there is too much interest in rich foods. Matters concerning finance are better left to the experts and not handled by the native.

Easy aspects. Popularity comes easily, as the native is so likeable. As with the conjunction, there will be business flair. A typical philosopher, but there can be a tendency to over-expansiveness.

Difficult aspects. Very similar to the opposition. A strong Saturn in the chart will be helpful, otherwise the native will be extravagant and over-indulgent. There is a tendency to let good opportunities slip away through laziness.

Saturn   *The conjunction.* Although Saturn has a stabilizing influence on the native, the 'hard' characteristics of that planet are emphasized. Life tends to be all work and duty—sometimes not accepted too graciously. The 'heavy father' attitude is extended to others, with criticism and lack of praise.

The opposition. In an otherwise good chart, this aspect will contribute a good balance between the emotional and practical characteristics, but there is often responsibility or disappointment concerning other members of the family. Sometimes the native experiences difficult childhood conditions.

Easy aspects. These give a sense of responsibility and a practical, patient outlook. Conscientiousness and ambition are both present and usually lead to success, but this never comes without hard work.

Difficult aspects. A great tendency to bottle-up the emotions can lead to health troubles. The native may lack confidence due to difficulties between himself and his parents. Partnerships are often formed with older people.

The conjunction. This contact gives originality and independence. Emotions are tense and the native tends to go to extremes. He is not easy to live with as he will use every means to get his own way. **Uranus**

The opposition. This can be helpful for development of the intuition. It encourages inventiveness and versatility.

Easy aspects. Intuitive and original, but moodiness is likely. There are often strong ideals, for which the native is willing to make sacrifices. Likely to be ambitious and inflexible.

Difficult aspects. Although the native can be extremely wilful and restless there is much mental activity and intelligence. These aspects often seem to work out better than the easy ones.

The conjunction. The emotions are strongly involved with both the Moon and Neptune. Sympathy and kindness are shown to others, together with practical help. The native is a good friend to have, though emotions may sometimes get the better of him. **Neptune**

The opposition. Emphasizes the fluctuating moods of the true Moon subject, causing tension. Can be woolly-minded unless counteracted by the rest of the chart.

Easy aspects. Good for all forms of inspiration, but the imagination needs to be kept within bounds. Difficulty in accepting his own limitations.

Difficult aspects. Self-deception is most common. Strong emotions also make the native subject to deception by others. Hunches are not to be trusted. The native is also capable of deceiving others.

The conjunction. Pluto's propensity to 'throw off' conditions, coupled with the fluctuations of the Moon, influence the native to act compulsively and unexpectedly. Changes of mood can result in wasted efforts. **Pluto**

The opposition. Restless and impulsive. Can 'play havoc' with nerves and emotions when sparked off by progressions.

Easy aspects. Hardly less easy to handle than the other aspects though they may be helpful for business.

Difficult aspects. Restlessness affects family life and relationships. Changes in life pattern may be forced on the native and prove disruptive. Native finds difficulty in releasing emotions, causing tension to build up.

183

In all these aspects, it is essential for the native to find positive ways to express emotions.

Ascendant *The conjunction.* If Moon is in twelfth house, the native will feel the need for privacy. There will be hidden depths in the character and a sense of self-containment (subject to the position of the Sun). In the first house, the emotional make-up will be that of the Ascending sign. There will be a tendency to worry.

The opposition. There may be difficulties in the marriage partnership, the native being particularly vulnerable to a stronger personality. However, it often works well, as the marriage partner is likely to be protective.

Easy aspects. The emotional nature combines well with the native's sense of his own worth. A happy home life (especially if Moon is in fourth house). The zodiacal sign will indicate the ways in which the emotions are well expressed.

Difficult aspects. Some difficulty in expressing the emotions. The outward personality does not portray the way the native feels, with consequent loss of self-confidence.

Midheaven *The conjunction.* The typical Cancerian professions are likely to be chosen as careers, but there may be indecision or several changes of job.

The opposition. The native will be happy in home and private life and have little interest in the career.

Easy aspects. Emotional and intuitive faculties are well used in connection with career and worldly affairs.

Difficult aspects. Emotional difficulties may relate to childhood conditions. House positions will indicate the likely causes.

ASPECTS TO MERCURY

Venus These planets can never be more than 76° apart. There are no major difficult aspects. The semi-sextile and semi-square are not very noticeable.

The conjunction. Venusian charm is combined with Mercury's emphasis on communications resulting, very often, in beautiful speaking voices and a good sense of balance in the use of words. The mind is composed and the nervous system calm.

The sextile is similar but both planets are gentle and the aspect may not be strong. It gives artistic ability to those engaged in craft work.

Mars *The conjunction.* Indicates an energetic mentality and quick wit, which may become rather too pointed at times. The nervous system may be over-stimulated and there is a tendency to hard mental work, which may become detrimental to health if care is not taken.

The opposition. Similar to the conjunction but with more likelihood of strain and overwork. The native often enjoys dangerous sports and can be too rash when indulging in them.

Easy aspects. The native is often a very good driver, particularly if practicality is also shown. The mind and nervous system are stimulated by the Mars contact, and the native has plenty of commonsense.

Difficult aspects. These can be a challenge and spur to mental accomplishments if rightly directed. Otherwise, the likelihood of nervous strain and overwork is increased and there may be much criticism of other people.

The conjunction. All the Mercury and Jupiter potentialities combine happily. Optimism, ability to study, and a relaxed attitude of mind are all indicated. Tolerance and broad-mindedness are also in evidence. **Jupiter**

The opposition. This aspect gives a good balance between the over-critical and the over-tolerant mind. There is originality of thought and ideas are never lacking.

Easy aspects. These can be rather weak, unless a strong Mars lends support, otherwise there may be laziness of thought and a lack of incentive to succeed. The native usually has a good sense of humour and facility with words.

Difficult aspects. The expansiveness of Jupiter is over-emphasized and judgement is poor. The native is usually more optimistic than conditions justify. Absent-mindedness is common.

The conjunction. The mind is controlled and practical. The native often benefits from further education as he tends to be a late developer, learning slowly but thoroughly. **Saturn**

The opposition. This often indicates a good balance between the Mercurial and the more practical nature. However, the native tends to underestimate his own mental capabilities, and suffers from lack of self-confidence.

Easy aspects. Much mental ability and the ambition to succeed produces a serious outlook. The native will be moral and honest.

Difficult aspects. The nervous system is not helped by the rigidity of the Saturn contact. The tendency is for the native to worry unduly because he expects too much of himself. These aspects emphasize the Virgo side of Mercury. While the native may be careful and methodical, he will be harsh with both himself and other people. A difficult aspect for personal relationships as shyness and lack of self-confidence is hidden by an abrupt and distant manner.

The conjunction. Originality and inventiveness are shown by this aspect. The native may be ahead of his time and become a leader in the realms of new thought and discoveries (especially of a scientific nature). This is a common aspect (together with the easy aspects) in the birth charts of astrologers. Great freedom of thought and action is demanded by the native. Stubbornness and wilfulness are common. **Uranus**

185

The opposition. Rebellion against accepted standards borders on the eccentric. There is great ability if it can be channelled in acceptable ways.

Easy aspects. Original, even brilliant, talent is found with these aspects, but the native is often preoccupied with his main interest and takes little notice of anything else—indeed, he often appears stupid in relation to the ordinary matters of life. Thoughts are well-expressed and intuition is good.

Difficult aspects. The native will not lack the originality and brilliance bestowed by the other aspects, but his tactless and abrupt manner will detract from his achievements. He has an exaggerated idea of his own importance. The aspects are not good for mental and nervous health as excessive expenditure of energy causes tensions.

Neptune *The conjunction.* This signifies the union of the mind with the 'higher mind'—or the inspiration. If well aspected it will encourage the development of the creative faculty and the native will be able to express this in accordance with the zodiacal sign. There may be some difficulty in separating the 'real' from the 'imagined'. The native will be sympathetic and gentle.

The opposition. Great sensitivity causes worry and apprehension. Much depends on the rest of the birth chart in all Neptune contacts, since it is so nebulous that it can work out in various ways.

Easy aspects. The fertile imagination should exteriorize easily in the creation of poetry, dancing, writing fiction, etc. The native may be mediumistic. Difficult conditions and harshness are extremely hurtful.

Difficult aspects. The native is perceptive and has all the Neptunian gifts, but self-deception and the deception of others is commonly found with these aspects.

Pluto *The conjunction.* This aspect usually conditions the mind to make changes without undue distress, and to throw off restrictions easily. The sign tenanted needs to be considered. In Leo, the native may try to dominate others.

The opposition. Enforced changes cause mental distress, and tensions need to be released.

Easy aspects. As for the conjunction. Likely to change his opinions suddenly.

Difficult aspects. The native often expresses an opinion on the spur of the moment, without giving consideration to the matter. Judgement tends to be poor, and there may be psychological difficulties.

Ascendant *The conjunction.* The mentality will be strongly emphasized according to the rising sign. Although versatility is likely there may be imbalance in the personality if the Sun occupies the same sign. If Mercury is in the twelfth house, there will be a need for privacy in connection with mental activities, and the native will be secretive about his plans.

The opposition. If Mercury falls in the seventh house, the native may be critical of partners. In the sixth, there is a tendency to worry unduly over health.

186

Easy aspects. These accentuate the mentality. Other people will see the native as an intellectual person, and he will get stimulation from discussions and ideas. The house tenanted will indicate the area of life in which this operates.

Difficult aspects. A worrying nature, with consequent strain on the nerves is the most likely manifestation of these aspects.

The conjunction. All the Mercurial types of career are likely. A lot of nervous and intellectual energy will be put into the effort to attain status.   ***Midheaven***

The opposition. The intellect is 'grounded' (sometimes through lack of education or ambition). The native may be uninterested in the career and choose to remain out of the limelight.

Easy aspects. The mind is oriented to making a successful career or the attainment of worthwhile objectives, and mental discipline is accepted.

Difficult aspects. There may be difficulties outside the control of the native which prevent him from realizing his objectives.

ASPECTS TO VENUS

The conjunction. In the normal way, Mars will be the stronger planet and this   ***Mars*** aspect will then indicate a tendency to short, sharp arguments. If Venus is the stronger by sign (or being chart ruler) the native is easily hurt by others. In any case, the sex life will be accentuated. Martian vitality and drive is expressed in likeable ways and the native is usually popular.

The opposition. Partnerships may be marred by frequent quarrels, and feelings are easily hurt.

Easy aspects. Very good for all types of relationships, which are very important to the native. Love and affection are easily expressed. The sex life is likely to be active, and tensions will occur if this is not so, unless the native can channel energy into other pursuits.

Difficult aspects. These can cause explosive situations in partnerships. Disappointments are common in this connection. As with the opposition, quarrels and hurt feelings result. The sexual life may be too intense for the native to handle.

The conjunction. All the Venusian and Jupiterian affectionate and generous traits   ***Jupiter*** make for popularity. Business will prosper, especially partnerships.

The opposition. The combination produces a lazy, relaxed attitude which must be judged by the character of the native as a whole.

Easy aspects. As for the conjunction. The native will not take risks. Good for business partnerships and for those who deal with the public.

Difficult aspects. The attitude is too easy-going and the native wants a luxurious life. Unless the rest of the chart adds strength, these aspects denote the typical 'playboy'.

Saturn   *The conjunction.* Here Saturn imposes his limitations on the love life and the affections. This may result from outside causes or from the native's own psychological make-up. Sacrifices and responsibilities may be forced on the subject in connection with other people.

The opposition. None of the Saturn/Venus contacts are particularly helpful, but at least with this aspect some balance may be experienced in that Saturn gives practicality to Venusian occupations, and especially business partnerships. There is no doubt, however, that it severely limits the expression of affection.

Easy aspects. As with the opposition, the best that can be said of these aspects is that they are helpful to business partnerships. Affections are not allowed full expression and marriage partnerships tend to be full of responsibilities.

Difficult aspects. The native may contribute largely to his difficulties by his own stern attitude to affection. He may inhibit the flow of his own emotions by a 'stiff upper lip' character. This can cause health difficulties in later life. Emotional relationships are subject to sacrifices, loss and responsibility. These are sometimes gladly undertaken for love of the person for whom the sacrifice is made. More often, they are a burden affecting the whole area of relationships.

Uranus   *The conjunction.* This contact adds excitement and originality to the emotions. The rest of the chart will show the likely result of this (e.g. whether it is expressed artistically in originality of design).

The opposition. This can vitalize an otherwise over-relaxed individual or cause nervous tension in a naturally emotional person. In both cases, personal freedom will be of great importance to the native and relationships may suffer in consequence.

Easy aspects. In many birth charts the effects of these aspects are hardly noticeable. Sensitivity is always present—especially to music and other arts. Humanitarian interests and an ability to get on well with groups of people are indicated.

Difficult aspects. Judgement in the choice of friends and partners often seems to be lacking and this results in upheavals of a distressing nature. Unconventional behaviour and an obsessive regard for personal freedom may also be indicated.

Neptune   *The conjunction.* Sensitivity can easily become over-sensitivity and this conjunction needs strength from other parts of the chart. Lack of practicality can result. The native will be kind and gentle and may be over-sensitive to the suffering of other people.

The opposition. Easily deceived about other people, with resulting disappointments.

Easy aspects. At its best, Neptune adds inspiration and sensitivity to all Venusian pursuits. The native is usually very artistic, but may lack the necessary drive to do anything about it. The tendency to daydream is often marked.

Difficult aspects. Disappointment occurs because daydreams do not materialize. Ideals are often impossibly high, and people are put on a pedestal. Emotions are confused.

The conjunction. All Pluto contacts add intensity to the natural Venusian feelings and affections. The conjunction, if well aspected, is helpful in business and financial affairs. Sudden and secretive love affairs are likely. If the conjunction receives difficult aspects, the sexual feelings may be repressed. *Pluto*

The opposition. The addition of intensity to the emotions result in tensions which need to be released. The native is highly strung generally, unless the rest of the chart contributes stability and restfulness.

Easy aspects. Good for financial ability, with a passionate enjoyment of life and its luxuries. Strongly sexed, but with genuine affection for partner.

Difficult aspects. Sexual life overactive in some cases. In others, the sexual emotions are inhibited by psychological difficulties.

The conjunction. All the creative, artistic Venusian traits will be emphasized in the nature of the rising sign. The native will be affectionate and charming, but tend to be possessive with others. In the first house, the emotional, affectionate nature will be the most important part of the personality. In the twelfth house, there will be more reserve in the display of affection, and a tendency to laziness. *Ascendant*

The opposition. In the seventh house, Venus is in its own house of partnerships and both marriage and business partnerships are likely to be successful. In the sixth house, health difficulties of a Venusian type may be experienced. The work is likely to be artistic.

Easy aspects. As with the conjunction, all the positive Venusian traits are emphasized. The warmth of the personality makes for popularity.

Difficult aspects. According to the rest of the chart, there may be difficulty in expressing affection. Venus is such a gentle contact that these aspects may not be noticeable.

The conjunction. All the Venusian types of career are likely. Success is indicated in business partnerships. *Midheaven*

The opposition. Shyness may be an inhibiting factor in a successful career, or the native may not be very interested in status and settle for a private, and more easy-going life. This aspect, where Venus is in the fourth house, sometimes indicates that there was a lack of affection in childhood.

Easy aspects. As for the conjunction. The love life is usually deeply satisfying.

Difficult aspects. Inhibition in the outward expression of affections. Shyness may be a positive drawback to a successful career.

ASPECTS TO MARS

The conjunction. Breadth of vision is added to the Martian energy and vitality. The native should be able to make money. Ability and decisiveness are present. *Jupiter*

The opposition. The native tends to get carried away by his own enthusiasm for big projects. Judgement may be too hasty.

Easy aspects. As for the conjunction. The native gets great enjoyment from life. The energy needs to be released in physical activity and in brain work.

Difficult aspects. The native tends to be too hasty. Restlessness is the most common manifestation of these aspects and extreme actions can result.

Saturn *The conjunction.* The limitation imposed on the Martian enthusiasm is not liked. It always causes frustration and, sometimes, actual suffering in the form of a limitation to the physical activity. Accident-proneness is common.

The opposition. This can bring practicality to the over-impetuous temperament. Often, however, it results in fluctuation of purpose, with activity and inactivity alternating.

Easy aspects. These are excellent in the charts of people who like a physical challenge. Harsh conditions, requiring endurance and discipline, are welcomed by such people. Mountaineers and explorers are of this breed. These aspects bestow organizing ability and qualities of leadership.

Difficult aspects. As with the opposition. Enthusiasm is not maintained. Energy tends to fluctuate.

Uranus *The conjunction.* Intensity is added to energy and this can be too much for the native to handle. Tension will always be present and the subject must learn to release this in physical activity. Self-will and intolerance are common.

The opposition. As for difficult aspects.

Easy aspects. As for the conjunction, but the native handles the 'mixture' better, with lots of energy and decisiveness. Vitality and physical strength are present and hard work is enjoyed.

Difficult aspects. Quarrels and intolerance can spill over into violence, unless control is shown elsewhere in the chart. Nervous tension is likely to be present, not helped by a tendency to overwork.

Neptune *The conjunction.* This aspect gives a powerful imagination and there is a love for the rhythms of poetry, music and dancing. Aspirations are high (sometimes too high). The Martian energy may be somewhat depleted by this contact.

The opposition. The energy may be directed towards rather nebulous projects and impractical aspirations.

Easy aspects. These give powerful use of inspiration and the native will be a leader in this field. The emotions are deep and there is genuine feeling for others.

Difficult aspects. The native may be unreasonably apprehensive, causing health difficulties. Sometimes there is the desire to escape by means of drugs or drink. A sensitive imagination may become morbid. Positive use of Neptunian activities— drama, rhythm, etc.—may help to overcome this.

The conjunction. Two strong, extrovert planets add up to a high level of energy **Pluto**
and emotion—sometimes more than the native can handle. A quick passionate
temper needs great control, and plenty of emotional outlets are essential if this
contact is not to cause trouble.

The opposition. Much the same as the conjunction, with due respect to the
signs tenanted.

Easy aspects. Enormous energy and emotional reserves, if used positively. The
native easily discards all that hinders him and makes changes with ease. He has
plenty of confidence in his ability to work hard and accomplish whatever he sets
out to do.

Difficult aspects. The native is often obsessional about his aims and will ignore
the rights and feelings of other people in order to achieve his objectives.

The conjunction. All the Martian traits will be strongly emphasized in the **Ascendant**
personality. Energy will be directed towards attaining objectives indicated by the
rising sign, which will give a very good idea of what the native really wants from
life. In the first house, vitality will be excellent. In the twelfth house, there will be
less frankness than is normal with a Martian native, and energy may be directed to
occult matters.

The opposition. In the seventh house, excellent for partnerships. Plenty of
energy and enthusiasm, though there may be sharp words at times. In the sixth
house, the health hazard is caused by a tendency to overwork.

Easy aspects. Energy is put into attaining objectives with every likelihood of
success. Vitality abundant.

Difficult aspects. Aggressive tendencies need to be positively controlled. The
native can be his own worst enemy, by projecting all the negative Martian traits
and making himself thoroughly unpopular.

The conjunction. The native is capable of a more-than-average day's work and **Midheaven**
this will be willingly undertaken if the work is enjoyed.

The opposition. Work which is disliked may be forced upon the native. Alternatively, the energies are directed to the private, rather than the public life.

Easy aspects. Ambitions are achieved without much difficulty, due to the
enthusiasm which is brought to them by the native.

Difficult aspects. The wrong type of work (or overwork) will cause strain or
tension.

ASPECTS TO JUPITER

Note. All the following aspects are within orb for a considerable period and will
apply to all born during that period. They should not be interpreted too personally
unless they receive aspects from the 'strong' planets, or are strongly placed.

Saturn *The conjunction.* This will only occur once in twenty-one years. Jupiter's broad and expansive outlook is well balanced by the practicality and caution of Saturn. Objectives will be achieved by sheer hard work and perseverance. Religious beliefs will be strongly held.

The opposition. Limitations are irksome and restlessness is common.

Easy aspects. As with the conjunction, the native is capable of achievements on a large scale. The need for discipline is recognized and even welcomed. These aspects are constructive and ambitions are usually realized.

Difficult aspects. As with the opposition, restlessness is likely and the native fails to attain his objectives because these are often too grandiose. He does not recognize his own limitations. These aspects can, however, be a source of strength when used by the native to discipline himself.

Uranus *The conjunction.* This occurs every fourteen years and, again, the aspect is within orb for some time. Restlessness is common and the urge for personal freedom is strong.

The opposition. See 'Difficult aspects'.

Easy aspects. Tolerance and broadmindedness are present, together with originality of vision.

Difficult aspects. The native may become completely unsettled and drift from place to place (or from job to job). He can also be far too outspoken. A determination to have his own way may inhibit relationships with others, despite his humanitarian outlook.

Neptune *The conjunction.* This occurs about every thirteen years. Neptunian inspiration and intuition influence Jupiter's philosophical and religious tendencies, and a positive interest in the occult is often shown. Music and poetry are liked.

The opposition. Mental confusion, especially on philosophical and religious subjects is possible. See also 'Difficult aspects'.

Easy aspects. Sympathy is expressed to help other people in practical ways. Privacy and secluded conditions are necessary to enable the native to 'recharge his batteries'. The energy is easily drained by other people.

Difficult aspects. There may be attraction to religious cults or practices which only serve to confuse the native. Sympathy to those in need can become overwhelming and needs to be counteracted by practical help. These aspects can be good and develop sensitivity in a positive way, provided the rest of the chart shows stability.

Pluto *The conjunction.* This occurs every thirteen years. The native is able to make new beginnings with very little difficulty.

The opposition. As for 'Difficult aspects'.

Easy aspects. Accentuates the desire, as well as the ability, to make new beginnings. The native has both mental and organizing ability.

Difficult aspects. Exploitation of others is a 'generation' tendency, and there is a lack of respect for resources and property.

The conjunction. A very optimistic, relaxed personality. All the positive Jupiter traits are very much in evidence, if the planet is in the first house. In the twelfth it indicates that privacy or retirement is necessary in order to develop the philosophical side of the nature, or for the deep study of which the native is capable. **Ascendant**

The opposition. In the seventh house, the partnership will benefit from relaxed and easy-going ways provided Jupiter is well aspected. If the opposition receives difficult aspects the partnership may not survive. In the sixth, the work may suffer from lack of application. Health needs to be watched to control the tendency to over-indulge.

Easy aspects. Enhances the personality. The native is 'friends with himself' and so able to relax and enjoy his life.

Difficult aspects. Over-expansion is the chief difficulty. The chart will show how this is likely to manifest.

The conjunction. The native is likely to be successful in his career, and to enjoy it. If his work is not also his hobby, he will not let it dominate his life. **Midheaven**

The opposition. Over-expansion may manifest as pomposity or an inflated opinion of his own importance.

Easy aspects. Optimism and an expectation of success in career matters. Financial gains are also likely.

Difficult aspects. As with the opposition. The manner may be over-expansive and insincere.

ASPECTS TO SATURN

The conjunction. Occurs every ninety-one years. This powerful combination will occur again in the late 1980s. It gives the native both determination and self-will. There is likely to be much originality of thought. The sign and house occupied will give a clue as to where the difficulties of reconciling the traits of these two planets are likely to lie. With the slow-moving planets these difficulties are likely to be life-long and, of course, to affect the whole generation. **Uranus**

The opposition. As for 'Difficult aspects'.

Easy aspects. Originality and initiative benefit by Saturnian practicality and patience. Good work likely to be done in scientific fields and with new techniques.

Difficult aspects. Nervous tension alternating with depression would seem to be the obvious result of these placings, but help should be sought from other areas of the chart, remembering that these aspects are, normally, for the whole generation.

Neptune *The conjunction.* This occurs about every thirty-six years. It was in Libra in 1952 and 1953 and occurs again in Capricorn in 1989 and 1990. The aspect is constructive, bringing Saturnian practicality and stability to the idealistic aspirations of Neptune. Much may be accomplished as substance should be given to seemingly impossible aims. It obviously favours the arts and all Neptunian pursuits.

The opposition. It seems likely that this aspect will not be good. The conflict between the inspirational and the material may prove difficult to resolve. Much depends upon which is the stronger planet in the chart. At best dreams are only realized by sheer hard work and sacrifice. This aspect may favour business affairs.

Easy aspects. As with the conjunction, high ideals are likely to be realized through constructive and practical ability.

Difficult aspects. Although the high ideals are present, there is likely to be confusion. Limitations are keenly felt with resulting emotional tension. Inability to express emotions may result in psychological difficulties. The tendency to live an escapist life and to be careless of practical, day-to-day affairs is common.

Pluto *The conjunction.* This occurs every ninety-two years, and it will be in Libra in 1982 and 1983. One would expect these two planets to be uneasy bedfellows and again, the aspect must be judged according to which is the most powerful planet in the chart. Remember, also, that these aspects must be generation influences.

The opposition, may work out better than the conjunction. At best, Saturn's practicality should impose some limitation on the restlessness of the Pluto connection.

Easy aspects. A likelihood that the native will be able to throw off inhibiting conditions and pave the way for better things.

Difficult aspects. As for the conjunction.

Ascendant *The conjunction.* In the first house, the personality will be very Saturnine. Serious mindedness, ambition, practicality and reliability can be expected. In the twelfth house, there will be a positive need for privacy. Shyness and lack of self-confidence are also likely to be present.

The opposition. In the seventh house, the marriage partnership is accepted with a great sense of responsibility. The partner may be much older than the native. In the sixth house, the health is likely to suffer (usually from one of the Saturnian ailments).

Easy aspects. The native is likely to achieve his ambitions by application and practicality.

Difficult aspects. Lack of confidence may be the worst feature of these aspects, which can otherwise be constructive.

The conjunction. Excellent for the big business man, who will be able to take responsibility. Not helpful for other facets of life, as the native may have little time for them. **Midheaven**

The opposition. Difficulties in achieving ambitions. In the fourth house, the lack of self-confidence may be due to childhood difficulties with the parents, who may have been overstrict.

Easy aspects. Good for the career, without inhibiting the native from enjoying other facets of his life.

Difficult aspects. As so often with Saturn, these can be constructive but they do put a limit on the achievements in career or public status.

ASPECTS TO URANUS

The conjunction. This only occurs every 170 years (approximately) and is next due in the 1990s. It adds up to originality combined with idealism and we should expect some greatly talented people to be born then. **Neptune**

The opposition. This seems likely to be a difficult aspect. Self will and unconventionality may be extreme—also self-delusion.

Easy aspects. Very much a generation influence, but the combination should produce a kindly, sympathetic and humanitarian personality.

Difficult aspects. As for the opposition. The emotions must have a positive outlet if they are not to be destructive.

The conjunction. This occurs every 115 years. The last one was in Virgo and was in orb for much of the 1960s. There is obviously a generation influence, but the potential of this aspect is enormous. Upheavals are certain, but if the rest of the chart has stabilizing influence these should be directed to the good of humanity. **Pluto**

The opposition. As for 'Difficult aspects'.

Easy aspects. As conjunction with even more likelihood that this powerful combination will be handled well.

Difficult aspects. Revolutionary tendencies may be misdirected or, if this aspect is 'strong' in the native's chart, there may be overwhelming emotional difficulties.

The conjunction. Originality, even to the point of genius, if other aspects are favourable. Inventiveness and great powers of leadership are shown by this aspect if Uranus is in the first house. In the twelfth, there will be secretiveness with possible emotional tension. The powerful urges of Uranus may find release in unconventional ways. **Ascendant**

The opposition. The native may be his own worst enemy. Emotional relationships are subject to his unpredictability and self-will. In the sixth house, the work may suffer similarly. Health difficulties are likely to be caused by sluggish circulation.

Easy aspects. The originality and independence of thought will be well used.

Difficult aspects. Emotional tensions are common. Similar to twelfth house position (see 'Conjunction').

Midheaven *The conjunction.* The career may be meteoric. Although originality, and even excellence will bring rewards, constant changes of career or self-will may negate them.

The opposition. Tensions, often acquired in childhood, may make the subject inclined to settle for a quiet life, rather than a career.

Easy aspects. The native should be able to reconcile the demands of his nature for freedom with his chosen career, which will probably call for originality and independence of thought.

Difficult aspects. Emotional tension tends to be aggravated by causes over which the native has no control.

ASPECTS TO NEPTUNE

Pluto The aspects are all 'generation influences', being in orb for long periods of time. They must be judged with due consideration of the rest of the chart, and to the placing of the aspect. Unless it is strong by sign or position it may be almost unnoticeable. If Neptune is the more important planet, the intuitive and occult side of the nature will be emphasized. If Pluto is dominant, secretiveness and restlessness will predominate.

Ascendant *The conjunction.* Much depends on the aspects to Neptune. If they are good, the positive attributes of the planet will predominate. Inspiration of the highest order is possible. In both first and twelfth houses there will be a tendency for the native to escape into daydreams. Other, and more dangerous, means of escape may be used if Neptune is afflicted.

The opposition. In the sixth house, the native should be aware of susceptibility to poisoning from drugs, drink or tainted water. Work, unless it calls for much imagination, may be erratic. In the seventh house, the partnership will be idealized and the native is subject to deception by others.

Easy aspects. The inspiration will be well utilized and may exteriorize in original artistic work.

Difficult aspects. Confusion and deception (including self-deception) are likely results of these aspects.

Midheaven *The conjunction.* The career is likely to concern inspirational writing, poetry, music or mediumship. There is a tendency to be unrealistic about how much can be achieved.

The opposition. The attitude to the career is changeable and confused. Over-sensitivity makes it difficult for the subject to cope with real life.

Easy aspects. The Neptunian attributes are used well and positively in matters concerned with the career or social standing.

Difficult aspects. As for the opposition.

ASPECTS TO PLUTO

Ascendant *The conjunction.* Intensity and the urge to make changes tend to disrupt the life pattern. In the twelfth house, these urges may remain unconscious and cause psychological difficulties, if not resolved.

The opposition. In the seventh house, disruptive changes are likely in the marriage partnership. In the sixth house, business affairs may be helped, but emotions need release.

Easy aspects. Helpful in releasing tensions and in making changes to discard old, outworn conditions.

Difficult aspects. Emotional release is difficult and intensity builds up as a result.

The conjunction. This aspect often signifies the business man who gets to the top **Midheaven** by the quickest route, and who is not overconcerned with who he treads underfoot on his way up. Ability and endurance are both present.

The opposition. The native is likely to take great risks to achieve his objectives.

Easy aspects. The ability to discard what is worthless and start again, together with a talent for organization are a positive help to the career.

Difficult aspects. As for the opposition. There may be difficulties imposed on the native in realizing his ambitions.

APPENDIX IV

RECOMMENDED READING

General

John Addey, *Astrology Reborn.*
Michel Gauquelin. *Astrology and Science,* Mayflower, 1972.
——. *Cosmic Clocks,* Paladin, 1973.
——. *Cosmic Influences on Human Behaviour,* Garnstone Press, 1974.
Warren Kenton. *Astrology: The Celestial Mirror,* Thames and Hudson, 1975.
Derek Parker. *The Question of Astrology,* Eyre and Spottiswoode, 1970.
J. A. West and J. G. Toonder. *The Case for Astrology,* Penguin, 1973.

Interpretation and Astrological Practice

C. E. O. Carter. *Astrological Aspects,* Fowler, 1969.
——. *The Foundations of Astrology,* Pythagorean Publications, 1960.
——. *The Principles of Astrology,* Theosophical Publishing House, 1969.
Sheila Geddes et al, *Synastry,* Astrological Association.
Linda Goodman. *Linda Goodman's Sun Signs,* Pan, 1972.
Alan Leo. *The Art of Synthesis,* Fowler, 1968.
Alan Oken. *As Above, So Below,* Bantam Books, 1974.
——. *The Horoscope, the Road and its Travellers,* Bantam Books, 1974.
Derek and Julia Parker. *Sun Signs,* Mitchell Beazley.

Assessing Future Trends

R. C. Davison. *The Technique of Prediction,* Fowler, 1955.
Chester Kemp. *Progressions,* Astrological Association.

Esoteric Astrology

C. E. O. Carter. *The Zodiac and the Soul,* Theosophical Publishing House, 1973.
Joan Cooke. *Wisdom in the Stars,*
I. M. Pagan. *From Pioneer to Poet,* Theosophical Publishing House, 1969.

David Evans. *Teach Yourself Astronomy,* Teach Yourself Books.   ***Astronomy***
The Sky at Night, The Planesphere, Daily Telegraph annual publications.

Equipment
and Charts

Birth chart forms (as used in this book): obtainable from the Faculty of Astro-
  logical Studies.
Ephemerides (*Raphael's*): published each year by W. Foulsham and Company
  Limited.
Geocentric longitudes for Mars, Jupiter, Saturn, Uranus and Neptune: obtainable
  from W. Foulsham and Company Limited.
Tables of houses for Great Britain and Northern Ireland: obtainable from W.
  Foulsham and Company Limited.
Perpetual noon date card: obtainable from L. N. Fowler Limited.
Pluto ephemeris 1851-2000: Ebertin.*
Pluto ephemeris 1840-1939: E. Benjamine.*
Time Changes in the U.S.A.: Doris Chase Doane.
Time Changes in Canada and Mexico, Time Changes in the World (excluding
  U.S.A., Canada and Mexico): Doris Chase Doane.

*Note. Pluto's positions were not listed in *Raphael's Ephemeris* until 1934.

APPENDIX V

RAPHAEL'S EPHEMERIS, TABLES OF HOUSES, POSITIONS OF PLUTO, TABLE OF PROPORTIONAL LOGARITHMS

PROPORTIONAL LOGARITHMS FOR FINDING THE PLANETS' PLACES

DEGREES OR HOURS

Min.	0	1	2	3	4	5	6	7	8	9	10	11	12	13	14	15	Min.
0	3.1584	1.3802	1.0792	.9031	.7781	.6812	.6021	.5351	.4771	.4260	.3802	.3388	.3010	.2663	.2341	.2041	0
1	3.1584	1.3730	1.0736	.9007	.7763	.6798	.5997	.5330	.4753	.4252	.3788	.3382	.3004	.2657	.2336	.2036	1
2	2.8573	1.3660	1.0720	.8983	.7745	.6784	.5985	.5320	.4744	.4236	.3780	.3368	.2992	.2646	.2325	.2032	2
3	2.6812	1.3590	1.0685	.8959	.7728	.6769	.5973	.5310	.4735	.4228	.3773	.3362	.2986	.2640	.2320	.2027	3
4	2.5563	1.3522	1.0649	.8935	.7710	.6755	.5961	.5300	.4726	.4220	.3766	.3355	.2980	.2635	.2315	.2022	4
5	2.4594	1.3454	1.0614	.8912	.7692	.6741	.5949	.5289	.4717	.4212	.3759	.3349	.2974	.2629	.2310	.2017	5
6	2.3802	1.3388	1.0580	.8888	.7674	.6726	.5937	.5279	.4708	.4204	.3752	.3342	.2968	.2624	.2305	.2012	6
7	2.3133	1.3323	1.0546	.8865	.7657	.6712	.5925	.5269	.4699	.4196	.3745	.3336	.2962	.2618	.2300	.2008	7
8	2.2553	1.3258	1.0511	.8842	.7639	.6698	.5913	.5259	.4690	.4188	.3737	.3329	.2956	.2613	.2295	.2003	8
9	2.2041	1.3195	1.0478	.8819	.7622	.6684	.5902	.5249	.4682	.4180	.3730	.3323	.2950	.2607	.2289	.1998	9
10	2.1584	1.3133	1.0444	.8796	.7604	.6670	.5890	.5239	.4673	.4172	.3723	.3316	.2944	.2602	.2284	.1993	10
11	2.1170	1.3071	1.0411	.8773	.7587	.6656	.5878	.5229	.4664	.4164	.3716	.3310	.2938	.2596	.2279	.1988	11
12	2.0792	1.3010	1.0378	.8751	.7570	.6642	.5866	.5219	.4655	.4156	.3709	.3303	.2933	.2591	.2274	.1984	12
13	2.0444	1.2950	1.0345	.8728	.7552	.6628	.5855	.5209	.4646	.4148	.3702	.3297	.2927	.2585	.2269	.1979	13
14	2.0122	1.2891	1.0313	.8706	.7535	.6614	.5843	.5199	.4638	.4141	.3695	.3291	.2921	.2580	.2264	.1974	14
15	1.9823	1.2833	1.0280	.8683	.7518	.6600	.5832	.5189	.4629	.4133	.3688	.3284	.2915	.2574	.2259	.1969	15
16	1.9542	1.2775	1.0248	.8661	.7501	.6587	.5820	.5179	.4620	.4125	.3681	.3278	.2909	.2569	.2254	.1965	16
17	1.9279	1.2719	1.0216	.8639	.7484	.6573	.5809	.5169	.4611	.4117	.3674	.3271	.2903	.2564	.2249	.1960	17
18	1.9031	1.2663	1.0185	.8617	.7467	.6559	.5797	.5159	.4603	.4109	.3667	.3265	.2897	.2558	.2244	.1955	18
19	1.8796	1.2607	1.0153	.8595	.7451	.6546	.5786	.5149	.4594	.4102	.3660	.3259	.2891	.2553	.2239	.1950	19
20	1.8573	1.2553	1.0122	.8573	.7434	.6532	.5774	.5139	.4585	.4094	.3653	.3252	.2885	.2547	.2234	.1946	20
21	1.8361	1.2499	1.0091	.8552	.7417	.6519	.5763	.5129	.4577	.4086	.3646	.3246	.2880	.2542	.2229	.1941	21
22	1.8159	1.2445	1.0061	.8530	.7401	.6505	.5752	.5120	.4568	.4079	.3639	.3239	.2874	.2536	.2223	.1936	22
23	1.7966	1.2393	1.0030	.8509	.7384	.6492	.5740	.5110	.4559	.4071	.3632	.3233	.2868	.2531	.2218	.1932	23
24	1.7781	1.2341	1.0000	.8487	.7368	.6478	.5729	.5100	.4551	.4063	.3625	.3227	.2862	.2526	.2213	.1927	24
25	1.7604	1.2289	0.9970	.8466	.7351	.6465	.5718	.5090	.4542	.4055	.3618	.3220	.2856	.2520	.2208	.1922	25
26	1.7434	1.2239	0.9940	.8445	.7335	.6451	.5706	.5081	.4534	.4048	.3611	.3214	.2850	.2515	.2203	.1917	26
27	1.7270	1.2188	0.9910	.8425	.7318	.6438	.5695	.5071	.4525	.4040	.3604	.3208	.2845	.2509	.2198	.1913	27
28	1.7112	1.2139	0.9881	.8404	.7302	.6425	.5684	.5061	.4516	.4032	.3597	.3201	.2839	.2504	.2193	.1908	28
29	1.6960	1.2090	0.9852	.8382	.7286	.6412	.5673	.5051	.4508	.4025	.3590	.3195	.2833	.2499	.2188	.1903	29
30	1.6812	1.2041	0.9823	.8361	.7270	.6398	.5662	.5042	.4499	.4017	.3583	.3189	.2827	.2493	.2183	.1899	30
31	1.6670	1.1993	0.9794	.8341	.7254	.6385	.5651	.5032	.4491	.4010	.3576	.3183	.2821	.2488	.2178	.1894	31
32	1.6532	1.1946	0.9765	.8320	.7238	.6372	.5640	.5022	.4482	.4002	.3570	.3176	.2816	.2483	.2173	.1889	32
33	1.6398	1.1899	0.9737	.8300	.7222	.6359	.5629	.5013	.4474	.3994	.3563	.3170	.2810	.2477	.2168	.1885	33
34	1.6269	1.1852	0.9708	.8279	.7206	.6346	.5618	.5003	.4466	.3987	.3556	.3164	.2804	.2472	.2164	.1880	34
35	1.6143	1.1806	0.9680	.8259	.7190	.6333	.5607	.4994	.4457	.3979	.3549	.3157	.2798	.2467	.2159	.1875	35
36	1.6021	1.1761	0.9652	.8239	.7174	.6320	.5596	.4984	.4449	.3972	.3542	.3151	.2793	.2461	.2154	.1871	36
37	1.5902	1.1716	0.9625	.8219	.7159	.6307	.5585	.4975	.4440	.3964	.3535	.3145	.2787	.2456	.2149	.1866	37
38	1.5786	1.1671	0.9597	.8199	.7143	.6294	.5574	.4965	.4432	.3957	.3529	.3139	.2781	.2451	.2144	.1862	38
39	1.5673	1.1627	0.9570	.8179	.7128	.6282	.5563	.4956	.4424	.3949	.3522	.3132	.2775	.2445	.2139	.1857	39
40	1.5563	1.1584	0.9542	.8159	.7112	.6269	.5552	.4947	.4415	.3942	.3515	.3126	.2770	.2440	.2134	.1852	40
41	1.5456	1.1540	0.9515	.8140	.7097	.6256	.5541	.4937	.4407	.3934	.3508	.3120	.2764	.2435	.2129	.1848	41
42	1.5351	1.1498	0.9488	.8120	.7081	.6243	.5531	.4928	.4399	.3927	.3501	.3114	.2758	.2430	.2124	.1843	42
43	1.5249	1.1455	0.9462	.8101	.7066	.6231	.5520	.4918	.4390	.3919	.3495	.3108	.2753	.2424	.2119	.1838	43
44	1.5149	1.1413	0.9435	.8081	.7050	.6218	.5509	.4909	.4382	.3912	.3488	.3102	.2747	.2419	.2114	.1834	44
45	1.5051	1.1372	0.9409	.8062	.7035	.6205	.5498	.4900	.4374	.3905	.3481	.3096	.2741	.2414	.2109	.1829	45
46	1.4956	1.1331	0.9383	.8043	.7020	.6193	.5488	.4890	.4365	.3897	.3475	.3089	.2736	.2409	.2104	.1825	46
47	1.4863	1.1290	0.9356	.8023	.7005	.6180	.5477	.4881	.4357	.3890	.3468	.3083	.2730	.2403	.2099	.1820	47
48	1.4771	1.1249	0.9330	.8004	.6990	.6168	.5466	.4872	.4349	.3882	.3461	.3077	.2724	.2398	.2095	.1816	48
49	1.4682	1.1209	0.9305	.7985	.6975	.6155	.5456	.4863	.4341	.3875	.3454	.3071	.2719	.2393	.2090	.1811	49
50	1.4594	1.1170	0.9279	.7966	.6960	.6143	.5445	.4853	.4333	.3868	.3448	.3065	.2713	.2388	.2085	.1806	50
51	1.4508	1.1130	0.9254	.7947	.6945	.6131	.5435	.4844	.4324	.3860	.3441	.3059	.2707	.2382	.2080	.1802	51
52	1.4424	1.1091	0.9228	.7929	.6930	.6118	.5424	.4835	.4316	.3853	.3434	.3053	.2702	.2377	.2075	.1797	52
53	1.4341	1.1053	0.9203	.7910	.6915	.6106	.5414	.4826	.4308	.3846	.3428	.3047	.2696	.2372	.2070	.1793	53
54	1.4260	1.1015	0.9178	.7891	.6900	.6094	.5403	.4817	.4300	.3838	.3421	.3041	.2691	.2367	.2065	.1788	54
55	1.4180	1.0977	0.9153	.7873	.6885	.6081	.5393	.4808	.4292	.3831	.3415	.3034	.2685	.2361	.2061	.1784	55
56	1.4102	1.0939	0.9128	.7854	.6871	.6069	.5382	.4798	.4284	.3824	.3408	.3028	.2679	.2356	.2056	.1779	56
57	1.4025	1.0902	0.9104	.7836	.6856	.6057	.5372	.4789	.4276	.3817	.3401	.3022	.2674	.2351	.2051	.1774	57
58	1.3949	1.0865	0.9079	.7818	.6841	.6045	.5361	.4780	.4268	.3809	.3395	.3016	.2668	.2346	.2046	.1770	58
59	1.3875	1.0828	0.9055	.7800	.6827	.6033	.5351	.4771	.4260	.3802	.3388	.3010	.2663	.2341	.2041	.1765	59

RULE.—Add proportional log. of planet's daily motion to log. of time from noon, and the sum will be the log. of the motion required. Add this to planet's place at noon, if time be p.m., but subtract if a.m. and the sum will be planet's true place. If Retrograde, subtract for p.m., but add for a.m.

What is the Long. of ☽ Jan. 21st, 1949 at 2.15 p.m.?

☽'s daily motion = 13° 42'

Prop. Log. of 13° 42' .... .2435

Prop. Log. of 2h. 15m. 1.0280

1.2715

☽'s motion in 2h. 15m. = 1° 17' or Log. 1.2715

☽'s Long. on Sept. 7th = 0 ♏ 0' +1° 17' = 1 ♏ 17'

The Daily Motions of the Sun, Moon, Mars, Venus and Mercury will be found on page: 26 to 28.

Table of Proportional Logarithms. (Reproduced from the RAPHAEL'S EPHEMERIS with permission of the publishers, W. Foulsham and Company Limited, Yeovil Road, Slough, Berkshire. © W. Foulsham & Co. Ltd.)

FULL MOON—June 10, 9h. 45m. 9s. p.m.

13

EPHEMERIS] JUNE, 1949

LAST QUARTER—June 18, 0h. 29m. 7s. p.m.

Raphael's Ephemeris. June 1949. (Reproduced from the RAPHAEL'S EPHEMERIS with permission of the publishers, W. Foulsham and Company Limited. Yeovil Road, Slough, Berkshire. © W. Foulsham & Co. Ltd.)

NEW MOON—June 26, 10h. 1m. 52s. a.m.

12

[RAPHAEL'S

JUNE, 1949

MIDNIGHT

FIRST QUARTER—June 4, 3h. 27m. 11s. a.m.

Raphael's Ephemeris. June 1949. (Reproduced from the RAPHAEL'S EPHEMERIS with permission of the publishers, W. Foulsham and Company Limited. Yeovil Road, Slough, Berkshire. © W. Foulsham & Co. Ltd.)

25

FULL MOON—December 10, 0h. 56m. 24s. a.m.

[EPHEMERIS] DECEMBER, 1954

D M	Venus. Lat.	Dec.	Mercury. Lat.	Dec.	Node.	☽ Long.	Mutual Aspects.

D M	☿ Long.	♀ Long.	♂ Long.	♃ Long.	♄ Long.	♅ Long.	♆ Long.	Lunar Aspects.

LAST QUARTER—December 17, 2h. 21m. 14s. a.m.

Raphael's Ephemeris, December 1954. (Reproduced from the RAPHAEL'S EPHEMERIS with permission of the publishers, W. Foulsham and Company Limited, Yeovil Road, Slough, Berkshire. © W. Foulsham & Co. Ltd.)

24

NEW MOON—December 25, 7h. 32m. 59s. a.m.

[RAPHAEL'S] DECEMBER, 1954

D M	Neptune. Lat.	Dec.	Herschel. Lat.	Dec.	Saturn. Lat.	Dec.	Jupiter. Lat.	Dec.	Mars. Lat.	Declin.

D M W	Sidereal Time. H. M. S.	☉ Long.	Dec.	☽ Long.	Lat.	Dec.	MIDNIGHT ☽ Long.	Dec.

FIRST QUARTER—December 3, 9h. 55m. 48s. a.m.

Raphael's Ephemeris, December 1954. (Reproduced from the RAPHAEL'S EPHEMERIS with permission of the publishers, W. Foulsham and Company Limited, Yeovil Road, Slough, Berkshire. © W. Foulsham & Co. Ltd.)

Raphael's Ephemeris, Tables of Houses, Positions of Pluto, Table of Proportional Logarithms

TABLES OF HOUSES FOR NEW YORK, Latitude 40° 43' N.

Tables of Houses for New York. (Reproduced from the RAPHAEL'S EPHEMERIS with permission of the publishers, W. Foulsham and Company Limited, Yeovil Road, Slough, Berkshire. © W. Foulsham & Co. Ltd.)

TABLES OF HOUSES FOR NEW YORK, Latitude 40° 43' N.

Tables of Houses for New York. (Reproduced from the RAPHAEL'S EPHEMERIS with permission of the publishers, W. Foulsham and Company Limited, Yeovil Road, Slough, Berkshire. © W. Foulsham & Co. Ltd.)

TABLES OF HOUSES FOR LONDON, Latitude 51° 32′ N.

Sidereal Time H.	M.	S.	10 ♎ °	11 ♎ °	12 ♏ °	Ascen ♐ °	′	2 ♑ °	3 ♒ °
12	0	0	0	27	17	3	23	8	21
12	3	40	1	28	18	4	4	9	23
12	7	20	2	29	19	4	45	10	24
12	11	0	3	♏	20	5	26	11	25
12	14	41	4	1	20	6	7	12	26
12	18	21	5	1	21	6	48	13	27
12	22	2	6	2	22	7	29	14	28
12	25	42	7	3	23	8	10	15	29
12	29	23	8	4	23	8	51	16	♓
12	33	4	9	5	24	9	33	17	2
12	36	45	10	6	25	10	15	18	3
12	40	26	11	6	25	10	57	19	4
12	44	8	12	7	26	11	40	20	5
12	47	50	13	8	27	12	22	21	6
12	51	32	14	9	28	13	4	22	7
12	55	14	15	10	28	13	47	23	9
12	58	57	16	11	29	14	30	24	10
13	2	40	17	11	♐	15	14	25	11
13	6	23	18	12	1	15	59	26	12
13	10	7	19	13	1	16	44	27	13
13	13	51	20	14	2	17	29	28	15
13	17	35	21	15	3	18	14	29	16
13	21	20	22	16	4	19	0	♒	17
13	25	6	23	16	4	19	45	1	18
13	28	52	24	17	5	20	31	2	20
13	32	38	25	18	6	21	18	4	21
13	36	25	26	19	7	22	6	5	22
13	40	12	27	20	7	22	54	6	23
13	44	0	28	21	8	23	42	7	25
13	47	48	29	21	9	24	31	8	26
13	51	37	30	22	10	25	20	10	27

Sidereal Time H.	M.	S.	10 ♏ °	11 ♏ °	12 ♐ °	Ascen ♐ °	′	2 ♒ °	3 ♓ °
13	51	37	0	22	10	25	20	10	27
13	55	27	1	23	11	26	10	11	28
13	59	17	2	24	11	27	2	12	♈
14	3	8	3	25	12	27	53	14	1
14	6	59	4	26	13	28	45	15	2
14	10	51	5	26	14	29	36	16	4
14	14	44	6	27	15	0 ♑	29	18	5
14	18	37	7	28	15	1	23	19	6
14	22	31	8	29	16	2	18	20	8
14	26	25	9	♐	17	3	14	22	9
14	30	20	10	1	18	4	11	23	10
14	34	16	11	2	19	5	9	25	11
14	38	13	12	2	20	6	7	26	13
14	42	10	13	3	20	7	6	28	14
14	46	8	14	4	21	8	6	29	15
14	50	7	15	5	22	9	8	♓	17
14	54	7	16	6	23	10	11	2	18
14	58	7	17	7	24	11	15	4	19
15	2	8	18	8	25	12	20	6	21
15	6	9	19	9	26	13	27	8	22
15	10	12	20	9	27	14	35	9	23
15	14	15	21	10	27	15	43	11	24
15	18	19	22	11	28	16	52	13	26
15	22	23	23	12	29	18	3	14	27
15	26	29	24	13	♑	19	16	16	28
15	30	35	25	14	1	20	32	17	29
15	34	41	26	15	2	21	48	19	♉
15	38	49	27	16	3	23	8	21	2
15	42	57	28	17	4	24	29	22	3
15	47	6	29	18	5	25	51	24	5
15	51	15	30	18	6	27	15	26	6

Sidereal Time H.	M.	S.	10 ♐ °	11 ♐ °	12 ♑ °	Ascen ♑ °	′	2 ♓ °	3 ♉ °
15	51	15	0	18	6	27	15	26	6
15	55	25	1	19	7	28	42	28	7
15	59	36	2	20	8	0 ♒	11	♈	9
16	3	48	3	21	9	1	42	2	10
16	8	0	4	22	10	3	16	3	11
16	12	13	5	23	11	4	53	5	12
16	16	26	6	24	12	6	32	7	14
16	20	40	7	25	13	8	13	9	15
16	24	55	8	26	14	9	57	11	16
16	29	10	9	27	16	11	44	12	17
16	33	26	10	28	17	13	34	14	18
16	37	42	11	29	18	15	26	16	20
16	41	59	12	♑	19	17	20	18	21
16	46	16	13	1	20	19	18	20	22
16	50	34	14	2	21	21	22	21	23
16	54	52	15	3	22	23	29	23	25
16	59	10	16	4	24	25	36	25	26
17	3	29	17	5	25	27	46	27	27
17	7	49	18	6	26	0 ♓	0	28	28
17	12	9	19	7	27	2	19	♉	29
17	16	29	20	8	29	4	40	2	♊
17	20	49	21	9	♒	7	2	3	1
17	25	9	22	10	1	9	26	5	2
17	29	30	23	11	3	11	54	7	3
17	33	51	24	12	4	14	24	8	5
17	38	12	25	13	5	17	0	10	6
17	42	34	26	14	7	19	33	11	7
17	46	55	27	15	8	22	6	13	8
17	51	17	28	16	10	24	40	14	9
17	55	38	29	17	11	27	20	16	10
18	0	0	30	18	13	30	0	17	11

Sidereal Time H.	M.	S.	10 ♑ °	11 ♑ °	12 ♒ °	Ascen ♈ °	′	2 ♉ °	3 ♊ °
18	0	0	0	18	13	0	0	17	11
18	4	22	1	20	14	2	39	19	13
18	8	43	2	21	16	5	19	20	14
18	13	5	3	22	17	7	55	22	15
18	17	26	4	23	19	10	29	23	16
18	21	48	5	24	20	13	2	25	17
18	26	9	6	25	22	15	36	26	18
18	30	30	7	26	23	18	6	28	19
18	34	51	8	27	25	20	34	29	20
18	39	11	9	29	27	22	59	♊	21
18	43	31	10	♒	28	25	22	1	22
18	47	51	11	1	♓	27	42	2	23
18	52	11	12	2	2	29	58	4	24
18	56	31	13	3	3	2 ♉	13	5	25
19	0	50	14	4	5	4	24	6	26
19	5	8	15	6	7	6	30	8	27
19	9	26	16	7	9	8	36	9	28
19	13	44	17	8	10	10	40	10	29
19	18	1	18	9	12	12	39	11	♋
19	22	18	19	10	14	14	35	12	1
19	26	34	20	12	16	16	28	13	2
19	30	50	21	13	18	18	17	14	3
19	35	5	22	14	19	20	3	16	4
19	39	20	23	15	21	21	48	17	5
19	43	34	24	16	23	23	29	18	6
19	47	47	25	18	25	25	9	19	7
19	52	0	26	19	27	26	45	20	8
19	56	12	27	20	28	28	18	21	9
20	0	24	28	21	♈	29	49	22	10
20	4	35	29	23	2	1 ♊	19	23	11
20	8	45	30	24	4	2	45	24	12

Sidereal Time H.	M.	S.	10 ♒ °	11 ♒ °	12 ♈ °	Ascen ♊ °	′	2 ♊ °	3 ♋ °
20	8	45	0	24	4	2	45	24	12
20	12	54	1	25	6	4	9	25	12
20	17	3	2	27	7	5	32	26	13
20	21	11	3	28	9	6	53	27	14
20	25	19	4	29	11	8	12	28	15
20	29	26	5	♓	13	9	27	29	16
20	33	31	6	2	14	10	43	♋	17
20	37	37	7	3	16	11	58	1	18
20	41	41	8	4	18	13	9	2	19
20	45	45	9	6	19	14	18	3	20
20	49	48	10	7	21	15	25	3	21
20	53	51	11	8	23	16	32	4	21
20	57	52	12	9	24	17	39	5	22
21	1	53	13	11	26	18	44	6	23
21	5	53	14	12	28	19	48	7	24
21	9	53	15	13	29	20	51	8	25
21	13	52	16	15	♉	21	53	9	26
21	17	50	17	16	2	22	53	10	27
21	21	47	18	17	4	23	52	10	28
21	25	44	19	19	5	24	51	11	28
21	29	40	20	20	7	25	48	12	29
21	33	35	21	22	8	26	44	13	♌
21	37	29	22	23	10	27	40	14	1
21	41	23	23	24	11	28	34	15	2
21	45	16	24	25	13	29	29	15	3
21	49	9	25	26	14	0 ♋	22	16	4
21	53	1	26	28	15	1	15	17	4
21	56	52	27	29	16	2	7	18	5
22	0	43	28	♈	18	2	57	19	6
22	4	33	29	2	19	3	48	19	7
22	8	23	30	3	20	4	38	20	8

Sidereal Time H.	M.	S.	10 ♓ °	11 ♈ °	12 ♉ °	Ascen ♋ °	′	2 ♋ °	3 ♌ °
22	8	23	0	3	20	4	38	20	8
22	12	12	1	4	21	5	28	21	8
22	16	0	2	6	23	6	17	22	9
22	19	48	3	7	24	7	5	23	10
22	23	35	4	8	25	7	53	23	11
22	27	22	5	9	26	8	42	24	12
22	31	8	6	10	28	9	29	25	13
22	34	54	7	12	29	10	16	26	14
22	38	40	8	13	♊	11	2	26	14
22	42	25	9	14	1	11	47	27	15
22	46	9	10	15	2	12	31	28	16
22	49	53	11	17	3	13	16	29	17
22	53	37	12	18	4	14	1	29	18
22	57	20	13	19	5	14	45	♌	19
23	1	3	14	20	6	15	28	1	19
23	4	46	15	21	7	16	11	2	20
23	8	28	16	23	8	16	54	2	21
23	12	10	17	24	9	17	37	3	22
23	15	52	18	25	10	18	20	4	23
23	19	34	19	26	11	19	3	5	24
23	23	15	20	27	12	19	45	5	24
23	26	56	21	29	13	20	26	6	25
23	30	37	22	♉	14	21	8	7	26
23	34	18	23	1	15	21	50	7	27
23	37	58	24	2	16	22	31	8	28
23	41	39	25	3	17	23	12	9	28
23	45	19	26	4	18	23	53	9	29
23	49	0	27	5	19	24	32	10	♍
23	52	40	28	6	20	25	15	11	1
23	56	20	29	8	21	25	56	12	2
24	0	0	30	9	22	26	36	13	3

Tables of Houses for London. (Reproduced from the RAPHAEL'S EPHEMERIS with permission of the publishers, W. Foulsham and Company Limited, Yeovil Road, Slough, Berkshire. © W. Foulsham & Co. Ltd.)

TABLES OF HOUSES FOR LONDON, Latitude 51° 32′ N.

Sidereal Time H.	M.	S.	10 ♈ °	11 ♉ °	12 ♊ °	Ascen ♋ °	′	2 ♌ °	3 ♍ °
0	0	0	0	9	22	26	36	12	3
0	3	40	1	10	23	27	17	13	3
0	7	20	2	11	24	27	56	14	4
0	11	0	3	12	25	28	42	15	5
0	14	41	4	13	25	29	17	15	6
0	18	21	5	14	26	29	55	16	7
0	22	2	6	15	27	0 ♌	34	17	8
0	25	42	7	16	28	1	14	18	8
0	29	23	8	17	29	1	55	18	9
0	33	4	9	18	♋	2	33	19	10
0	36	45	10	19	1	3	14	20	11
0	40	26	11	20	1	3	54	20	12
0	44	8	12	21	2	4	33	21	13
0	47	50	13	22	3	5	12	22	14
0	51	32	14	23	4	5	52	23	15
0	55	14	15	24	5	6	30	23	15
0	58	57	16	25	6	7	9	24	16
1	2	40	17	26	6	7	50	25	17
1	6	23	18	27	7	8	30	26	18
1	10	7	19	28	8	9	9	26	19
1	13	51	20	29	9	9	48	27	19
1	17	35	21	♊	10	10	28	28	20
1	21	20	22	1	10	11	8	28	21
1	25	6	23	2	11	11	48	29	22
1	28	52	24	3	12	12	28	♍	23
1	32	38	25	4	13	13	8	1	24
1	36	25	26	5	14	13	48	1	25
1	40	12	27	6	14	14	28	2	25
1	44	0	28	7	15	15	8	3	26
1	47	48	29	8	16	15	48	4	27
1	51	37	30	9	17	16	28	4	28

Sidereal Time H.	M.	S.	10 ♉ °	11 ♊ °	12 ♋ °	Ascen ♌ °	′	2 ♍ °	3 ♍ °
1	51	37	0	9	17	16	28	4	28
1	55	27	1	10	18	17	8	5	29
1	59	17	2	11	19	17	48	6	♎
2	3	8	3	12	19	18	28	7	1
2	6	59	4	13	20	19	9	8	2
2	10	51	5	14	21	19	49	9	2
2	14	44	6	15	22	20	29	9	3
2	18	37	7	16	22	21	10	10	4
2	22	31	8	17	23	21	51	11	5
2	26	25	9	18	24	22	32	11	6
2	30	20	10	19	25	23	14	12	7
2	34	16	11	20	25	23	55	13	8
2	38	13	12	21	26	24	36	14	9
2	42	10	13	22	27	25	17	15	10
2	46	8	14	23	28	25	58	15	11
2	50	7	15	24	29	26	40	16	12
2	54	7	16	25	29	27	22	17	12
2	58	7	17	26	♌	28	4	18	13
3	2	8	18	27	1	28	46	18	14
3	6	9	19	27	2	29	28	19	15
3	10	12	20	28	3	0 ♍	12	20	16
3	14	15	21	29	3	0	54	21	17
3	18	19	22	♋	4	1	36	22	18
3	22	23	23	1	5	2	20	22	19
3	26	29	24	2	6	3	2	23	20
3	30	35	25	3	7	3	45	24	21
3	34	41	26	4	7	4	28	25	22
3	38	49	27	5	8	5	11	26	23
3	42	57	28	6	9	5	54	27	24
3	47	6	29	7	10	6	38	27	25
3	51	15	30	8	11	7	21	28	25

Sidereal Time H.	M.	S.	10 ♊ °	11 ♋ °	12 ♌ °	Ascen ♍ °	′	2 ♍ °	3 ♎ °
3	51	15	0	8	11	7	21	28	25
3	55	25	1	9	12	8	5	29	26
3	59	36	2	10	12	8	49	♎	27
4	3	48	3	10	13	9	33	1	28
4	8	0	4	11	14	10	17	2	29
4	12	13	5	12	15	11	2	2	♏
4	16	26	6	13	16	11	46	3	1
4	20	40	7	14	17	12	30	4	2
4	24	55	8	15	17	13	15	5	3
4	29	10	9	16	18	14	0	6	4
4	33	26	10	17	19	14	45	7	5
4	37	42	11	18	20	15	30	8	6
4	41	59	12	19	21	16	15	8	7
4	46	16	13	20	21	17	0	9	8
4	50	34	14	21	22	17	45	10	9
4	54	52	15	22	23	18	30	11	10
4	59	10	16	23	24	19	16	12	11
5	3	29	17	24	25	20	3	13	12
5	7	49	18	25	26	20	49	14	13
5	12	9	19	25	27	21	35	14	14
5	16	29	20	26	28	22	20	15	14
5	20	49	21	27	28	23	6	16	15
5	25	9	22	28	29	23	51	17	16
5	29	30	23	29	♍	24	37	18	17
5	33	51	24	♌	1	25	23	19	18
5	38	12	25	1	2	26	9	20	19
5	42	34	26	2	3	26	55	21	20
5	46	55	27	3	4	27	41	21	21
5	51	17	28	4	4	28	27	22	22
5	55	38	29	5	5	29	13	23	23
6	0	0	30	6	6	30	0	24	24

Sidereal Time H.	M.	S.	10 ♋ °	11 ♌ °	12 ♍ °	Ascen ♎ °	′	2 ♎ °	3 ♏ °
6	0	0	0	6	6	0	0	24	24
6	4	22	1	7	7	0	47	25	25
6	8	43	2	8	8	1	33	26	26
6	13	5	3	9	9	2	19	27	27
6	17	26	4	10	10	3	5	27	28
6	21	48	5	11	10	3	51	28	29
6	26	9	6	12	11	4	37	29	♐
6	30	30	7	13	12	5	23	♏	1
6	34	51	8	14	13	6	9	1	2
6	39	11	9	15	14	6	55	2	3
6	43	31	10	16	15	7	40	2	4
6	47	51	11	16	16	8	26	3	4
6	52	11	12	17	16	9	12	4	5
6	56	31	13	18	17	9	58	5	6
7	0	50	14	19	18	10	43	6	7
7	5	8	15	20	19	11	28	7	8
7	9	26	16	21	20	12	14	8	9
7	13	44	17	22	21	12	59	8	10
7	18	1	18	23	22	13	45	9	11
7	22	18	19	24	23	14	30	10	12
7	26	34	20	25	24	15	15	11	13
7	30	50	21	26	25	16	0	12	14
7	35	5	22	27	25	16	45	13	15
7	39	20	23	28	26	17	30	13	16
7	43	34	24	29	27	18	15	14	17
7	47	47	25	♍	28	18	59	15	18
7	52	0	26	1	29	19	43	16	19
7	56	12	27	2	29	20	27	17	20
8	0	24	28	3	♎	21	11	18	20
8	4	35	29	4	1	21	56	18	21
8	8	45	30	5	2	22	40	19	22

Sidereal Time H.	M.	S.	10 ♌ °	11 ♍ °	12 ♎ °	Ascen ♎ °	′	2 ♏ °	3 ♐ °
8	8	45	0	5	2	22	40	19	22
8	12	54	1	5	3	23	24	20	23
8	17	3	2	6	3	24	7	21	24
8	21	11	3	7	4	24	50	22	25
8	25	19	4	8	5	25	34	23	26
8	29	26	5	9	6	26	18	23	27
8	33	31	6	10	7	27	1	24	28
8	37	37	7	11	8	27	44	25	29
8	41	41	8	12	8	28	26	26	♑
8	45	45	9	13	9	29	8	27	1
8	49	48	10	14	10	29	50	27	2
8	53	51	11	15	11	0 ♏	32	28	3
8	57	52	12	16	12	1	15	29	4
9	1	53	13	17	12	1	58	♐	4
9	5	53	14	18	13	2	39	1	5
9	9	53	15	18	14	3	21	1	6
9	13	52	16	19	15	4	3	2	7
9	17	50	17	20	16	4	44	3	8
9	21	47	18	21	16	5	26	3	9
9	25	44	19	22	17	6	7	4	10
9	29	40	20	23	18	6	48	5	11
9	33	35	21	24	18	7	29	5	12
9	37	29	22	25	19	8	9	6	13
9	41	23	23	26	20	8	50	7	14
9	45	16	24	27	21	9	31	8	15
9	49	9	25	28	22	10	11	9	16
9	53	1	26	28	23	10	51	9	17
9	56	52	27	29	23	11	32	10	18
10	0	43	28	♎	24	12	12	11	19
10	4	33	29	1	25	12	53	12	20
10	8	23	30	2	26	13	33	13	20

Sidereal Time H.	M.	S.	10 ♍ °	11 ♎ °	12 ♎ °	Ascen ♏ °	′	2 ♐ °	3 ♑ °
10	8	23	0	2	26	13	33	13	20
10	12	12	1	3	26	14	13	14	21
10	16	0	2	4	27	14	53	15	22
10	19	48	3	5	28	15	33	15	23
10	23	35	4	5	29	16	13	16	24
10	27	22	5	6	29	16	52	17	25
10	31	8	6	7	♏	17	32	18	26
10	34	54	7	8	1	18	12	19	27
10	38	40	8	9	2	18	52	20	28
10	42	25	9	10	2	19	31	20	29
10	46	9	10	11	3	20	11	21	♒
10	49	53	11	11	4	20	50	22	1
10	53	37	12	12	4	21	30	23	2
10	57	20	13	13	5	22	9	24	3
11	1	3	14	14	6	22	49	24	4
11	4	46	15	15	7	23	28	25	5
11	8	28	16	16	7	24	8	26	6
11	12	10	17	17	8	24	47	27	8
11	15	52	18	17	9	25	27	28	9
11	19	34	19	18	10	26	6	29	10
11	23	15	20	19	10	26	45	♑	11
11	26	56	21	20	11	27	25	0	12
11	30	37	22	21	12	28	5	1	13
11	34	18	23	22	13	28	44	2	14
11	37	58	24	23	13	29	24	3	15
11	41	39	25	23	14	0 ♐	3	4	16
11	45	19	26	24	15	0	43	5	17
11	49	0	27	25	15	1	23	6	18
11	52	40	28	26	16	2	3	6	19
11	56	20	29	27	17	2	43	7	20
12	0	0	30	27	17	3	23	8	21

Tables of Houses for London. (Reproduced from the RAPHAEL'S EPHEMERIS with permission of the publishers, W. Foulsham and Company Limited, Yeovil Road, Slough, Berkshire. © W. Foulsham & Co. Ltd.)

TABLES OF HOUSES FOR LIVERPOOL, Latitude 53° 25′ N.

Sidereal Time.	10 ♈	11 ♉	12 ♊	Ascen ♋	2 ♌	3 ♍	Sidereal Time.	10 ♉	11 ♊	12 ♋	Ascen ♌	2 ♍	3 ♎	Sidereal Time.	10 ♊	11 ♋	12 ♌	Ascen ♍	2 ♎	3 ♏
H. M. S.	°	°	°	° ′	°	°	H. M. S.	°	°	°	° ′	°	°	H. M. S.	°	°	°	° ′	°	°
0 0 0	0	9	24	28 12	14	3	1 51 37	0	10	18	17 32	5	28	3 51 15	0	9	12	7 55	28	25
0 3 40	1	10	25	28 51	14	4	1 55 27	1	11	19	18 11	6	29	3 55 25	1	10	13	8 37	29	26
0 7 20	2	12	25	29 30	15	4	1 59 17	2	12	20	18 51	6	♎	3 59 36	2	11	13	9 20	♏	27
0 11 0	3	13	26	0♉ 9	16	5	2 3 8	3	13	21	19 30	7	1	4 3 48	3	12	14	10 3	1	28
0 14 41	4	14	27	0 48	17	6	2 6 59	4	14	22	20 9	8	2	4 8 0	4	12	15	10 46	2	29
0 18 21	5	15	28	1 27	17	7	2 10 51	5	15	22	20 49	9	2	4 12 13	5	13	16	11 30	2	♏
0 22 2	6	16	29	2 6	18	8	2 14 44	6	16	23	21 28	9	3	4 16 26	6	14	17	12 13	3	1
0 25 42	7	17	♋	2 44	19	9	2 18 37	7	17	24	22 8	10	4	4 20 40	7	15	18	12 56	4	2
0 29 23	8	18	1	3 22	19	10	2 22 31	8	18	25	22 48	11	5	4 24 55	8	16	18	13 40	5	3
0 33 4	9	19	1	4 1	20	10	2 26 25	9	19	25	23 28	12	6	4 29 10	9	17	19	14 24	6	4
0 36 45	10	20	2	4 39	21	11	2 30 20	10	20	26	24 8	12	7	4 33 26	10	18	20	15 8	7	5
0 40 26	11	21	3	5 18	22	12	2 34 16	11	21	27	24 48	13	8	4 37 42	11	19	21	15 52	7	6
0 44 8	12	22	4	5 56	22	13	2 38 13	12	22	28	25 28	14	9	4 41 59	12	20	21	16 36	8	7
0 47 50	13	23	5	6 34	23	14	2 42 10	13	23	29	26 9	15	10	4 46 16	13	21	22	17 20	9	7
0 51 32	14	24	6	7 13	24	14	2 46 8	14	24	29	26 49	15	10	4 50 34	14	22	23	18 4	10	8
0 55 14	15	25	6	7 51	24	15	2 50 7	15	25	♌	27 29	16	11	4 54 52	15	23	24	18 48	11	9
0 58 57	16	26	7	8 30	25	16	2 54 7	16	26	1	28 10	17	12	4 59 10	16	24	25	19 32	12	10
1 2 40	17	27	8	9 8	26	17	2 58 7	17	27	2	28 51	18	13	5 3 29	17	24	26	20 17	12	11
1 6 23	18	28	9	9 47	26	18	3 2 8	18	28	2	29 32	19	14	5 7 49	18	25	26	21 1	13	12
1 10 7	19	29	10	10 25	27	19	3 6 9	19	29	3	0♍13	19	15	5 12 9	19	26	27	21 46	14	13
1 13 51	20	♊	11	11 4	28	19	3 10 12	20	♊	4	0 54	20	16	5 16 29	20	27	28	22 31	15	14
1 17 35	21	1	11	11 43	28	20	3 14 15	21	♋	5	1 36	21	17	5 20 49	21	28	29	23 16	16	15
1 21 20	22	2	12	12 21	29	21	3 18 19	22	1	5	2 17	22	18	5 25 9	22	29	♍	24 1	17	16
1 25 6	23	3	13	13 0	♍	22	3 22 23	23	2	6	2 59	23	19	5 29 30	23	♌	1	24 46	18	17
1 28 52	24	4	14	13 39	1	23	3 26 29	24	3	7	3 41	23	20	5 33 51	24	1	1	25 30	18	18
1 32 38	25	5	15	14 17	1	24	3 30 35	25	4	8	4 23	24	21	5 38 12	25	2	2	26 15	19	19
1 36 25	26	6	15	14 56	2	25	3 34 41	26	5	9	5 5	25	22	5 42 34	26	3	3	27 0	20	20
1 40 12	27	7	16	15 35	3	25	3 38 49	27	6	10	5 47	26	22	5 46 55	27	4	4	27 45	21	21
1 44 0	28	8	17	16 14	3	26	3 42 57	28	7	10	6 29	27	23	5 51 17	28	5	5	28 30	22	21
1 47 48	29	9	18	16 53	4	27	3 47 6	29	8	11	7 12	27	24	5 55 38	29	6	6	29 15	23	22
1 51 37	30	10	18	17 32	5	28	3 51 15	30	9	12	7 55	28	25	6 0 0	30	7	7	0 0	23	23

Sidereal Time.	10 ♋	11 ♌	12 ♍	Ascen ♎	2 ♏	3 ♏	Sidereal Time.	10 ♌	11 ♍	12 ♎	Ascen ♎	2 ♏	3 ♐	Sidereal Time.	10 ♍	11 ♎	12 ♎	Ascen ♏	2 ♐	3 ♑
H. M. S.	°	°	°	° ′	°	°	H. M. S.	°	°	°	° ′	°	°	H. M. S.	°	°	°	° ′	°	°
6 0 0	0	7	7	0 0	23	23	8 8 45	0	5	2	22 5	18	21	10 8 23	0	2	25	12 28	11	19
6 4 22	1	8	7	0 45	24	24	8 12 54	1	6	2	22 48	19	22	10 12 12	1	3	26	13 6	12	20
6 8 43	2	9	8	1 30	25	24	8 17 3	2	7	3	23 30	20	23	10 16 0	2	4	27	13 45	13	21
6 13 5	3	9	9	2 15	26	25	8 21 11	3	8	4	24 13	20	24	10 19 48	3	4	27	14 25	14	22
6 17 26	4	10	10	3 0	27	26	8 25 19	4	8	5	24 55	21	25	10 23 35	4	5	28	15 4	15	23
6 21 48	5	11	11	3 45	28	28	8 29 26	5	9	6	25 37	22	26	10 27 22	5	6	29	15 43	16	24
6 26 9	6	12	12	4 30	29	29	8 33 31	6	10	7	26 19	23	27	10 31 8	6	7	29	16 22	16	25
6 30 30	7	13	13	5 15	29	♐	8 37 37	7	11	7	27 1	24	28	10 34 54	7	8	♏	17 0	17	26
6 34 51	8	14	13	6 0	♏	1	8 41 41	8	12	8	27 43	25	29	10 38 40	8	9	1	17 39	18	27
6 39 11	9	15	14	6 44	1	2	8 45 45	9	13	9	28 24	25	♐	10 42 25	9	10	2	18 17	18	28
6 43 31	10	16	15	7 29	2	3	8 49 48	10	14	10	29 6	26	1	10 46 9	10	11	3	18 55	19	29
6 47 51	11	17	16	8 14	3	4	8 53 51	11	15	11	29 47	27	1	10 49 53	11	11	3	19 34	20	♑
6 52 11	12	18	17	8 59	4	5	8 57 52	12	16	11	0♏29	28	2	10 53 37	12	12	4	20 12	21	1
6 56 31	13	19	18	9 43	4	6	9 1 53	13	17	12	1 9	28	3	10 57 20	13	13	4	20 52	22	2
7 0 50	14	20	18	10 27	5	6	9 5 53	14	18	13	1 50	29	4	11 1 3	14	14	5	21 30	22	3
7 5 8	15	21	19	11 11	6	7	9 9 53	15	19	14	2 31	♐	5	11 4 46	15	15	6	22 8	23	3
7 9 26	16	22	20	11 56	7	8	9 13 52	16	19	15	3 11	1	6	11 8 28	16	16	7	22 46	24	4
7 13 44	17	23	21	12 40	8	9	9 17 50	17	20	15	3 52	1	7	11 12 10	17	16	7	23 25	25	5
7 18 1	18	24	22	13 24	8	10	9 21 47	18	21	16	4 32	2	8	11 15 52	18	17	8	24 4	26	6
7 22 18	19	24	23	14 8	9	11	9 25 44	19	22	17	5 12	3	9	11 19 34	19	18	9	24 42	26	7
7 26 34	20	25	23	14 52	10	12	9 29 40	20	23	18	5 52	4	10	11 23 15	20	19	9	25 21	27	10
7 30 50	21	26	24	15 36	11	13	9 33 35	21	24	18	6 32	5	11	11 26 56	21	20	10	25 59	28	11
7 35 5	22	27	25	16 20	12	14	9 37 29	22	25	19	7 12	5	12	11 30 37	22	21	11	26 38	29	12
7 39 20	23	28	26	17 4	13	15	9 41 23	23	26	20	7 52	6	13	11 34 18	23	21	11	27 16	♑	13
7 43 34	24	29	27	17 47	14	16	9 45 16	24	27	21	8 32	7	14	11 37 58	24	22	12	27 54	1	14
7 47 47	25	♍	28	18 30	14	17	9 49 9	25	28	23	9 11	8	15	11 41 39	25	23	13	28 33	1	15
7 52 0	26	1	28	19 13	15	18	9 53 1	26	28	24	9 51	8	16	11 45 19	26	24	14	29 11	2	16
7 56 12	27	2	29	19 56	16	19	9 56 52	27	29	24	10 30	9	17	11 49 0	27	25	14	29 49	3	17
8 0 24	28	3	♎	20 40	17	19	10 0 43	28	♎	24	11 9	10	17	11 52 40	28	26	15	0♐ 30	4	18
8 4 35	29	4	1	21 23	17	20	10 4 33	29	1	24	11 49	11	18	11 56 20	29	26	16	1 9	5	20
8 8 45	30	5	2	22 5	18	21	10 8 23	30	2	25	12 28	11	19	12 0 0	30	27	16	1 48	6	21

TABLES OF HOUSES FOR LIVERPOOL, Latitude 53° 25′ N.

Sidereal Time.	10 ♎	11 ♎	12 ♏	Ascen ♐	2 ♑	3 ♒	Sidereal Time.	10 ♏	11 ♏	12 ♐	Ascen ♐	2 ♒	3 ♓	Sidereal Time.	10 ♐	11 ♐	12 ♑	Ascen ♒	2 ♓	3 ♉
H. M. S.	°	°	°	° ′	°	°	H. M. S.	°	°	°	° ′	°	°	H. M. S.	°	°	°	° ′	°	°
12 0 0	0	27	16	1 48	6	21	13 51 37	0	21	8	23 6	8	27	15 51 15	0	17	4	24	15	26	7
12 3 40	1	28	17	2 27	7	22	13 55 27	1	22	9	23 55	9	28	15 55 25	1	18	5	25	41	28	8
12 7 20	2	29	18	3 6	8	23	13 59 17	2	23	10	24 43	10	♈	15 59 36	2	19	6	27	11	♈	9
12 11 0	3	♏	18	3 46	9	24	14 3 8	3	24	10	25 33	12	1	16 3 48	3	20	7	28	41	2	10
12 14 41	4	0	19	4 25	10	26	14 6 59	4	25	11	26 23	13	2	16 8 0	4	21	8	0♓14	4	12
12 18 21	5	1	20	5 6	10	26	14 10 51	5	26	12	27 14	15	4	16 12 13	5	22	9	1 50	5	13
12 22 2	6	2	21	5 46	11	27	14 14 44	6	26	14	18 4	16	6	16 16 26	6	23	10	3 30	7	14
12 25 42	7	3	21	6 26	12	29	14 18 37	7	27	13	28 59	18	6	16 20 40	7	24	11	5 13	9	15
12 29 23	8	4	22	7 6	13	♒	14 22 31	8	28	14	29 52	19	8	16 24 55	8	25	12	6 58	11	17
12 33 4	9	4	23	7 46	14	1	14 26 25	9	29	15	0♒46	20	9	16 29 10	9	26	13	8 45	13	18
12 36 45	10	5	24	8 27	15	2	14 30 20	10	♐	16	1 41	22	10	16 33 26	10	27	14	10 38	15	19
12 40 26	11	6	24	9 8	17	3	14 34 16	11	1	17	2 37	23	11	16 37 42	11	28	15	12 32	17	20
12 44 8	12	7	25	9 49	17	5	14 38 13	12	2	18	3 33	25	13	16 41 59	12	29	16	14 31	19	22
12 47 50	13	8	26	10 30	18	6	14 42 10	13	4	18	4 31	26	14	16 46 16	13	♑	18	16 33	20	23
12 51 32	14	9	26	11 12	19	7	14 46 8	14	5	19	5 29	28	16	16 50 34	14	1	19	18 40	22	24
12 55 14	15	9	27	11 54	20	8	14 50 7	15	6	20	6 29	♒	17	16 54 52	15	2	20	20 50	24	25
12 58 57	16	10	28	12 36	21	10	14 54 7	16	7	21	7 30	1	18	16 59 10	16	3	21	23 0	26	26
13 2 40	17	11	28	13 19	22	11	14 58 7	17	8	22	8 32	3	20	17 3 29	17	4	22	25 18	28	28
13 6 23	18	12	29	14 2	23	12	15 2 8	18	9	22	9 35	5	21	17 7 49	18	5	24	27 42	♉	29
13 10 7	19	13	♐	14 46	23	13	15 6 9	19	10	23	10 39	6	22	17 12 9	19	6	25	0♈ 8	3	♊
13 13 51	20	13	1	15 28	25	15	15 10 12	20	11	24	11 45	8	23	17 16 29	20	7	26	2 37	3	1
13 17 35	21	14	1	16 12	27	16	15 14 15	21	12	25	12 52	10	25	17 20 49	21	8	28	5 10	5	3
13 21 20	22	15	2	16 56	♑	18	15 18 19	22	13	26	14 1	11	26	17 25 9	22	9	29	7 46	6	4
13 25 6	23	16	3	17 40	1	19	15 22 23	23	14	27	15 11	13	27	17 29 30	23	10	♒	10 24	8	5
13 28 52	24	17	4	18 26	3	20	15 26 29	24	15	28	16 23	14	28	17 33 51	24	11	2	13 7	10	6
13 32 38	25	17	4	19 11	4	21	15 30 35	25	16	29	17 37	15	♈	17 38 12	25	12	3	15 52	11	7
13 36 25	26	18	5	19 57	5	22	15 34 41	26	16	♑	18 53	17	1	17 42 34	26	13	4	18 38	13	8
13 40 12	27	19	6	20 44	7	23	15 38 49	27	17	1	20 10	18	2	17 46 55	27	14	6	21 27	15	9
13 44 0	28	20	7	21 31	8	24	15 42 57	28	18	2	21 29	20	4	17 51 17	28	15	7	24 16	16	10
13 47 48	29	21	7	22 18	9	26	15 47 6	29	19	4	22 51	21	5	17 55 38	29	16	9	27 5	18	12
13 51 15	30	21	8	23 6	8	27	15 51 15	30	21	5	24 15	26	7	18 0 0	30	17	11	0 0	19	13

Sidereal Time.	10 ♑	11 ♑	12 ♒	Ascen ♈	2 ♉	3 ♊	Sidereal Time.	10 ♒	11 ♓	12 ♈	Ascen ♉	2 ♊	3 ♋	Sidereal Time.	10 ♓	11 ♈	12 ♉	Ascen ♊	2 ♋	3 ♌
H. M. S.	°	°	°	° ′	°	°	H. M. S.	°	°	°	° ′	°	°	H. M. S.	°	°	°	° ′	°	°
18 0 0	0	17	11	0 0	19	13	20 8 45	0	23	4	5 45	26	13	22 8 23	0	3	22	6 54	22	8
18 4 22	1	18	12	2 52	21	14	20 12 54	1	25	6	7	9 27	14	22 12 12	1	4	23	7	42	23	9
18 8 43	2	20	14	5 43	23	15	20 17 3	2	26	7	8 31	28	16	22 16 0	2	5	25	8	29	23	10
18 13 5	3	21	15	8 33	24	16	20 21 11	3	27	8	9 50	29	17	22 19 48	3	7	26	9	16	24	11
18 17 26	4	22	17	11 22	25	17	20 25 19	4	29	9	11 8	♋	18	22 23 35	4	8	27	10	3	25	12
18 21 48	5	23	19	14 8	27	18	20 29 26	5	♓	10	12 23	1	17	22 27 22	5	9	29	10	49	26	13
18 26 9	6	24	20	16 53	28	19	20 33 31	6	1	11	13 37	2	8	22 31 8	6	11	♋	11	34	26	14
18 30 30	7	25	22	19 36	30	20	20 37 37	7	3	12	14 49	3	1	22 34 54	7	12	1	12	19	27	14
18 34 51	8	26	23	22 16	♉	21	20 41 41	8	4	13	15 59	4	18	22 38 40	8	13	3	13	4	28	15
18 39 11	9	27	25	24 50	2	22	20 45 45	9	5	14	17 8	5	20	22 42 25	9	14	4	13	48	29	16
18 43 31	10	29	27	23	4	23	20 49 48	10	7	15	18 16	6	21	22 46 9	10	16	4	14	32	29	17
18 47 51	11	♒	28	29	52	5	24	20 53 51	11	8	17	19 22	8	22	22 49 53	11	17	5	15	15	♌	18
18 52 11	12	1	♈	2 8	18	6	25	20 57 52	12	10	18	20 27	9	23	22 53 37	12	18	7	15	59	1	18
18 56 31	13	2	2	4 39	8	26	20	21 1 53	13	11	19	21 31	10	24	22 57 20	13	19	8	16	41	2	19
19 0 50	14	4	4	6 56	9	27	23	21 5 53	14	12	20	22 33	11	25	23 1 3	14	20	9	17	24	2	20
19 5 8	15	5	9	10	10 28	24	21 9 53	15	14	21	23 34	12	26	23 4 46	15	22	10	18	6	3	21
19 9 26	16	6	8	11 29	21	14	25	21 13 52	16	15	23	24 31	13	27	23 8 28	16	23	11	18	48	4	22
19 13 44	17	7	10	13 27	12	2	26	21 17 50	17	16	24	25 30	14	28	23 12 10	17	24	12	19	30	5	23
19 18 1	18	8	11	15 27	4	26	21 21 47	18	17	25	26 25	15	29	23 15 52	18	25	13	20	11	5	23
19 22 18	19	9	13	17 28	15	2	21	21 25 44	19	19	26	27 22	16	♌	23 19 34	19	27	14	20	52	6	24
19 26 34	20	11	15	19 22	16	3	21 29 40	20	20	28	8 28	19	1	23 23 15	20	28	15	21	33	6	25
19 30 50	21	12	17	21 14	17	4	21 33 35	21	22	29	8 52	19	2	23 26 56	21	29	16	22	14	7	26
19 35 5	22	13	19	23 2	18	6	21 37 29	22	22	♊	0♊29	20	3	23 30 37	22	♉	17	22	54	8	27
19 39 20	23	15	21	24 51	20	7	21 41 23	23	24	1	1 16	21	4	23 34 18	23	1	18	23	34	9	27
19 43 34	24	16	23	26 30	20	7	21 45 16	24	25	2	1 54	22	4	23 37 58	24	2	19	24	14	9	28
19 47 47	25	17	25	28 10	21	8	21 49 9	25	26	2	2 46	18	4	23 41 39	25	3	20	24	54	10	29
19 52 0	26	18	26	29 46	22	9	21 53 1	26	28	15	2 37	19	5	23 45 19	26	5	21	25	35	11	♍
19 56 12	27	20	28	1♉19	23	10	21 56 52	27	29	18	4 27	20	6	23 49 0	27	6	22	26	14	11	1
20 0 24	28	21	♈	2 50	24	11	22 0 43	28	♈	5	17 20	7	23 52 40	28	7	22	26	55	12	2
20 4 35	29	22	2	4 19	25	12	22 4 33	29	2	21	5 21	8	23 56 20	29	8	23	27	33	13	3
20 8 45	30	23	4	5 45	26	13	22 8 23	30	3	22	6 54	22	8	24 0 0	30	9	24	28	12	14	3

THE POSITION OF PLUTO (♇) IN 1949.

Date	Long.	Lat.	Dec.
Jan. 1	16 Ω 6	7 N45	23 N24
11	15 ℞54	7 47	23 30
21	15 41	7 49	23 35
31	15 27	7 50	23 41
Feb. 10	15 13	7 51	23 46
20	14 59	7 51	23 50
Mar. 2	14 46	7 51	23 54
12	14 34	7 51	23 57
22	14 24	7 50	24 0
April 1	14 16	7 49	24 1
11	14 11	7 48	24 1
21	14 8	7 46	24 1
May 1	14 D 7	7 45	24 0
May 11	14 Ω11	7 N43	23 N57
21	14 17	7 42	23 54
31	14 25	7 41	23 51
June 10	14 35	7 40	23 46
20	14 48	7 39	23 42
30	15 2	7 38	23 37
July 10	15 18	7 38	23 32
20	15 35	7 38	23 26
30	15 53	7 38	23 21
Aug. 9	16 11	7 38	23 16
19	16 30	7 39	23 11
29	16 47	7 39	23 7
Sept. 8	17 4	7 40	23 3
Sept. 18	17 Ω20	7 N44	23 N 0
28	17 34	7 46	22 57
Oct. 8	17 47	7 48	22 56
18	17 57	7 51	22 55
28	18 4	7 54	22 55
Nov. 7	18 9	7 57	22 56
17	18 11	8 0	22 59
27	18 ℞10	8 3	23 2
Dec. 7	18 8	8 6	23 6
17	18 0	8 8	23 10
27	17 52	8 11	23 15
Jan. 1	17 46	8 12	23 18

THE POSITION OF PLUTO (♇) IN 1954.

Date	Long.	Lat.	Dec.
Jan. 1	24 Ω43	9 N58	22 N39
11	24 32	10 0	22 45
21	24 20	10 2	22 51
31	24 6	10 4	22 58
Feb. 10	23 51	10 5	23 4
20	23 36	10 6	23 9
Mar. 2	23 22	10 6	23 14
12	23 9	10 5	23 18
22	22 57	10 3	23 22
Apr. 1	22 47	10 1	23 24
11	22 39	9 58	23 25
21	22 34	9 58	23 24
May 1	22 32	9 58	23 24
May 11	22 Ω33	9 N56	23 N22
21	22 36	9 54	23 19
31	22 42	9 52	23 15
June 10	22 51	9 50	23 10
20	23 2	9 48	23 5
30	23 16	9 46	22 59
July 10	23 31	9 45	22 52
20	23 48	9 45	22 46
30	24 6	9 44	22 39
Aug. 9	24 25	9 45	22 33
19	24 44	9 45	22 27
29	25 3	9 46	22 21
Sept. 8	25 22	9 47	22 16
Sept. 18	25 Ω39	9 N49	22 N12
28	25 56	9 52	22 8
Oct. 8	26 10	9 54	22 5
18	26 23	9 57	22 4
28	26 34	10 1	22 3
Nov. 7	26 40	10 4	22 5
17	26 46	10 8	22 8
27	26 48	10 11	22 12
Dec. 7	26 47	10 15	22 16
17	26 43	10 19	22 22
27	26 36	10 22	22 22
Jan. 1	26 32	10 23	22 25

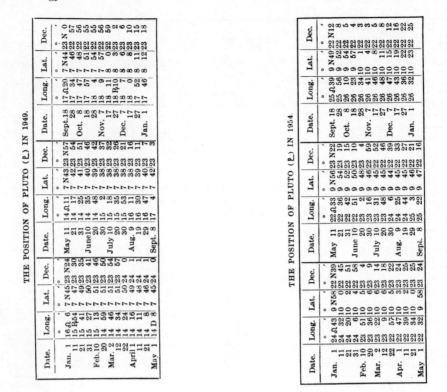

Position of Pluto in 1949 and 1954. (Reproduced from the RAPHAEL'S EPHEMERIS with permission of the publishers, W. Foulsham and Company Limited, Yeovil Road, Slough, Berkshire. © W. Foulsham & Co. Ltd.)

INDEX